Shipwrecks of Lake Michigan

Benjamin J. Shelak

TRAILS BOOKS

Black Earth, Wisconsin

Library of Congress Control Number: 2002114603
ISBN: 1-931599-21-1

Editor: Stan Stoga
Copy Editor: David Wright
Designer: John Huston
Cover Photo: Courtesy of the Wisconsin Maritime Museum
Back Cover Photo: Courtesy of the Eastland Memorial Society

Printed in the United States of America by McNaughton & Gunn.

08 07 06 05 04 03   6 5 4 3 2 1

Trails Books, a division of Trails Media Group, Inc.
P.O. Box 317 • Black Earth, WI 53515
(800) 236-8088 • e-mail: books@wistrails.com
www.trailsbooks.com

To my wife, Jo Ann, and our sons, Ian and Andrew.
You are the reason I love to write.

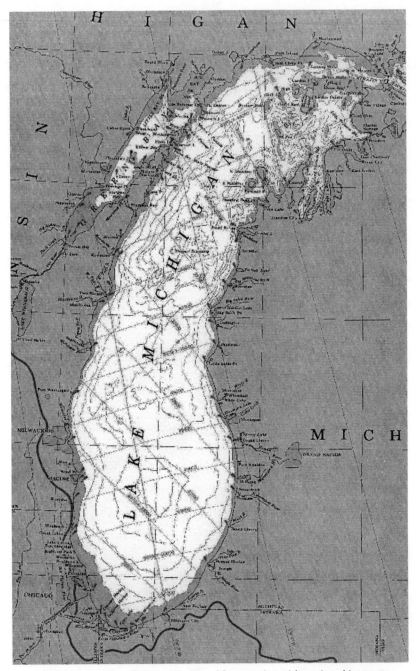

Lake Michigan shoreline.— *Courtesy of the National Oceanographic and Atmospheric Administration*

contents

PREFACE

My purpose in writing *Shipwrecks of Lake Michigan* was two-fold. After living throughout the Great Lakes region for many years and becoming familiar with them, I developed a lasting fascination with these great expanses of water. While the necessities of my professional life dictated that I leave the Great Lakes for the mid-Atlantic region, my love for their beauty has grown, lending credence to the saying that "absence makes the heart grow fonder." After watching my library of Great Lakes books grow, I decided to work on a project about the upper Midwest, and it is this undertaking that led to a work on Lake Michigan shipwrecks.

My interest in writing about Lake Michigan satisfies the second purpose of this book. A tremendous amount of excellent literature exists that describes shipwrecks on Lake Michigan, but all these descriptions are presented in the context of Great Lakes wrecks in general. There are books that examine shipwrecks of the four other Great Lakes, but none that are exclusively devoted to telling the story of Lake Michigan's maritime disasters. This book is my attempt to correct what I view as a deficiency and to give readers a coherent picture of these wrecks.

Shipwrecks of Lake Michigan also seeks to go beyond mere description. While the crux of this work is to portray the events of actual wrecks, I've tried to present them within the context of the development of the Great Lakes, particularly Lake Michigan. This is done in the belief that an understanding of a shipwreck is more meaningful and instructive if it's set against a historical backdrop: the region's industrial and agricultural development, the rise of lake ports, the introduction of new means of transportation such as rail, the impact of immigration, and other important historical forces. These factors help explain why a vessel was sailing at a specific time of the year with a particular cargo between two specific ports, and why it was at a given location at a specific time when it was lost.

Most of the book is divided into chapters representing nine regions around Lake Michigan. These chapters follow the same pattern. Each begins with a brief examination of the forces that shaped the development of each region as a center of maritime activity. Following this are descriptions of significant wrecks that occurred within that geographic location. These stories tell of disasters involving significant loss of life or property, or that were particularly harrowing. Each section concludes with a brief look at other famous and lesser-known shipwrecks in the region. I sincerely hope that you enjoy *Shipwrecks of Lake Michigan*. With you, I share an enduring appreciation of the Great Lakes.

ACKNOWLEDGMENTS

I want to thank all of those who assisted in researching this project. I am especially grateful to a number of authors who have allowed material from their works to be referenced in *Shipwrecks of Lake Michigan*.

Among these is Paul J. Creviere, Jr., author of *Wild Gales and Tattered Sails*, for making available information from his book detailing the shipwrecks and history of the Door County area from Kewaunee, Wisconsin, to Michigan's Upper Peninsula. A wealth of information on Lake Michigan shipwrecks was also obtained from *Terrifying Steamboat Stories* and *Schooners in Peril*, both by James Donahue. Another invaluable source was the encyclopedic reference of over 3,700 Great Lakes shipwrecks in the book by David Swayze entitled *Shipwreck!*

A great deal of detailed information on specific events was also provided by Wes Oleszewski in his excellent books *Sounds of Disaster; Lighthouse Adventures, Mysteries and Histories of the Great Lakes,* and *Ghost Ships, Gales and Forgotten Tales.*

Brendon Baillod, president of the Great Lakes Shipwreck Research Foundation and author of numerous articles pertaining to Great Lakes wrecks, provided information on quite a few of the shipwrecks described in this work including the freighters *Appomattox, Frank O'Connor,* and *Prins Willem V;* the steamers *Lady Elgin* and *Sebastopol;* the schooner *Edna* and the lumber hooker *Three Brothers.*

Mary Bonevelle and Karl Sup, both founders of the Eastland Memorial Society, Craig Rich, author of various articles on the *Alpena, Andaste, Chicora,* and *Ironsides,* and Rick Drews, who provided information on the *David Dows, Material Service Barge,* and *Sebastopol,* have all graciously allowed their works to be referenced. Added to this list is Bill Wangemann, Sheboygan historian and alderman, who provided information on the *Lottie Cooper,* the *R.H. Becker,* and the *Phoenix* disasters. Also, Ms. Boneville and Mr. Sup have allowed the reproduction of a number of photographs for this work, for which I would like to additionally thank them.

I also wish to thank Ted Wachholz and other members of the Eastland Disaster Historical Society who patiently reviewed the chapter on the *Eastland* and supplied additional information pertaining to this wreck.

Thanks for the photographs in this book go to Molly Biddle of the Wisconsin Maritime Museum in Manitowoc; the Beaver Island Historical Society; the Michigan Maritime Museum; and the employees of the Library of Congress for their assistance. I would also like to acknowledge the help of the National Oceanographic and Atmospheric Administration, a division of the U.S. Department of Commerce, for all of the maps contained within *Shipwrecks of Lake Michigan*.

A special note of thanks goes to Frederick Stonehouse, who patiently edited this work and provided a tremendous amount of information related to Great Lakes maritime history and Lake Michigan shipwrecks. His considerable knowledge and efforts on this work have proven invaluable. Mr. Stonehouse is considered by many, including myself, to be the premier historian of the Great Lakes.

I am also very grateful to the staff at Trails Media Group for publishing *Shipwrecks of Lake Michigan* and for guiding the project through the process of getting it into print.

Finally, I would like to thank my wife, Jo Anne, and my entire family for reviewing portions of this book and offering their support.

Great effort has been taken to ensure that the information contained in *Shipwrecks of Lake Michigan* is as accurate as possible. Any errors should be attributed solely to the author.

OUR INLAND SEAS

Throughout Lake Michigan's history of human settlement, this vast inland sea has never failed to leave the region's inhabitants with anything less than a profound sense of awe and respect. Whether it is a first-time visitor or someone raised along its shores, Lake Michigan's stark beauty leaves an indelible print on one's soul.

In summer, crowds of anglers stand along the piers and docks of Lake Michigan's coastal communities. This is also the time of year when families visit parks and other recreational areas that dot the lakeshore. Common sights include those of children wading into the cold lake water or building sand castles along the shoreline. Freighters ply their trade from port to port while sharing the waters with the smaller leisure craft that venture away from their harbor homes during the warmer months.

By fall, there are fewer brave souls fishing along the lake. The crash of tremendous breakers against the concrete piers and steel breakwaters makes it impossible to go far in search of fish. The water is too cold for swimming and sailboats are more a rarity than a commonplace sight. Violent storms are a frequent occurrence during this season, further inhibiting sporting activities along the lakefront. Quite often only the silhouettes of ore boats can be seen against the stark horizon, braving the fierce autumn gales.

Winter's Arctic-spawned winds, drifting snow, and ice-choked harbors often prevent even the larger freighters from leaving their berths where they lay immobile until spring. Coast Guard icebreakers like the *Mackinac* smash their way through the crusts of ice, carving pathways into choked harbors that allow easier means of access.

COMMERCIAL DEVELOPMENT

Despite the vagaries of its weather and often-treacherous sailing conditions, the lure of Lake Michigan has always attracted adventurers, merchants, and settlers. The lake's location as a gateway to the west and its proximity to abundant natural resources are the two major factors that led its development as a vital means of transportation for the country. The region became an ideal place to raise families, find employment, or operate a business.

As the westernmost of the Great Lakes, Michigan and Superior were gateways to the rich soil and abundant natural resources of the Midwest and, later, to the West's expanding frontier. The two lakes enabled goods and people to finish their journey by boat from New York, Pennsylvania, and Ohio via lakes Ontario, Erie, and Huron. Reaching the western lake ports, these settlers, merchants, and commodities either remained in Wisconsin, Michigan, Illinois,

Indiana, and Canada or continued farther west toward the Rocky Mountains and Pacific Ocean.

Due to the early remoteness of Lake Michigan and Lake Superior, they were the last of the lakes to develop a commercial maritime presence. Before this was possible it was first necessary to bring settlers to what was at one time an untamed frontier. In Lake Michigan's favor was the ease of travel from Lake Huron: they both stand at 577 feet above sea level. Lake Superior, on the other hand, lies 600 feet above sea level. Prior to construction of the Soo Locks, navigating the St. Mary's River between Lake Huron and Lake Superior was difficult and dangerous. At one point the river dropped by as much as 21 feet. Vessels and cargo had to take an overland route around the rapids. It was far easier to enter the warmer and more hospitable waters of Lake Michigan, which remained open to maritime traffic longer during the year.

In the late seventeenth and early eighteenth centuries, French voyageurs established several small ports, such as Green Bay, on Lake Michigan. These were essentially forts and fur trading communities, such as Fort Michilimackinac in the Straits of Mackinac or Fort Dearborn at what was to become Chicago, as well as the trading center of Green Bay. Commerce led to the development of cities like Chicago, Milwaukee, and Frankfort, Michigan, while the subsequent increase in shipbuilding aided cities such as Manitowoc and Manistee to grow.

The development of these communities was one of the first steps in settling the entire region. Isolated from the more populated East Coast until the early part of the nineteenth century, the 1,600 miles of Lake Michigan shoreline was a forbidding environment to tame. It is precisely for this reason that only isolated trading posts and forts existed in the region. Nevertheless, individuals such as Jean Baptiste Point du Sable, who founded Chicago in 1779, were establishing the roots of what would one day be mighty commercial centers.

As the small towns and burgeoning cities around Lake Michigan began to flex their muscles in the latter part of the eighteenth and the early part of the nineteenth centuries, commercial connections to the East were required to satisfy consumer needs. This necessity encouraged shipping and the construction of lake boats.

Lake Michigan's geography, as well as its vast size, made it ideally suited to the task. It is roughly 118 miles wide and 307 miles long. The lake displaces 1,180 cubic miles of water, averages 279 feet in depth with the lowest point descending to 925 feet, has approximately 22,300 square miles of surface water, and includes a drainage basin of rivers and smaller lakes almost twice as large as that of its entire area of surface water. Navigating these vast waters was a necessity if people and goods were to be efficiently and safely transported through the region. It was through this process that the lake trade on Lake Michigan was established and developed. Disasters went hand in hand with increasing traffic on the lake.

THE PRICE OF PROGRESS

Heavy lake traffic inevitably led to the growing numbers of wrecks, and over the years the cost has been enormous. An accounting of the cost of the vessels, the value of their cargoes and, most tragically of all, the number of lives lost to the Great Lakes can never be fully established. It is estimated that more than 10,000 vessels have been destroyed and approximately 30,000 people have perished on the lakes. Even these numbers may fall far short of the totals.

In addition, an estimated $800 million in salvageable property lies at the bottom of the lakes. Some of the lost cargoes in Lake Michigan include lumber, coal, gravel, iron ore, china, railroad ties, automobiles, general merchandise, hardware and machine tools, liquor, juke boxes, marble, Christmas trees, and perishables such as grain, fruit, and salt. There are also three locomotive engines resting at the bottom of Lake Michigan. Two washed off the brig *Clarion* during a storm in 1851. The remaining engine was rolled overboard by the crew of the barge *Arcturus* during a storm in the spring of 1853 to prevent the boat from capsizing.

Sailors and passengers alike rest together in the cold depths of the lakes. Unlike the corrosive effects of salt water, the cold waters of the Great Lakes preserve the remains of the boats and their passengers in an ice water grave. Toward the bottom of the lake, the temperature remains roughly 39° Fahrenheit or 4° Celsius. This cold water deters destructive bacteria and encourages the phenomenon of frozen mummification or soapification.

Part of the uncertainty in determining the exact number of lives lost to ice, fire, gale, and other causes lies in the nature of the lake trade itself. Seeking just enough money to get by on, temporary crew members would often sign up for a few voyages or a single trip. Few records remain to document their names or passing. A schooner might carry a regular crew of eight but have taken on an additional number. Passengers whose presence was either not reported or poorly recorded may also have booked passage. Even when accurate records were kept and when passenger manifests survived, only some of those lost would be listed in the newspapers as having perished. Accounts differed.

Despite the terrible risks and tragic losses, the Great Lakes hold sway over the imaginations and dreams of those who live near their shores. The full story of the modern Great Lakes began 20,000 years ago during the Pleistocene Ice Age. The tales of Lake Michigan's shipwrecks comprise a small and recent chapter of this grand saga. But to those who share a love affair with the lakes, their stories are anything but insignificant.

CHAPTER

2

FROM SAIL TO STEAM

The first European to set sail through the waters of the Great Lakes region was Jean Nicolet who, in 1634, mistakenly believed that he had found the fabled lands of Cathay, as China was then known. Several days in the company of friendly Winnebago Indians on the shores of Green Bay were enough to convince Nicolet that he had made a mistake in his search for a new route to China.

THE "BIG CUT"

The country that Nicolet discovered was filled with white pine, white and black spruce, balsam fir, and hardwoods such as birch and cedar. This was the land of the Menominee, Winnebago, and Potawatomi. Later, these Native Americans would trade with French voyageurs and settlers.

When massive tracts of virgin forest were obliterated between 1840 and 1890, the era of the "Big Cut," the forest ecology of the region was severely affected. In the middle of the nineteenth century, much of the Great Lakes basin was 60 percent eastern hemlock. By the latter half of the twentieth century, eastern hemlock would come to comprise less than 1 percent of the region's forested area. Due to past lumbering practices, the sights of verdant forests that have held mariners in awe since the times of Jean Nicolet have been gradually altered, until today a mixed pine-oak forest exists throughout the region.

But the "Big Cut" and the tremendous amount of shipping that took place would never have occurred were it not for the settlers who put down roots in this country in their search for a better life. The regional flavor of these early men and women can still be seen, for example, in the architecture of Norwegian-settled Sister Bay, Wisconsin, or the Moravian and Norwegian influences of nearby Ephraim. Washington Island, just off the tip of the Door Peninsula, is home to the oldest Icelandic settlement in the United States. Michigan's Upper Peninsula is well known for its mix of Finns, Irish, Italians, and other groups. Lower Michigan has great numbers of Poles, Germans, and Dutch, and few cities can claim greater ethnic diversity than Chicago. Waves of immigrants have brought new ideas and a solid work ethic to the shores of Lake Michigan. What exists today is built on the firm foundation of pioneering spirit and work.

EARLY SAILING VESSELS

There have been many significant changes in ship design, construction, and the types of craft sailing the inland seas since La Salle's *Griffon* graced these waters. This 45-ton bark carries the dubious honor of being the first decked vessel to be lost on the upper Great Lakes; it met its fate in 1679, presumably close to Wisconsin's Death's Door passage between the Door Peninsula and Washington Island.

By the early 1800s, triple-masted barkentines and double-masted brigantines were plying the lake trade. The barkentine differed in construction from the earlier barques in the way the rigging was designed and used. Whereas a barque carried square sails on all but the aftermast, which was fore-and-aft rigged, the barkentine only carried square sails on the foremast, the remaining masts being all fore-and-aft rigged. A further distinction can be made between brigantines with square rigging on the foremast and fore-and-aft rigging on the aftermast, and brigs that had both masts square rigged.

Designed to sail before the wind, square-rigged vessels were ideal for the wide-open expanse of the oceans but proved less than perfect for the enclosed spaces of the Great Lakes, where tacking was necessary. For this reason, by mid-century these early craft were largely replaced with schooners, which were capable of sailing across the wind. Adaptations of the schooner included shallow drafted scow schooners and schooner barges, both of which were rigged for sail. The schooner was in constant competition with the lake steamers, but several generations would pass before sail was completely replaced. The age of working sail on the Great Lakes quite possibly came to a close with the loss of the schooner *Our Son*.

The *Our Son*, built in 1875, foundered 20 miles from Sheboygan on September 26, 1930. The triple-masted schooner, listed with the official number of 14437, was owned by W. Schlosser of Milwaukee when it became waterlogged during a storm and foundered. A load of pulpwood was lost but the crew was saved by the self-unloader *William Nelson*.

THE AGE OF STEAM

The emergence of steam on the Great Lakes began long before the *Our Son*, having its origins in the construction of the steamers *Ontario* and *Walk-In-The-Water*. The *Ontario* was built on Lake Ontario in 1818, *Walk-In-The-Water* at Black Rock later that same year. The first steamship to dip its paddles into the waters of Lake Michigan did so in 1826 or 1827. In 1832, Chicago witnessed the power of steam for the very first time. The following year a steamer traveling from Buffalo, New York, to Chicago completed the voyage in twenty-five days. By 1854, the same journey was accomplished in four days. A new era in Great Lakes maritime travel had dawned, and it was the age of steam.

As steam replaced sail, passenger travel on the lakes increased, and it could be a daunting and hazardous undertaking. *Walk-In-The-Water*, *Phoenix,* and

Niagara are just three examples of passenger steamers that met unfortunate ends in the early days of lake travel. Of these, only *Walk-In-The-Water* was destroyed without any casualties, although the survivors were forced to spend the night, ankle deep in freezing water in their rooms until the storm abated and they could abandon the stranded steamer. Despite the discomfort and dangers associated with lake travel, people were still willing to serve as crew members or seek passage on board the growing numbers of vessels.

At the same time, more finished goods were flowing from the eastern reaches of the Great Lakes to the western lakes. Raw materials, including timber, copper, and iron moved in the opposite direction, creating a prosperous symbiotic relationship. Along the way vessels would stop at Cleveland, Detroit, Mackinac Island, Manitowoc, and numerous other ports to refuel and take on supplies. Safe havens, such as Washington Island or Beaver Island, were often used during foul weather, enabling passengers and crews to wait out a storm in greater safety than that available on the open lakes.

With steam came a variety of different types of lake boats. There were stern- and side-wheelers, whalebacks that bore a striking resemblance to the hull of a shallow-drafted freighter turned turtle, propellers, and a variety of others. All proudly traversed the length and breadth of the lakes. In addition to these there were large, flat-bottomed and harbor-bound lighters which were used to load and unload freight.

In 1869, the first modern lake freighter, the 210-foot-long *R.J. Hackett*, was built. The *Hackett* had all its machinery placed near the aft, thereby leaving the decks clear. This distinct silhouette has become the standard for modern lakers ever since. The *Hackett* was the first lake boat able to carry ore and grain below decks in a watertight hold. The freighter was fitted with hatches to ease the loading of cargo. These features were incorporated into other freighters that used them to good effect. As for the *Hackett*, like so many of its peers, the freighter's remains rest in the waters of Green Bay, where it burned and sank in 1905.

THE HAZARDS OF STEAM

As ship traffic grew on the Great Lakes throughout the nineteenth century, it is hardly surprising that the number of wrecks increased. One of the reasons was the growth of steam-powered vessels. Steam brought with it speed and reduced the reliance on wind, but it also brought new problems. The early steamers could explode or catch fire with little provocation and even less warning. With the tremendous increase in maritime activity, especially steam-powered vessels, the number of wrecks grew at an amazing rate, culminating in the

The Southerner, an example of a mid-nineteenth-century steamer.— *Courtesy of the Library of Congress*

1880s with more than 300 wrecks.

Obtaining accurate information on the number of wrecks during the nine-teenth and early twentieth centuries however, is impossible. Nevertheless, a survey of existing records shows that the second half of the nineteenth century produced a disproportionately large percentage of Great Lakes shipwrecks.

The nature of accidents underwent a change as well. While the occasional sail-powered schooner or bark caught fire, the vast majority of disasters caused by fire are generally attributed to steamers and other vessels that relied on a source of power other than wind. Steam also resulted in more frequent on-board explosions. These incidents were the result of dangerously high boiler pressure and the onboard storage of flammable or other volatile cargoes such as gasoline, varnish, or dynamite. Quite often these goods were stored near the boilers or stack.

With the advent of radar and sonar in the mid-twentieth century, other ves-sels and underwater obstructions could be located in heavy storms and thick fogs. Vessels no longer become stranded (the most common cause of all ship-wrecks on the Great Lakes) or involved in collisions with a frequency that was once commonplace.

Despite the dangers inherent in working or seeking passage on board the early steamers, they were generally much safer than their wind-driven counter-parts. From the beginnings of travel on Lake Michigan to the present, vessels powered by steam, coal, oil, or gas account for nearly one-third of all shipwrecks.

DECADE OF LOSS	PERCENT OF SAMPLE TOTAL BY DECADE
Prior To 1800:	0.12
1800s:	0.00
1810s:	0.06
1820s:	0.06
1830s:	1.79
1840s:	3.58
1850s:	12.94
1860s:	13.06
1870s:	12.22
1880s:	19.20
1890s:	16.70
1900s:	7.87
1910s:	5.61
1920s:	2.03
1930s:	2.03
1940s:	1.19
1950s:	0.72
1960s:	0.18
1970s:	0.30
1980s:	0.30
1990s:	0.06
Total:	100.00

But schooners, schooner barges, scow schooners, barks, brigs, and sloops contributed to roughly the other two-thirds of all wrecks, nearly twice as many as vessels fitted with an onboard power plant. Of these vessels reliant on wind, approximately 83 percent were schooners; but this figure increases if schooner barges and scow schooners are included. Barges and other craft that are strictly towed contribute around one percent to the total number of wrecks on Lake Michigan.

REASONS FOR LOSS ON LAKE MICHIGAN

TYPE	PERCENT OF SAMPLE TOTAL
Stranded:	45.47
Capsized or foundered:	33.54
Fire or explosion:	13.19
Collision:	7.42
Scuttled:	0.25
Piracy:	0.13

Given the tremendous change within the past 200 years in ship design and technology, one wonders what the future holds for boats. Despite continuing improvements it is unlikely that human beings will ever tame Mother Nature or calm her fickle moods. As long as people sail the lakes, they will do so knowing that disaster can strike at any moment and from any quarter.

CHAPTER

3

NATURE'S FURY

The men and women who work the Great Lakes do so with the knowledge that disaster can strike with little warning. Weather, fire, collisions, and other accidents have contributed to the destruction of hundreds of strong and proud boats. There is no solace in tragedy, whatever the cause. Nature's angry gales and foaming water have destroyed many of the vessels that have braved these waters. Others have come face to face with destiny as the result of navigational error or from the sudden and devastating effects of fire. On occasion, and regardless of weather, a boat might beach upon a shoal and break apart by wave action. The Great Lakes are a vast theater in which the weather, strong currents, collisions, and circumstance have played a role in the destruction of countless vessels.

Weather-related events have been the cause of the most widespread destruction on the lakes. They are constantly battered by storm action but there are a few storms that stand out in history due to their wide-ranging impact, the large loss of shipping and crews, and extensive inland damage.

Any time of the year, the waters of the Great Lakes can be whipped to a savage fury. As winds pick up, rolling swells become pronounced. If the wind continues to strengthen, the waves become peaked; a phenomenon referred to as "Christmas trees," and most visible on the horizon. As conditions worsen, the peaks may actually be blown from the waves and visibility reduced to zero by the blinding spray.

GREAT LAKES WEATHER

The pattern of seasonal changes in the Great Lakes Basin has its origins in two air masses that sweep across the region. From the south, warm, humid air pushes up from the Gulf of Mexico, while at the same time cold, dry air sweeps down from the Arctic.

During the lazy days of summer, the cooler air blowing in from the Canadian northwest influences the weather in the northern lakes. As this occurs, warm air arriving from the Gulf of Mexico affects the southern reaches of the Great Lakes. This peaceful coexistence of air masses allows for calm water and pleasant days.

By fall, rapid movement of air masses from both north and south vie for dominance. This clash of fronts produces high winds and severe weather. It was during one such autumn storm in 1975 that the *Edmund Fitzgerald*, a modern freighter, was lost off Whitefish Point in Lake Superior.

In winter, the lakes are influenced by three air masses. These weather features are the occasional warm front blowing up from the Gulf of Mexico, the freezing tendrils of Arctic air reaching their long fingers south, and an additional air mass, known as an Alberta Clipper, driven in from Canada's Pacific coast.

The Arctic air, known as an "Arctic blast" by those living in the Great Lakes region, arrives over the lakes as a dry air mass. Upon reaching water, this air picks up moisture. As a consequence, the leeward shores of the lakes may receive relatively little precipitation, while the windward sides may be buried under a heavy layer of snow. This phenomenon is referred to by meteorologists as "lake-effect snow."

The region's severe cold occasionally causes Lake Erie to freeze. The shallowest of the five Great Lakes (with an average depth of 62 feet), Erie is the only one to commonly experience this ice cover. As a consequence, cars and trucks often drive between the mainland and islands or venture out for a day of ice fishing. The bottom of the lake is littered with vehicles and equipment left behind by foolhardy adventurers who misjudged the strength of the ice and the suddenness of the spring thaw.

Spring, like fall in the Great Lakes, is a time of overcast days and severe thunderstorms. As in autumn, this is brought about by rapidly contending air masses. The warm Gulf air is the hammer to the Arctic's anvil. In between are the lakes, which can be subjected to fierce beatings as these forces converge.

As recently as the early twentieth century, some captains would sail in the treacherous months in hopes of getting their cargo to market and reaping a profit. This was certainly the case with the *Rouse Simmons*, famous as the "Christmas Tree Ship," which sank off Sheboygan, Wisconsin, with a load of fir trees in November 1912 while en route to Milwaukee. Even today, ice-jammed harbors and severe weather force a mariner to pay heed to the seasonal variability in weather.

Such weather can produce waves of 30 feet or more. One can easily imagine the thoughts and fears of the early sailors as their schooners or tugs slipped into a deep trough while mountains of roiling water loomed off port and starboard. Early sailors and passengers could not rely on radar, satellite imagery, or marine weather forecasts. Theirs was an uncertain world. It was, and still is, common for vessels to leave port during the morning hours and in fine weather, only to be subjected to gale-force winds by mid-afternoon. Even with today's technological advances, it is possible for a vessel to succumb to the fury of a lake storm.

Gradually, with the advent of shipbuilding technology and improved weather forecasting techniques, wrecks have declined in number.

Early well-known Great Lakes storms include one in November 1842 that led to 20 wrecks on the Canadian side of Lake Erie. This was followed by another nasty blow five years later. But such damage pales in comparison to that caused by the gale that blew across the Great Lakes basin for four days in November 1867. This storm was responsible for at least 97 wrecks!

One of the worst blows to strike Lake Michigan was the Alpena Storm of October 16, 1880. The storm was named for the wooden side-wheeler *Alpena*, which went down near Holland, Michigan. The last known sighting of the passenger boat, which carried between 60 and 101 people at the time, was off Racine, Wisconsin. Wreckage washed up along the Michigan shoreline for at least four years, yet the *Alpena*'s final resting-place remains a mystery.

The Wisconsin side of Lake Michigan was subjected to a merciless beating during the Alpena Storm. When the schooner *Josephine Lawrence* went ashore at Baileys Harbor, the captain, his wife, and their son barely made it to safety. Other losses include two scows that broke free of their tug and washed up near Algoma. Farther south, near Two Rivers, a steam barge foundered in shallow water.

Other wrecks included the small two-masted schooner *Ebeneezer*, which ran ashore at Mud Bay near Baileys Harbor. At Jacksonport, not far from where the *Ebeneezer* grounded, the schooner *Perry Hannah* stranded close to the piers. The *Hannah*'s cargo of hemlock ties was recovered.

Two more schooners and a bark were destroyed that day. The two-masted schooner *Peoria*, carrying a load of lumber, was wrecked near Baileys Harbor, in the vicinity of the *Josephine Lawrence* and *Ebeneezer*. The 237-gross-ton *Reciprocity*, 124 feet in length with a beam of 27 feet, struck bottom at Stoney Creek near Algoma. The crew lowered the ship's yawl and reached shore safely.

The other states bordering Lake Michigan faired substantially better. Indiana escaped relatively unharmed, while the only recorded loss for Illinois was the schooner *David A. Wells*, which went down with a load of iron ore and eight crew.

Despite suffering fewer wrecks than Wisconsin, Michigan accounts for nearly all of the lives lost during the Alpena Storm. At least fourteen crew members or passengers surrendered their lives to the lake that day around Wisconsin and Illinois, but as many as another 100 may have died when the *Alpena* disappeared with all hands.

The final loss that day was the *Two Friends,* a three-masted bark built in 1873 by McDermond at Port Burwell, Ontario. Carrying a load of salt, the *Two*

Friends struck a reef just north of the Door Peninsula. The crew found refuge in the rigging until they were rescued. The ship was salvaged in 1881 and saw later use as a schooner until retiring from service as the steamer *Pewaukee*.

Although most lake storms occur in autumn, spring weather can also provide a nasty turn. This was the case with the gale of May 1894. By the time this front was finished with the Great Lakes, 27 lives and at least 37 boats were lost.

The year 1905 was particularly bad for autumn storms on the Great Lakes. The huge storm that laid the region waste was two smaller storms, with the first cold front striking on November 19 and the second on the following day and 48 hours. Twenty-eight vessels were lost in these three days. The region had no sooner recovered when it was blasted by another blow on November 28. Thirty vessels were wrecked in Lake Superior alone. Fortunately, the shorelines of Lake Michigan were relatively untouched.

While the Alpena Storm is considered to be the most damaging gale to strike Lake Michigan, it is the Big Storm of 1913 that is regarded as the worst, in terms of sheer power and destruction, to lash the Great Lakes.

Friday evening, November 9, saw a strong wind blowing across Canada toward the western edge of Lake Superior, with snow showers so heavy that whiteout conditions blanketed the region. By Saturday the wind was tearing at Lake Superior with speeds of up to 68 miles per hour. Any vessel on the lake headed for shelter, while those already docked in port remained at their berths.

The first boat to fall victim to the storm was the steam propeller *Louisiana,* 267 feet long, with a beam of 40 feet and a displacement of 1,929 gross tons. A wood vessel, the *Louisiana* was running under steam power as it set out from Milwaukee for Escanaba, Michigan, to pick up a load of iron ore. When the steamer ran into the Big Storm, it desperately sought shelter, finally blowing ashore on Washington Island at about 2 a.m. on November 10. Adding to the trials of the crew, fire was discovered in the hold. Despite the crew's efforts, the fire raged out of control and the *Louisiana* was abandoned. All seventeen crew members safely reached the island.

The *Louisiana* was not the only boat to wreck near Washington Island. The following day, the two-masted schooner barge *Halstead* foundered, taking the crew to its grave. Built as a three-masted schooner, the *Halstead* was 40 years old at the time of its destruction.

The Big Storm is aptly named. By the time the winds died down on the eleventh, 19 boats were lost and 52 were damaged. The human toll was 248 sailors dead, of whom 186 were from Cleveland. For 16 hours, the average wind speed was 60 miles per hour, with towering waves. The blinding snows and raging winds knocked out communications, rail service, and lights across the region. The hardest hit lakes were Huron and Erie, where shoreline communities were buried beneath a blanket of snow. The Big Storm was truly the storm of storms.

One of the Big Storm's enduring mysteries involves the *Charles S. Price*. The *Price* was a modern wood freighter completed in 1910 by American Ship Building in Lorain, Ohio; it was built strongly enough that everyone felt it could withstand anything nature might throw. The *Price* capsized on Saturday, November 10, 1913, in Lake Huron, with 28 on board. When discovered, the freighter had turned upside down, hiding the vessel's name from view. Divers discovered the ship's identity before the *Price* sank days later.

What makes this story so unusual is the fact that crew members of the *Price* were discovered wearing life preservers from the steel freighter *Regina*, another ship lost in the Big Storm. It would appear as though some of the crew of the *Price* were taken on board the *Regina*, which carried a crew of 20, before the *Regina* sank. But how was this possible in such conditions? A theory at the time maintained that the two vessels collided in blinding snow. As the facts came in, this was ruled out. Not only had the *Regina* foundered in southern Lake Huron, approximately 15 miles from the *Price*'s resting place, which was closer to the Port Gratiot lighthouse, but the *Price*'s hull betrayed no evidence of damage indicating a collision. This story is one of many tales that haunts the Great Lakes.

This was not the last of the region's great storms. There was the Armistice Day Storm of 1940, with winds of up to 100 miles per hour. By the time the November 11 had passed, more than 70 men had died. Two freighters, the *William B. Davock* and the *Anna C. Minch*, both foundered near Pentwater, Michigan, taking with them their crews. Joining them was the fishing tug *Indian*, which foundered off South Haven with five on board.

More recently, there was the storm called the Witch of November, which claimed the *Edmund Fitzgerald* in November of 1975.

OTHER WEATHER HAZARDS

While storms have caused their havoc on the lakes, other weather-related phenomena have contributed to numerous disasters. Heavy fog has resulted in boats driving up on shore or played a role in collisions, often with loss of life.

Fires along the coasts have also played a part in the destruction of many vessels. Some forest fires, such as the great Peshtigo Fire of October 8, 1871, produced so much smoke that boats were unable to find their way in the haze. Burning embers, caught by the wind, reportedly started fires among the sails. The Peshtigo Fire destroyed more than one million acres and killed four times as many people as the Chicago Fire, which occurred the same day. Despite being less destructive, the Chicago conflagration is more well known.

Through the years, newspaper reports and other documents often neglected to mention the contribution of foul weather to the destruction of many vessels. Stories of founderings and capsizings were rather sparsely provided in the local news, and the fact that these were caused by driving rain, blinding snow, heavy fog, high winds, and rough seas is often passed over. Despite a lack of comprehensive wreck descriptions, at least half of all of Lake Michigan's shipwrecks stem from poor weather. It is more likely that two-thirds to three-quarters of all shipwrecks on Lake Michigan are partly or entirely the consequence of nature's fury.

WHEN DO WRECKS OCCUR?

Not surprisingly, the worst seasons for destructive storms are late summer and autumn. The peak month, as those who live along the lakes realize, is November. By winter, modern freighters are often in port for overhaul, where they await spring. Until the first quarter of the twentieth century, schooners and steamers would sometimes risk sailing during this dangerous time. After all, there was money to be made. But it came at a great price: in cargo, ships, and human lives. It was an unforgiving trade during an unforgiving season, but the promise of profit was often enough to undertake such risks.

Despite these occasional winter ventures, most ships remained in harbor. As an obvious consequence, there were relatively few wrecks during January and February. In April and May, modern freighters and the schooners of old resumed work. This period also coincides with changing air patterns in the region. It is a time of renewed shipping and violent storms, reflected in the number of shipwrecks during these two months.

Summer is a period of calmer weather and smoother water, of relative peace from the storms of spring and autumn. And so it is the busiest shipping season of the year. But summer is all too brief and before long the gales return, leaving in their wake a history of battered wrecks and lost lives.

Although severe storms, sudden squalls, driving rain, and blinding snow continue throughout the Great Lakes today, the losses are no longer as terrible as they once were. While the beautiful lines that are the hallmark of the age of sail no longer grace the lakescape, the steel freighters of today have proven significantly more capable of handling the capricious nature of the Great Lakes.

PERCENTAGE OF SHIPWRECKS ON LAKE MICHIGAN BY MONTH

MONTH	PERCENTAGE OF SHIPWRECKS
January	0.74 %
February	0.20 %
March	1.75 %
April	5.74 %
May	7.29 %
June	4.72 %
July	6.01 %
August	7.15 %
September	13.77 %
October	21.46 %
November	24.83 %
December	6.34 %

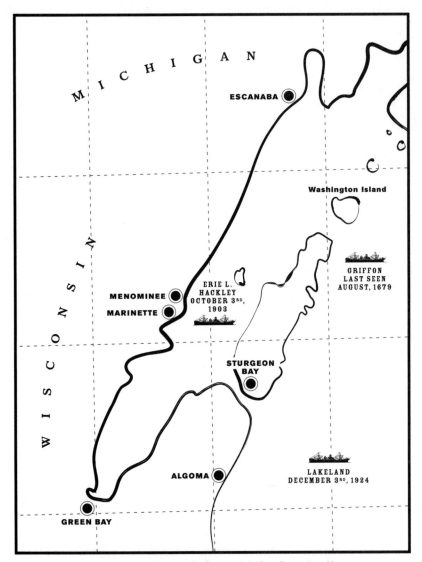

Northern Wisconsin shoreline from Kewaunee and the Door Peninsula to Marinette.
—*Courtesy of the National Oceanographic and Atmospheric Administration*

CHAPTER

4

NORTHERN WISCONSIN

The shape of Wisconsin resembles a glove, with the Door Peninsula serving as the thumb that extends to grip the waters of Lake Michigan. Nestled in the crook between thumb and forefinger is the port city of Green Bay, named for the stretch of water between the Door Peninsula and the rest of Wisconsin. For anyone who has ever viewed the bay in calm weather, it is aptly named.

The waters from Kewaunee up and around Washington Island then back down to Green Bay and toward Marinette are littered with rocks, shoals, and battered wrecks. The coastline often rises from the lake with sudden cliffs that can catch a vessel off guard in bad weather. These granite bluffs and underwater hazards, plus unpredictable wave action, have led to the wrecking of countless vessels of all sizes.

Long before the coming of the Europeans, local Indians knew the six-mile expanse of water between the Door Peninsula and Washington Island. It was the Native Americans who gave this place its name—Death's Door. The French adopted the name and referred to this treacherous stretch of water as *Porte des Mort*. Strong currents and waves have claimed everything from Indian canoes to schooners and steamers.

Possibly the first vessel to be lost in Death's Door Passage, indeed in Lake Michigan, was the French bark *Griffon,* which was last observed heading through the passage during a storm. Whether or not the *Griffon* met its fate in Death's Door is a matter of speculation.

I THE GRIFFON

The first decked vessel to be lost to the Great Lakes was the *Frontenac*, a French brig built for the fur trade and exploration. Built in 1678, the *Frontenac* was destroyed by a storm a year later at Cape Enrage, near the Niagara River. The second wreck of a decked ship in the lakes, and the first in the Upper Lakes, was the *Griffon*. Ironically, the *Griffon* was built by the same man responsible for the construction of the *Frontenac*, Rene Robert Cavalier, also known as Sieur de La Salle.

La Salle was the sort of man of whom the history paints a mixed portrait. He can best be described as both adventurous and exceedingly stubborn. In the end, it was these two qualities that led to his downfall.

Born in Rouen, France, in 1643, La Salle entered the Jesuit novitiate as a youth. By the time he was 23, La Salle had abandoned the religious life and traveled to Canada, where he began to make a name for himself. Whether the decision to leave the clergy was La Salle's is open to debate. Another version states that he was released for reasons of "mental instability." In 1673, nine years after leaving France, La Salle became commander of Fort Frontenac at Kingston, Ontario. This commission was granted by order of Count Frontenac, the Governor of New France.

An ambitious individual, La Salle became a member of the French nobility, expanding his interests in the New World through trade and the establishment of a series of forts. After the destruction of the *Frontenac*, LaSalle ordered a new vessel built.

The ship was *Le Griffon*, or simply *Griffon*. Construction began on January 22, 1679, at the mouth of the Niagara River by Henri de Tonti, a LaSalle aide. The vessel was named after the mythological beast, half eagle and half lion, that appears in the Frontenac coat of arms. The vessel was thought to be more than 60 feet long, weighing between 40 and 60 tons, and was equipped with five small cannon.

In August 1679, La Salle led an expedition across the Great Lakes in the newly finished *Griffon*. The journey took him and his crew through the Straits of Mackinac, between Michigan's Upper and Lower Peninsulas, arriving in Green Bay.

On board was Father Louis Hennepin, a Franciscan friar who maintained a journal of La Salle's expeditions. Father Hennepin's chronicles provide insight into the early years of European exploration and settlement in North America. Despite the tremendous amount of information provided by Father Hennepin, modern historians suspect that a great deal of his accuracy and detail were mixed with a flair for overstatement.

There has been a lot of conjecture about the disappearance of the *Griffon*. What little is known is that La Salle, Hennepin, and a contingent of men remained in Green Bay while the ship set off for the Straits of Mackinac in September 1679 under the command of Captain Luc Dare. The *Griffon*, loaded with furs that La Salle hoped would help pay off his debts, was last seen as it sailed into the teeth of a storm in Death's Door.

In its wake, the *Griffon* has left one of the most enduring Lost Dutchman legends on the Great Lakes. People have sought the remains of the *Griffon* for decades, but the circumstances surrounding the bark's loss, as well as the vessel's resting place, remain a mystery.

The fate of the *Griffon* is haunted by supposition. Various conclusions have been drawn as to its last hours. Some claim that the crew mutinied, while others maintain that a storm claimed ship and crew. A report written in 1680 by a Jesuit priest, Father La Potherie, states that the vessel was destroyed by Odawa Indians.

The location of the *Griffon* is unknown. Claims as to the bark's discovery have been made since the first settlers moved into the Great Lakes area. With advances in science, it is possible to more accurately date the remains of wrecked ships. As a consequence, wreckage found at Mississagi Passage near Manitoulin Island on Lake Huron and in Georgian Bay near Tobermory, Ontario, has been ruled out as being the *Griffon*. Tests have confirmed that these wrecks occurred much later than the *Griffon*'s first, and final, voyage.

Another eerie aspect of its disappearance involved Captain Luc Dare. Apparently, he was a huge man, and a massive skull later found in a cave near one of the sites where the *Griffon* is assumed to have been lost was thought to be his. The skull was subsequently lost, supposedly by being knocked off a pier.

Eventually, La Salle was given the task of exploring and colonizing between the Great Lakes and the Gulf of Mexico. Searching by sea for the Mississippi River in 1684, but unable to find the waterway's outlet to the ocean, La Salle landed in Texas. Attempting to reach the Mississippi River by going across the untamed wilderness, La Salle and his men forged ahead on three separate occasions. In the end, his men mutinied and he was murdered.

Less than a century later, the French and Indian War changed the political and social landscape of the eastern United States. In 1763, France lost a huge tract of land to the British, who gained not only territory but also the fruits of French exploration. History was repeated the following decade, only this time it was to be the citizens of the United States who rose up to acquire their right to nationhood from England.

Despite all that France lost in the mid-eighteenth century, the maps, journals, accounts, and histories, as well as the *Griffon*, mark this passage in a nation's history.

II THE ERIE L. HACKLEY

The largest loss of life along northern Wisconsin's Lake Michigan coast up to 1903 was attributed to the sinking of the *Erie L. Hackley*. The *Hackley,* a wood propeller steamer built in 1882 by J. Arnold of Muskegon Michigan, was 79 feet long, with a 17-foot beam, and 5 feet of depth. Total, the boat was 20 net tons and 55 gross tons burden and was assigned an official number of 135615. The vessel's original owner was Seth Lee of Muskegon and the *Directory of Marine Interests of the Great Lakes* for 1884 indicates that the *Hackley* was used as a yacht. This was a very different purpose than the one for which the steamer was eventually destined.

In the spring of 1903, the *Hackley* was purchased for $3,000 by Captain Joseph Vorous, Henry Robertoy, Orin Bowin, and Edgar Thorp. As a result of this purchase, the *Erie L. Hackley* became part of the recently formed Fish Creek Transportation Company; a product of Captain Vorous' efforts. Nicknamed the *Egg Harbor Express,* the *Erie L. Hackley* ferried passengers and freight along a route from Sturgeon Bay to Marinette and Menominee, back across Green Bay to Egg Harbor and Fish Creek, and then on to Washington Island. Other stops included Ephraim, Sister Bay, and Ellison Bay.

This was a new job for the 21-year-old *Hackley* and one it was marked by a lack of distinction. In early September 1903, the *Hackley* damaged the shaft coupling for its propeller. Two weeks later the steamer's boiler gave out near Menominee, and yet another week later saw the *Hackley* stranded at its dock due to high winds.

At 5:45 p.m. on October 3, the *Hackley* set off from Menominee to Egg Harbor. On board were Captain Vorous and Orin Bowin, who served as the steamer's engineer. The trip nearly included Captain Vorous' sister, but the captain felt uneasy about this run and was unwilling to allow his sister passage. This decision probably saved the woman's life.

Only fifteen minutes after departing Menominee, the eight crew members and eleven passengers of the *Hackley* were in a desperate fight for their lives. A sudden storm blew up, driving into the *Hackley* with such savagery that it was later termed a tornado.

Making a run for Green Island, Captain Vorous intended to find shelter on the lee side of the island. East of Green Island, disaster struck: The cabin was ripped from the deck. What happened next occurred so quickly that there was no time for anyone to find a life preserver. Battered by the high winds and rough water, the *Erie L. Hackley* made straight for the bottom of Green Bay.

Abandoned by their boat to the angry waters of Lake Michigan, the passengers and crew desperately clung to whatever wreckage they could find. It wasn't until later on the morning of October 4 that the steamer *Sheboygan*, under the command of Captain Asa Johnson, chanced by and rescued eight people. Eleven others were not so fortunate. Included in this number were two of the *Hackley*'s owners, Captain Vorous and Henry Robertoy. Orin Bowin, the engineer, reached land safely.

A pair of tugboats, the *Leona R.* and *Pilgrim*, searched for the wreck of the *Erie L. Hackley* by using a chain strung between the two vessels. Although it was determined that the remains of the *Hackley* had, in fact, been found, the depth at which the wreck lay precluded plans to dive on the steamer. For this reason, the bodies of eight of those lost in the incident were not recovered at that time.

This decision to abandon the *Erie L. Hackley* and the bodies of those lost to Lake Michigan was made in December, the same month that a board of inquiry determined that the condition of the *Hackley* was not at fault. Given the suddenness and savagery of the storm, the cause of the *Hackley*'s destruction was ruled a tornado.

Even though it was thought that the *Leona R.* and *Pilgrim* had located the wreck, the remains of the *Erie L. Hackley* remained lost for another 77 years, until divers located the steamer in June of 1980. The following year, the skeletal remains of two people were discovered and brought to the surface. This was part of a failed attempt to raise the *Hackley*.

Rather than bury the remains, the bodies languished in a Sturgeon Bay mortuary due to a lack of funds for internment. No relatives could be found to claim the two unidentifiable bodies and no one was willing to pay for a burial. Furthermore, due to the law, the remains could not be returned to the lake, since this was considered "polluting." Finally, five years later, a group of individuals gave their time and efforts to the forgotten victims of the *Hackley*.

On May 10, 1986, an 1898 horse-drawn hearse brought the two victims of the *Erie L. Hackley* to a site donated by the Bayside Cemetery Association. The bodies were interred in a handmade oak coffin and rest beneath the solitude of encircling pines.

III THE LAKELAND

When the Globe Iron Works of Cleveland launched the *Cambria* in 1887, it was considered the largest freighter then working the lakes. The *Cambria* was 280 feet overall in length, was 40 feet in beam, and had a draft of 20 feet. In addition, the *Cambria* was a grand 1,878 gross tons burden. Built with a steel hull and fitted with three masts, the *Cambria* was a transition between old and new. The steel hull reflected the shape of things to come, but the auxiliary masts indicated a reluctance to part with tried and true methods. Despite this hesitancy, the *Cambria* was the first freighter on the Great Lakes outfitted with a triple-expansion engine.

The *Cambria* went through three owners as a freighter, during which time it set several cargo records. The first owner was the Mutual Transportation Company, based in Escanaba. The *Cambria* was subsequently managed by the Hanna firm and the Pittsburgh Steamship Fleet.

The Thomson Transportation Company eventually acquired the *Cambria*. While under Thomson ownership, the vessel underwent several substantial changes. Its name was changed to *Lakeland*, and the vessel was converted from a freighter to a handsome passenger and freight steamer in 1901. The *Lakeland*'s home port while in the employ of Thomson Transportation was Port Huron, Michigan, on Lake Huron.

The long black hull and white cabins made the ship's outline a distinct and impressive sight on the lakes. In 1924, after the summer passenger season was long over, the *Lakeland,* under the command of Captain John T. McNeely, arrived in Chicago with a cargo of new automobiles. The freight was unloaded and the *Lakeland* headed back into Lake Michigan for Detroit on December 2.

Given the severity and unexpected nature of storms during late autumn, Captain McNeely wisely kept the western coast of Lake Michigan in sight. Traveling light, the crew of the *Lakeland* was treated to an uncomfortable journey, which would not have been the case had the freighter been carrying cargo and riding lower in the water.

By evening, Captain McNeely hove to inside the Sturgeon Bay canal. Sheltering in the canal that Tuesday night, the *Lakeland* set off again the following morning. No sooner had it resumed the voyage to Detroit than it was discovered that the freighter was leaking heavily. By now the ship was ten miles from the Sturgeon Bay canal.

The Lakeland.—*Courtesy of the Wisconsin Maritime Museum*

Wisely, Captain McNeely turned the *Lakeland* around and ordered the pumps into action. When it was realized that ship and crew would never reach the Sturgeon Bay canal, an SOS was issued. Only essential members of the crew were kept on board. The rest entered the lifeboats, which were promptly lowered.

The car ferry *Ann Arbor No. 6*, making its regular run between Ludington and Manitowoc, was the first boat on the scene. A Coast Guard cutter out of Sturgeon Bay joined the rescue efforts. By this point the *Lakeland* was listing 45 degrees to port. Captain Robert Anderson, commanding the crew of the cutter, ordered the remaining crew of the *Lakeland* to abandon ship. They were safely taken aboard the *Ann Arbor*.

Half an hour after the last of the 26 crew members had abandoned the *Lakeland,* the battered vessel began its descent, stern first, into 35 fathoms of water. The vessel's death throes were apparent to the survivors. As the *Lakeland* sank, its lights flickered beneath the waves. Added to this farewell were the muffled explosions of escaping air. Portions of the *Lakeland*'s hatch covers and cabins were blown 40 feet into the air as it disappeared.

This was not the end of the *Lakeland* affair, however. Sixteen insurance companies sued its owners in federal court in Cleveland, Ohio. At stake was the issue of whether the *Lakeland,* worth $500,000 and insured for $450,000, had been deliberately scuttled. If this proved to be the case, the insurance companies would not be liable to the Thomson Transportation Company for the insured value.

There was strong evidence to suggest wrongdoing. Professional saltwater divers were brought in. Diving on the wreck, they discovered two interesting facts. The first was that the *Lakeland* lay on a ledge with the forward third of the boat resting over deep water. The more important finding, and the only one of interest to the jury, was the fact that the seacocks were open.

The case was tried in court, but the jury remained deadlocked and the matter was eventually dropped. In a second trial, the insurance companies accused Thomson Transportation and the *Lakeland*'s officers of deliberately scuttling the boat. The shipping firm denied knowledge of criminal activity and may have attempted to shift the burden of proof to the boat's officers.

The argument offered by Thomson Transportation was simple. The company claimed to have no knowledge of deliberate wrongdoing and, therefore, was not at fault. In addition, any illegal action on the part of the boat's officers, without the knowledge of their employers, was an equally noncontentious issue before the law. In either instance, the *Lakeland* was covered by insurance. In any event, the case could not be proved one way or the other, and Thomson was exonerated.

Today, the *Lakeland* lies in 210 feet of water approximately seven miles east of the Sturgeon Bay canal. The cause of its loss may never be known.

OTHER SIGNIFICANT WRECKS

Long before the French arrived in northern Wisconsin, Potawatomi Indians forced the Cape Indians from the northern end of what is now known as the Door Peninsula. The Cape Indians found refuge on Detroit Island in Death's Door but were intent on reclaiming their original lands. The Cape Indians sent two braves to their former grounds with instructions to light a fire when the time to attack the Potawatomi was right. The two Cape Indians were captured and forced to reveal their plans. On a night when storm clouds obscured the moon and stars, the Potawatomi lit a bonfire. The Cape Indians, mistakenly believing that their spies had set the signal, crossed Death's Door. With a storm front advancing, the waters were rough and a number of canoes capsized. Tossed into the violent surf, some of the Cape Indians drowned. The surviving Cape Indians, on reaching shore, were quickly dispatched by the waiting Potawatomi, thus earning the waters at the tip of the Door Peninsula the name "Door of Death." Based on this story, the Wisconsin State legislature gave Door County its name in 1851. This Indian tale serves as another example of how treacherous Door Peninsula waters can be.

One of the very first casualties in this area was the *Toledo*, a brig that may also hold the honor of being the very first wreck at Ahnapee, or present-day

Algoma. The *Toledo* became stranded at the mouth of the Wolf River. Such was the desolate nature of the region at the time that the *Toledo* was paid a visit by the only settler in the area, Bradford White, who rendered what assistance he could to the crew.

The first *known* vessel lost in Death's Door was the *Leland*, a schooner that stranded on shore in 1855. Later that same year the schooner *Windham*, carrying a load of lumber, stranded close to where the *Leland* went aground. The *Windham* was last observed being battered by wave action. The following year, the two-masted schooner *Maria Hilliard* was destroyed after stranding on yet another bar in Death's Door.

Death's Door would claim another victim before the 1850s came to a close. On June 7, 1859, the double-masted brig *Columbia* entered Death's Door in the face of driving rain blowing in from the north. The *Columbia*'s captain, Jacob Hansen, found temporary refuge at Plum Island, but the rain soon turned to snow. Striking back into the storm, the boat was soon in danger of washing ashore. In desperation, Hansen ordered the first anchor dropped, but the iron broke and the anchor was lost. The second anchor fared no better, disappearing beneath the waves. When the 177-ton *Columbia* finally struck shore, it did so close enough to the trees that the entire crew was able to clamber with near impunity from the rigging into the branches and safety. A tug was sent five days later to salvage the *Columbia,* but by this time a second storm had destroyed the craft. The *Columbia* is remembered as being the vessel that brought out the first load of copper from Lake Superior's Keweenaw Peninsula and the first shipment of iron ore from the Superior fields. The *Columbia* also carried the first locomotive to Michigan's Upper Peninsula, which was delivered to Marquette in 1857.

GREEN BAY

While the original Indian name for Green Bay is uncertain, the early French referred to this beautiful expanse of water as *Baye des Puans* or the Bay of Bad Odors. The fur town and trading center of Green Bay was simply known as *La Baye*. French explorers and missionaries were the first Europeans to explore the area, and their cultural imprints are evident today. They came seeking a new route to the Orient or the opportunity to convert the local inhabitants to Christianity. As commerce blossomed throughout the lake region, voyageurs and trappers consorted with Native American women and fathered children with them. Thus, a Metis society developed in the region.[1]

[1] The word metis is French in origin and means of mixed blood.

While the eastern half of the new country was experiencing rapid growth and development, the *Baye des Puans* remained little affected. This peaceful, even idyllic life was drastically altered 20 years later. In 1824, the U.S. government supplied *La Baye* with the Honorable James Doty, a circuit court judge. No sooner had he settled into his new role than Doty set about charging the town's male inhabitants with fornication and adultery for living outside the bounds of legally recognized marriage with Native American women. Apparently, the Indian customs pertaining to cohabitation and marriage were too loose for Doty's strict views. A culture established nearly 200 years in the past was irrevocably changed.

It was 30 years after Judge Doty took up residence in Green Bay that tragedy struck a family named Perrigo. On November 17, 1854, the *Little Sarah*, a schooner en route from Big Suamico to Oconto, experienced a stiff wind blowing in from the northwest. On board the *Little Sarah* were Danforth Perrigo, his wife, and two or three children who were moving to Oconto, Wisconsin. The Perrigo's family possessions amounted to some furniture, clothing, and a box of carpenter's tools. At about 2:30 p.m., the *Little Sarah*, carrying a load of freight and 15 passengers, capsized in the icy waters of Green Bay. The crew and passengers clung to the vessel's side until a local fisherman was able to sail the one and a half miles between the *Little Sarah* and shore. It was during this wait that one of the young Perrigo girls lost her grip on the hull and drowned. The survivors reached safety, but the Perrigo family, in addition to losing a daughter, also lost their possessions. It was a cruel way to begin a new life in Oconto. The remains of the *Little Sarah* were later found beached and picked over by thieves.

LATE NINETEENTH-CENTURY WRECKS

By 1869, the schooner was the undisputed king of the lakes. Although many other types of vessels were operating at that time, including the occasional bark, it was the schooner that was the most common sight on the horizon. Early on July 3, 1869, the schooner *J. G. McCullough*, bound for Kenosha from Escanaba with a load of pig iron, collided with the bark *Pensaukee* off Clay Banks. The blow was a fatal one for the six-year-old *McCullough*. The foremast and mainmast broke, shattering the lifeboat and a cabin. The *McCullough* could have survived this damage, but water was streaming into the hold. As luck would have it, the watch was in the middle of being changed and the entire crew was on deck. The crew safely reached the *Pensaukee* before the *J. G. McCullough* sank twenty minutes later in 200 feet of water.

Before 1869 was out, six more vessels were fated to meet their end in these waters. Interestingly, nearly all wrecked not far from the *McCullough*. The schooner *Gray Eagle* followed 14 days after the *McCullough*, stranding at Whitefish Bay. Of the five remaining boats, three were destroyed at Bailey's Harbor. The *Ocean Wave*, a two-masted scow schooner carrying a load of building stone, struck some debris, and quickly foundered about 15 miles southeast of Bailey's Harbor. The crew managed to launch the lifeboat before the *Ocean Wave* sank in 360 feet of water.

The 93-foot schooner *Fairfield*, traveling light, sank in a storm on September 29. Having sunk near the Bailey's Harbor light, the *Fairfield* was quickly joined by the schooners *Magic* and *Blue Bell*. These boats were salvaged, but the *Fairfield* was abandoned and quickly broke up.

The month prior to the destruction of the *Fairfield*, the schooner *Art Palace* stranded during a storm at Green Bay. The *Art Palace* was an example of the sometimes unexpected cargoes carried by lake boats. The *Art Palace* was nothing less than a brothel carrying a cargo of prostitutes. All employees, referred to as "model artists," as well as the crew, were able to safely reach land.

If ever there were a ship prone to misfortune, it would have to be the scow schooner *Ella Doak*. The *Ella Doak* was also known, somewhat unkindly, as the *Queen of the Beach*. In September 1872, the *Ella Doak* capsized prior to stranding on the beach at Port Washington. Two months later, the *Ella Doak* drove up on the beach at Algoma. The *Ella Doak* was quickly worked loose and continued on its way to Kewaunee, whereupon the schooner ran into the pier. The next two years saw the *Ella Doak* run ashore at South Manitou Island in 1873 and Sheboygan in 1874. The final blow to the luckless schooner was dealt on August 5, 1875. Caught by a storm, the *Ella Doak* was tossed ashore at Hedgehog Harbor, which overlooks Plum Island from the very tip of Door County. As is true with many place names around Lake Michigan, Hedgehog Harbor was eventually renamed. Today, it is known as Gills Rock. Efforts to salvage the scow schooner were begun but abandoned. The *Ella Doak* became another Wisconsin wreck.

Perhaps one of the best descriptions of how treacherous and difficult it is to navigate the waters of Death's Door was noted by the keeper of the Pilot Island lighthouse, who stated that eight large schooners stranded or wrecked in the area in a period of one week during the autumn of 1872.

Almost ten years after the *McCullough-Pensaukee* incident, another early morning collision cost yet another boat its life. This time it was the *Daniel Lyons*, which was lost due east of Foscoro, a community north of Algoma. The *Lyons*, a schooner with a cargo of wheat, was struck on the starboard side by the schooner *Kate Gillet*. The blow was strong enough for the *Kate Gillet* to plough halfway through the *Lyons*. After the two vessels were pried apart, the *Lyons* sank immediately in about 110 feet of water. Similar to the *McCullough*, all of the crew of the *Lyons* reached the safety of the vessel responsible for the accident.

Of the *William Livingstone, Jr.* it can be truly said that it was a work of art. Certainly, the *Livingstone* was one of the finest displays of the shipbuilders' craft ever seen on the lakes. Graceful and elegant, its lines suggested a grander purpose than its role as a tug. No expense was spared in the *Livingstone*'s construction. By the time the tug was launched, the *Livingstone* was worth $30,500. Stout oak imported from Canada was used in the construction of the hull, while amenities in the staterooms included such features as fine carpeting, marble wash stands, and steam heat. The *Chicago Tribune* went so far as to claim that the *William Livingstone, Jr.* was the fastest and most powerful tug on the lakes.

Sadly, the *Livingstone* was a mere youth of six when it sank off the shores of Cana Island in about 250 feet of water on October 4, 1880. Nor did the *Livingstone*'s end come easily. In fact, the crew's frantic and heroic efforts served to keep the boat afloat until a nearby tug could be hailed.

Around noon, it was discovered that the engine shaft had torn a hole below the waterline. A temporary patch of blankets failed to prevent the lake water from pouring in. The pumps also quit. Finally, as the cold water reached the boilers, the *Livingstone*'s engine went dead. At this point the crew abandoned the boat for the safety of the *Mauntee*, one of two consorts in its care. Shortly after a line was tied between the *William Livingstone, Jr.* and the tug *Favorite*, the *Livingstone* went to the bottom. Its death throes lasted nearly four hours, but not one member of the crew was lost.

October of that year saw a number of wrecks wash ashore or founder in mid-lake. Twelve days after the *Livingstone* sank, the Alpena Storm ravaged the lake-front, taking with it the *Perry Hannah, Josephine Lawrence, Ebeneezer, Reciprocity,* and *Two Friends*. The *Two Friends*, a bark, was the only nonschooner to be wrecked during this savage one-day period.

Either the proximity to land, the brave actions of the local lifesaving crew, assistance from another vessel, or prompt and efficient manning of the lifeboats was usually enough to save most, if not all, of the crew. Despite favorable odds of surviving a wreck, not every accident has been free of tragedy. A tremendous number of lives have been claimed by Lake Michigan, sometimes including all hands.

One such incident involved the *D.A. Van Valkenburg*, a three-masted schooner built in 1866 by Albert Little of Tonawanda, New York.[2] The 539-ton *Van Valkenburg* was laden with a cargo of corn and was en route from Chicago

---

[2] Other sources state that the D.A. Van Valkenburg was a bark.

to Buffalo when the boat sailed into the teeth of a storm on September 15, 1881. The sole survivor, Thomas Breen, claimed that something was wrong with the compass, which may account for the *Van Valkenburg* drifting off course.

At about seven o'clock that evening, the *Van Valkenburg* ran hard aground on the rocks at Whitefish Point, roughly ten miles north of Sturgeon Bay. The crew took to the boat's yawl, but waited for calmer seas before heading to shore. While waiting for their chance to escape the *Van Valkenburg*, all nine crew members were thrown into the lake when the yawl capsized. Breen awoke on shore and wandered into Jacksonport, briefly to the north, where he was helped by townspeople.

In the days to come, the *Van Valkenburg* gave up enough of its cargo to provide many of Jacksonport's citizens with corn for the winter. As for the *Van Valkenburg*, it seems as though the schooner was ill fated to wreck where it did. Only the previous year, the *Van Valkenburg* had been forced ashore during the Alpena Storm at Whitefish Bay, just two miles south of its final resting place.

Although steamers were by now a familiar sight on the Great Lakes, none had yet gone down in Death's Door. The first steamer to accept this dubious honor was the 50-foot *Fawn*. The *Fawn* was a wooden tug loaded with a cargo of lumber. On August 8, 1888, the *Fawn* foundered in Death's Door.

Four years after the loss of the *Fawn* and approximately one hour before midnight on October 27, 1892, the 138-foot schooner *J. C. Gilmore* blew onto Pilot Island. The keeper of the Pilot Island light, Martin Knudsen, attempted to aid the crew. Despite Knudsen's efforts at a quick rescue, the crew waited on board the stricken vessel for the winds to die down and the seas to calm.

The following day the 31-year-old three-masted schooner *A. P. Nichols* ran ashore on Pilot Island, fewer than 100 feet from where the *J. C. Gilmore* sat. By coincidence, both wrecks were also less than 100 feet from the scow schooner *Forest,* which stranded during a storm the previous year. The battered wreck of the *Forest* found employment as a playhouse for the children on the island.

The *A. P. Nichols* had its first brush with disaster during the Great Chicago Fire of 1871. In 1872, the *Nichols* suffered additional damage during a storm in which the schooner was declared lost. Despite being given up in 1872, the *A. P. Nichols* returned to service, only to be heavily damaged a third time after washing ashore in 1888 close to Detour, Michigan. October 28, 1892 would not be as kind to the schooner.

Captain David Clow, Jr. was making for the safety of Plum Island when the shifting winds put the *A. P. Nichols* on a course with Pilot Island. Releasing the 1,400-pound anchor its full length of 600 feet, Captain Clow tried to prevent grounding in the shallow waters of Pilot Island. Unable to find purchase on the lake bottom, the anchor was dragged along by the schooner toward the island.

At 8 p.m., Knudsen, his two assistants, and wife Theresa heard the sound of the *A.P. Nichols* washing ashore. They went outside and sized up the situation. The *Nichols* was being subjected to a tremendous beating and was in danger of breaking up. Knudsen and an assistant went aboard the wreck of the *Forest*, where the lighthouse keeper climbed onto the bow as far as possible. In doing so, Knudsen put his life in considerable danger because one slip from his spray-lashed perch and he would fall between the two vessels, where he would be crushed.

Ignoring his safety, Martin Knudsen helped Captain Clow over to the *Forest*. Following Captain Clow was his 320-pound father, Captain David Clow, Sr. This left six additional crew members, including the female cook, on board the *A.P. Nichols*. These people were helped over one by one.

Due to the severity of the weather, it was two weeks before the crews of the *Gilmore* and *Nichols* could leave Pilot Island and its brave lighthouse keeper. For his selfless actions, Martin Knudsen was awarded a gold medal by the Lifesaving Benevolent Association of New York and a Second Class or Silver Medal by the U.S. Government.

An interesting, almost comical venture involved the *Australasia* en route from Cleveland to Manitowoc. A steam powered vessel, the *Australasia* was abandoned by its crew near Whitefish Bay when a fire was discovered the evening of October 18, 1896. A short while later, the *Australasia* was boarded by crewmembers of the tug *Leathem,* who finished the meal left by the departing crew of the *Australasia.* An attempt to tow the *Australasia* to safety failed as the hawser connecting the two vessels burned through. The *Australasia* was finally abandoned by the crew of the *Leathem,* who then sailed into Jacksonport, where they discovered the crew of the doomed freighter in a rather drunken state. Both crews headed back for the *Australasia,* at which point a fistfight broke out.

The *Australasia,* a wood bulk freighter, was built by Jas. Davidson and was 12 years old at the time of its loss. The cargo of 2,200 tons of soft coal was largely salvaged, as were the boilers, engines, and most equipment.

Two years after the wrecking of the *Australasia,* the wood freighter *Keystone* was making the voyage from Cleveland to Manitowoc with a cargo of coal. The *Keystone,* originally built as a bark in 1866 by Hitchcock and Gibson of Buffalo, now sported a propeller. The propeller was part of the repair work and modifications made to the *Keystone* in 1880 following salvage operations after an 1875 wrecking at Buffalo.

On December 4, 1897, the *Keystone,* under the command of Captain Carelton Graves, went ashore just north of Two Rivers during a raging blizzard. So did the schooner barge *Joseph G. Masten.* The *Keystone* was worked off the shore, but the *Masten* was wrecked. The *Masten* had been under the tow of the steamer *George W. Morley,* which escaped disaster that day only to catch fire and strand herself the following day just off Evanston, Illinois. Despite this series of mishaps, there were no fatalities.

Having wrecked twice, the *Keystone* was now taking its load of coal to Manitowoc so the citizens of this Wisconsin port town could heat their homes. It was still September, well before the harshest days of winter settled over the northern Midwest, but the stockpiles of coal were gradually being built up all around the lakes in expectation of the looming cold weather.

Still under the command of Captain Graves, the *Keystone* passed through the Straits of Mackinac from Lake Huron and entered the waters of Lake Michigan. Either near Waugoschance Point or at Big Summer Island the *Keystone* went ashore and burned to the waterline. Despite the fact that the entire crew escaped the wrecked *Keystone,* the location where the steamer was destroyed has been lost. Helping make this an uncharted loss is the fact that the *Keystone* appears to have been far off course. The few news articles describing the *Keystone* do not satisfactorily shed light on its last location, but at least one newspaper pointed to Big Summer Island.

TWENTIETH-CENTURY DISASTERS

Captain Graves continued serving on the Great Lakes until a storm on April 12, 1907, struck the lumber hooker *Arcadia.* Captain Graves was the pilot on this voyage when the *Arcadia* disappeared off Big Sable Point. It has been surmised that a boiler explosion took the *Arcadia* and its crew of 14 to the bottom of Lake Michigan, but the true cause, as is often the case, was never determined.

In another irony, reminiscent of the *D.A. Van Valkenburg* lost 20 years earlier, the schooner *Peoria* seemed fated to wreck at a predetermined location. During a severe storm on November 10, 1901, the *Peoria* washed ashore at Baileys Harbor near where the vessel had wrecked during the Alpena Storm of 1880. At times the lake seems to possess a flair for the theatric as well as the ironic.

In 1928, four years after the *Lakeland* disaster (recounted earlier in this chapter), the freighter *M.J. Bartelme* became stranded on the southeastern side of Cana Island. The *Bartelme,* built as the *John J. McWilliams* in 1895, was 352 feet in length and 45 feet in beam and was renamed the *Central West* in 1916 before receiving its final name in 1928. This was the same year it grounded with a load of ballast.[3] Traveling from Ashtabula to Milwaukee, the *Bartelme* ran into a thick fog on October 4. Unable to see Cana Island in the gloom, the *Bartelme* grounded on a shoal. What was not destroyed by wave action was eventually salvaged.

---

[3] Other sources state that the M.J. Bartelme carried a cargo of coal.

Earlier in the twentieth century, four schooners, the *Pride, Berwyn, Seaman,* and *Resumption,* were victims of the treacherous waters of Death's Door. There are similarities between the *Berwyn* and the *Seaman.* Both schooners were stranded during storms on November 15, 1908. The *Seaman* was carrying a load of slabs and 3,000 bushels of potatoes when the vessel went ashore on Pilot Island. Sixty years old at the time of its destruction, the *Seaman* is described in David Swayze's book *Shipwreck!* as "the oldest working sailing vessel afloat at the time of her loss."

The *Berwyn,* originally christened the *R. C. Crawford,* followed a brief eight days later. The *Berwyn* was a bulk freight schooner being towed by the steam barge *Walter Vail.* Reports regarding the *Berwyn*'s destruction state that both vessels were caught in either a heavy fog or a sudden gale. They went ashore on the south side of Plum Island. The *Walter Vail* managed to work free, but the *Berwyn* eventually broke up on a reef and was lost.

A large number of vessels were destroyed in the grip of Death's Door, but Door County itself has more than 250 miles of coastline, the most of any county in the United States. Moreover, much of this coastline is treacherous in any weather. Victims claimed by the Door coastline include the *R. J. Hackett,* described earlier as being the first freighter to bear modern lines, and the *Lilly Amiot,* a gas launch destroyed by a horrific explosion.

The *Lilly Amiot* started its career in 1873 as a schooner. Built in Cheboygan, Michigan, the *Lilly Amiot* was constructed with a length of 47 feet, a beam of 12 feet, and a draft of 5 feet. This design was eventually altered to accommodate a modern gas engine, a process that entailed cutting a foot from the *Lily Amiot*'s length and reducing the overall net tonnage. On June 6, 1905, the *Lilly Amiot* was in Ellison Bay with a load of general freight, dynamite, and gasoline. Reports differ as to the nature of the *Lilly Amiot*'s destruction. Some state that the small boat struck a reef and exploded. A more likely account claims that the owner of the *Lilly Amiot* discovered a leak and lit a match to examine it. Fire quickly broke out. Cut loose, the *Lilly Amiot* drifted until an explosion, heard up to 15 miles away, destroyed it. Taken together, the two accounts suggest that the *Lily Amiot* may have struck a reef after first being set adrift in flames. On colliding with the reef, the vessel may have disappeared in a sudden, disintegrating ball of fire.

Even the most famous sailing event on the Great Lakes, the Chicago to Mackinac Race, was not immune to disaster. On July 23, 1911, the sailing yacht *Vencedor* was competing in the race to Mackinac when a storm blew the yacht off course. The vessel wound up on Fisherman Island, where the crew was rescued. The *Vencedor* was not as lucky and was battered to pieces by wave action.

Shortly after World War I, the wood steamer *Frank O'Connor*, laden with 3,000 tons of coal, entered the waters of Lake Michigan via the Straits of Mackinac. The date was September 29, 1919, and the *Frank O'Connor* was bound for the port of Milwaukee.

Originally christened the *City of Naples*, the *O'Connor* and its two sister ships, the *City of Genoa* and the *City of Venice* were built in 1892 by Captain James Davidson in West Bay City, Michigan. The *O'Connor* was 301 feet in length and had a 43-foot beam and a 20-foot depth. It weighed 1,772 net tons and displaced 2,109 gross tons.

At a time when other shipbuilders were struggling to convert their plant and labor forces to producing new steel-hulled vessels, Captain Davidson prudently stuck with what he and his people knew best—wood-hulled boats.

Several years after being in the service of Captain Davidson, the *O'Connor* was sold to the Gilchrist Transportation Line, at which time the deck was raised 18 inches in order to increase the amount of ore the *O'Connor* could carry. Still bearing the name *City of Naples*, the *Frank O'Connor* went through several other owners including Norris & Company, based in Chicago; the Tonawanda Iron and Steel Company of Tonawanda, New York; and finally the O'Connor Transportation Company.

Originally an employee of the Tonawanda Iron and Steel Company, James O'Connor struck out on his own in 1916. Purchasing the *City of Naples*, O'Connor renamed the freighter after his son, Frank. When the United States entered World War I, Frank enlisted and was sent to France to fight the armies of Kaiser Wilhelm. On May 3, 1918, the younger O'Connor was killed in battle.

Almost a year after the war ended and its namesake dead, the steamer *Frank O'Connor* approached the Door Peninsula under the command of Captain William Hayes, the son-in-law of James O'Connor. At 4 p.m., while still east of Cana Island, fire broke out toward the bow.

Responding to the threat, Captain Hayes ordered the *O'Connor* toward land. The freighter never made it. Several miles off of Cana Island, Captain Hayes ordered the seacocks opened and the crew into the lifeboats. By these two actions, Captain Hayes intended to save the crew and as much of the *O'Connor* as possible for eventual salvage. Better to flood the stricken vessel and extinguish the flames than to allow the $30,000 cargo to be destroyed by the fire.

As smoke billowed over the stricken freighter, Oscar Knudson, keeper of the Cana Island light, spied the telltale sign of trouble on the horizon. Knudson and his assistant, Louis Pecon, manned a powerboat and went to aid the crew of the *O'Connor*. Towing the lifeboats to safety, Knudson and Pecon were joined by the Coast Guard, which rendered additional assistance.

Due to the quick actions of Captain Hayes, the crew of the *O'Connor* and the operators of the Cana Island light, there were no casualties. The ship sank in about 70 feet of water, and although a salvage attempt managed to remove roughly 700 tons of coal from the wreck, the effort was abandoned. Today, the *Frank O'Connor* is an attraction for divers.

Even though shipwrecks occurred less often in later years, the occasional accident continued to haunt the region. Other wrecks of the twentieth century include the yacht *Francis IV* in 1927 and the catamaran *Buccaneer* in 1981. Clearly, the lakes remain a power that cannot be taken for granted.

A more recent wreck was the diesel-powered tug *Bridgebuilder X*. The fate of the *Bridgebuilder X* is another example of the mysteries in which the lakes are steeped. Bound for South Fox Island from Sturgeon Bay, the *Bridgebuilder X* simply vanished, taking both crew members. The circumstances surrounding their disappearance, like that of so many others, have yet to be determined.

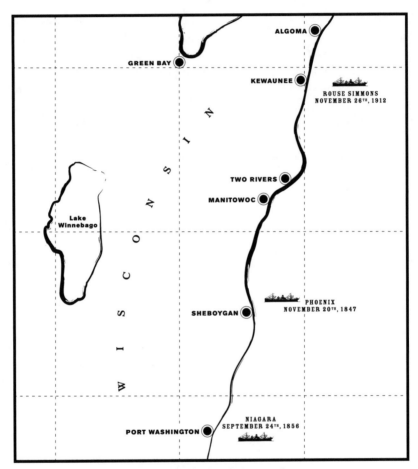

Central Wisconsin shoreline from Sheboygan to Kewaunee.
−Courtesy of the National Oceanographic and Atmospheric Administration

CENTRAL
WISCONSIN

Central Wisconsin is a region of maritime commerce and shipbuilding. The lake cities of Two Rivers, Kewaunee, Manitowoc, and Sheboygan are known to professional and recreational boaters. The history of this area has its roots firmly planted in the lake trade and early waves of European migration.

During the eighteenth century, the Neshotah Indians chose to establish a village along Lake Michigan. French fur traders subsequently named this village *Deux Riviers* or Two Rivers. The fur trade gave way to lumbering with the construction of a sawmill in 1837. Given its prime location on the shores of Lake Michigan, Two Rivers gradually became an important fishing and manufacturing town. One of the most famous things for which Two Rivers is known is the invention of the ice cream sundae, first dished out in 1881.

American Indians and French traders once peacefully shared the area of Manitowoc. The name Manitowoc is an Indian name that means, *Home of the Great Spirit.* With the conclusion of the Seven Years War, the territory today known as Wisconsin passed from the French to the British, who in turn surrendered it to the fledgling United States government.[1] The first of the new settlers to Manitowoc arrived in 1836. Fifteen years later, Manitowoc was incorporated as a village. By 1870, Manitowoc was a city with a thriving industrial center and an established shipbuilding industry. The first schooner built in Manitowoc was the *Citizen,* constructed in 1847. Companies such as Burger Boats have their origins during this era. Burger originally built schooners for the lake trade, but shifted production with changes in technology and ship design. By 1941, Burger moved entirely to a wartime footing. Twenty-eight submarines and various other craft came out of the yards of a company that is known today for luxury yachts.

South of Manitowoc is the Indian settlement of Sheboygan. Because of Sheboygan's location in the middle of the state, combined with a good harbor, the city grew quickly during the 1800s. Between 1844 and 1847, the population increased from 77 to almost 700. The lake trade grew at an equally fast pace. The harbor provided safe refuge, while immigrants found the city's location ideal for reaching points north and south and for traveling west.

With central Wisconsin's economic boom and the region's "anything goes" character during this time, it is no surprise that numerous shipwrecks and great loss of life were the result. Early nineteenth-century Lake Michigan was not governed by the same safety regulations that would later be standard procedures. Travel on the lakes was akin to driving down an eight-lane highway with-

---

[1] The Seven Years War was fought primarily in Europe by England and France. The French and Indian war was the New World extension of this conflict.

out speed limits or dividing lines. The use of Sheboygan by thousands of immigrants to spread across the West made it inevitable that some great tragedy would eventually strike innocent passengers. This happened in 1847 with the burning of the *Phoenix,* one of the first documented wrecks in the central Wisconsin region.

I THE PHOENIX

In the Egypt of the pharoahs, the phoenix was a fabled bird destined to perish in the flames of its own funeral pyre. Ascending from the ashes, the phoenix was reborn, thereby continuing its eternal cycle of life and death. Tragically for those on board the *Phoenix,* this passenger steamer was fated to die by fire but never to rise.

On its fateful voyage in 1847, the *Phoenix* was carrying a cargo of immigrants and their families from northern Europe. These were men, women, and children fleeing religious persecution in Holland. As religious reform swept Europe, many people escaped to the New World where they could practice their faith as they chose. In Holland, the reform movement was shaking the foundations of the Dutch State Church. Civil authorities strongly discouraged notions of reform. Confronted with a hostile environment, those in the reform movement left their country for a better life where freedom of religion and inexpensive land were available. Many settled along the shores of Lake Michigan and further inland, bringing with them a new and rich culture to the Midwest. The more than 200 immigrants on board the *Phoenix* desired the same thing.

The vessel incorporated the latest concepts in propulsion. Most steamers on the lakes at this time were side-wheelers, but the *Phoenix* was a departure from the norm. Possessing twin screws powered by a steam engine, the steamer was built in Buffalo in 1845, two years after the first propeller-driven vessel, the *Vandalia,* graced the waters of the Great Lakes. The *Phoenix* was a sizable vessel, with a length of 140 feet, a beam of 22 feet, and a depth of 10 feet. It displaced 302 gross tons.[2]

The *Phoenix* was under the command of Captain G. B. Sweet, an experienced skipper who, by all accounts, was well acquainted with the lakes. On

---

[2] Another source states that the Phoenix was built by G. Jones of Cleveland and was 155 feet in length with a beam of 24 feet and a displacement of 350 tons. This is most likely a reference to the repairs that were made after the Phoenix sustained heavy damage in a collision with the steamer Troy in 1845.

November 11, 1847, Captain Sweet watched as his boat was loaded with the last of its freight. In addition to the immigrant passengers, the cargo included molasses, coffee, and hardware. As Captain Sweet edged the *Phoenix* away from the dock in Buffalo, the passengers and crew, unaware of what fate had in store, set off on a journey that few would survive.

Crossing Lake Erie en route to Fairport due east of Cleveland, the *Phoenix* suffered the first accident of the voyage and an ominous harbinger of later events. Fracturing his knee in a fall, Captain Sweet was carried to his room, where he stayed in bed for the remainder of the journey. The first mate, H. Watts, took over and the *Phoenix* continued on its way.

Throughout much of the steamer's voyage across Lake Erie, the *Phoenix* was plagued by poor weather. Nature smiled warmly on the passengers for the journey between Cleveland and Detroit, but by the time the *Phoenix* entered Lake Huron, dark clouds hid the sun. Huron was an angry, roiling sea. Minor damage was done to the *Phoenix* but few, if any, of the passengers braved the slick, heaving decks and were therefore unaware of the beating to which the steamer was being subjected. Many were too seasick to leave their rooms.

The weather lightened briefly as the *Phoenix* headed though the Straits of Mackinac, but Lake Michigan proved no better than its neighbor to the east. The *Phoenix* sheltered at Beaver Island, northeast of the Door Peninsula, for several days until the winds died down and the seas grew substantially calmer.

Continuing south along Lake Michigan's western shore, the *Phoenix* reached the port of Manitowoc. The vessel pulled into the harbor just before midnight on Saturday, November 20, when most of the inhabitants were asleep. Delaying until the winds brought in by a new front settled, the *Phoenix* departed Manitowoc on midnight of the following day.

While the *Phoenix* was at berth, first mate Watts unloaded that portion of the cargo consigned to Manitowoc. While there, a few passengers and some of the crew went on a brief, unscheduled shore leave. As the *Phoenix* was being unloaded, a supply of cordwood was taken on board for fuel.

When some of the crew returned to the *Phoenix* and prepared to get under way, they apparently did so after visiting several of the local taverns. Years later, the granddaughter of one of the survivors remembered her grandfather admonishing her never to drink because they had lost family on the *Phoenix* due to the irresponsibility of drunken crew members.

The *Phoenix* departed Manitowoc at 1 a.m. Sunday. The night was clear and bright. After traveling hundreds of miles across storm-tossed lakes, the passengers were now blessed with a peaceful night's sleep. They had braved religious persecution, the Atlantic Ocean, and three churning lakes. They were nearing the end of a voyage that would lead them to a new life and now, less than thirty miles from their final port of Sheboygan, and in peaceful seas, disaster struck.

The first person to sense the danger was one of the first-class passengers, an Irishman and an engineer by trade, who was traveling with his wife and their two children. Waking up about 1:30 a.m., he detected an unusual sound coming from the ship's engines. He went below and informed the engineer that something was wrong. His warnings were ignored, possibly because some of the crew were drunk, and he was forcibly ejected. Sensing that the engine and boilers were in serious trouble, he gathered his family together and placed them in a lifeboat. They were among the handful of passengers who survived the night.

At about 2 a.m., one of the firemen noticed that the wooden ceiling over one of the ship's boilers had overheated and caught fire. Efforts to fight the initial blaze proved futile as the fire quickly spread out of control. Captain Sweet was alerted and ordered the three steam pumps on board the *Phoenix* into full operation. Soon, streams of water were desperately pouring from the fire hoses. Despite the crew's best efforts, thick, black smoke filled the passageways. Coughing, passengers and crew came out on deck in various stages of undress. Some of the men were used in a bucket brigade, but their bid to stem the flames was hopeless.

First mate Watts ordered the ship's helmsman to steer the *Phoenix* for shore. If they could reach the sandy beaches north of Sheboygan, or even get closer to shore, some lives could be saved. As the fire billowed out of control, the engine room was abandoned. Unable to maintain the boilers, the crew could do nothing to prevent steam pressure from being lost. The *Phoenix* came to a dead stop nine miles from Sheboygan and five miles from land.

Much like the *Titanic* 70 years later, the first-class passengers received priority seating when the lifeboats were lowered into the freezing waters. Still suffering from a broken knee, Captain Sweet was placed into one of the lifeboats and survived. As this was accomplished, flames leapt more than 200 feet over the decks. The *Phoenix* was a blazing inferno. People dove, their clothing in flames, into the frigid water. One woman ran back to her cabin to find a shawl for her baby and did not return. Two sisters named Hazelton, coming home to Sheboygan from a school in the East, stood on the side of the steamer, joined hands, and leaped into the lake, where they drowned.

The passengers and crew had few options. Those who survived were already in the lifeboats. Some clung to the rigging, which burned through and dropped the helpless passengers into the flames on deck. Others jumped overboard, hoping to cling to the side of the *Phoenix*, to find a raft of some sort, or to be taken aboard one of the small boats already floating in the lake. Fearing for their own lives, many of those in the lifeboats tore the fingers of drowning men, women, and children from the gunwales. Survivors recalled a young girl who was pushed back into the water, where she drowned.

As the boats were being lowered, a seat was offered to David Blish, a businessman from Kenosha.[3] Known and respected, Blish had everything to live for. A successful businessman with a wife and four young children, he could very well have taken the proffered seat. He declined. Instead, Blish did everything in his power for those still alive on the doomed steamer. When it was no longer possible to remain on board, he went over the railing with a child under each arm. Once in the water he hung on to a piece of wreckage for as long as possible until disappearing beneath the waves.

The engineer, the ship's clerk, and a passenger survived by holding onto the ship's rudder chains and one of the ship's fenders that was floating in the water. Others were not so fortunate. Hypothermia can claim a life in less than ten minutes. Many of the survivors thrashed about in the water or held onto wreckage until exhaustion and exposure took their toll.

The water was filled with the dead and dying. Shattered and charred wreckage floated everywhere. Anything that could float was thrown overboard for use as a raft. The scene was like some horrible nightmare out of Dante's *Inferno*, in which the water and the faces of those in the lifeboats heading for shore reflected the red glare of the flames.

On shore, a justice of the peace, Judge Morris, awoke from his slumber. Like the Irish engineer now in one of the lifeboats, Morris woke for some inexplicable reason and with a sense that things were not right. Going to his window, he at first mistook the fire on the placid waters for the rising sun. Coming to his senses, he realized that a large ship was in flames.

Running to Sheboygan's harbor, Morris boarded the steamer *Delaware*. Soon the ship's entire crew was awake, but the boilers were cold and it took some time to build up a head of steam. Nearby, the captain of the schooner *Liberty* also woke to discover the ship burning out on the lake. Without wind to power their vessel, the *Liberty*'s crew manned their ship's boat and headed for the stricken vessel.

By the time the crews of the *Liberty* and the *Delaware* reached the scene, there was little left of the *Phoenix* apart from a hulk burned to the waterline. The three men clinging to the fender and rudder chain near the stern were plucked from the water. They and the 43 people who had reached shore in the lifeboats were the only survivors.

[3] Kenosha was known as Southport at the time.

The men of the *Delaware* circled the *Phoenix,* but it was soon grimly apparent that there was nothing else they could accomplish. Five bodies were taken from the water, and the *Delaware* took the *Phoenix* and the small boat from the *Liberty* in tow. Approaching Sheboygan, part of the fore section of the *Phoenix* broke off. With it went the ship's safe, rumored to have contained a small fortune. Given the fact that hundreds of people brought their life savings to America from Holland, that is possible. The safe has never been recovered.

Although there were a number of accusations and rumors following the incident, most are groundless and unjust. Much was made of the fact that Captain Sweet did not go down with his ship. While this is true, he was disabled and physically placed in a lifeboat early in the disaster. Sadly, he lived the rest of his life in poor mental health as a result of the accident.

After the surviving crew members of the *Phoenix* reached Sheboygan, they were accused of drunkenness and dereliction of duty by an outraged public, so much so that they feared for their lives. For their safety, they were taken to Manitowoc by the *Delaware.* En route, those on board noticed many bodies floating near the scene of the accident. Despite the fact that crew members of the *Delaware* and the *Phoenix* implored him to retrieve the bodies, the captain refused. This action resulted in his losing the respect of people within the maritime community, but the criticism was probably unjust. Because the *Delaware* had already picked up five bodies at the scene, the captain could not be accused of being superstitious about carrying corpses on board his ship.

Due to his efforts the morning of the accident, the captain should be regarded as brave and selfless. By speeding to the scene of a blazing inferno, he placed himself and his crew in harm's way. Even though by the time he reached the *Phoenix* the dead steamer was a smoldering ruin, it was impossible to know that when he left Sheboygan.

The burning of the *Phoenix* spawned several rumors, none of them kind. Two persist to this day regarding the drunken state of some crew members and the possibility that they robbed some of the passengers. The latter argument is most likely false, the former probably true in at least several cases.

Another rumor concerns James Berry, coroner for the city of Sheboygan. It was said that Berry found a substantial amount of gold in the remains of the *Phoenix.* True or not, Berry was also a farmer and shortly thereafter ordered a herd of Holstein cattle. These cattle were something new to Wisconsin and the present day Holstein industry has its origins in James Berry.

The true death toll from the *Phoenix* will never be known. According to the ship's clerk, who survived by hanging on to the rudder chain, at least 250 perished. This is at odds with the owners, who state that not more than 190 died.

The lower number may be the result of the company's unwillingness to admit that the *Phoenix* may have been overloaded. No matter the number, across the Atlantic in Holland, church bells rang throughout the land for friends and family who had perished. In some cases, entire families were wiped out. For years afterward, Dutch immigrants stopped settling in the area.

The survivors left a deep and lasting impression on Wisconsin. Many had lost family members, and some were totally impoverished, since their possessions went down with the *Phoenix*. But they were taken care of by the people of Sheboygan and the surrounding communities. With the same spirit that brought them thousands of miles to the Midwest, the survivors worked hard, acquired land, and established businesses. Of the 25 who remained in the central Wisconsin region, their present-day legacy to the state is 8,000 descendents.

II THE NIAGARA

In a tale reminiscent of the *Phoenix*, the *Niagara* was yet another lake boat destined to perish by fire. At the time of its last voyage in 1856, the *Niagara* was one of many side-wheel steamers engaged in the profitable business of carrying passengers and cargo from lake port to lake port. Built in 1845 by Bidwell & Banta of French Creek, New York, the 473 ton *Niagara* was 192 feet in length, 27 feet at the beam, and possessed a draft of 9 feet. One of the longest steamers in the world at the time of its construction, the *Niagara* was also one of the first of the "palace steamers."

"Palace steamers" were side-wheel steamers known for their expensive apartments. These vessels were luxury liners of 1,000 or more net tons and were built with such extravagant features as stained glass domes, beautifully designed fittings, plush carpets, and parlors.

Owned by the Collingwood Line, the *Niagara* was a familiar sight on the lakes. This boat, like many of its peers at the time, helped build a new country by bringing thousands of German and Scandinavian immigrants to the Midwest. Steamers such as the *Niagara* are credited with carrying roughly half of Wisconsin's immigrants to the shores of the Badger State.

On September 24, 1856, the *Niagara* was en route from Collingwood, Ontario, to Chicago. The skipper of the *Niagara*, Captain Fred S. Miller, brought his charge into the port of Sheboygan, where many passengers disembarked. This fact undoubtedly saved many lives. No official accounting of the number of passengers exists, but an estimated 140 remained on board. Shortly after leaving Sheboygan, fire broke out. The cause was never determined, but the *Niagara* was carrying flammable merchandise and this may have played a role in the unfolding drama.

Captain Miller had only been in his stateroom for a short time when he awoke to the panicked cries of "Fire! Fire!" He saw to it that a fire hose was hooked up and put into use. Once the fire hose was in operation, Captain Miller headed for the pilothouse. In an attempt to save as many lives as possible, the *Niagara*'s captain ordered the wheelman to set a course for land. This may have been a fatal mistake. The speed of the *Niagara* as the steamer hurried toward the shoreline fueled the fire, which leaped across the deck and superstructure. The alternative would have been to allow the *Niagara* to go dead in the water.

Providing little time for passengers and crew to react, the flames spread quickly. This was the result of the flames reaching contraband flammable goods, which were stored in the hold. A stiff wind served to fan the flames. Originating amidships, the fire effectively cut the steamer in half, preventing families separated at the bow and stern ends from coming to one another's aid. Whatever could have been done to save lives is a matter of hindsight. The *Niagara* was destined never to reach land. As the flames raged out of control, doors and anything that could float were thrown into the cold waters of Lake Michigan.

People dangled over the sides, clinging to the doomed vessel by ropes. The fire quickly burned through the hemp lines. Many passengers temporarily escaped the flames, only to drown moments later. According to one source, "People were hanging like trout on a line."

The confusion and panic can only be imagined as the flames consumed the superstructure. Panic cost more lives than the fire itself. The crew attempted to reach the lifeboats but was unable to pass through the fire. Passengers tried to lower the boats, but haste and lack of familiarity with handling the lifeboats were a recipe for disaster. As a consequence of these efforts, some of the lifeboats capsized, throwing occupants into the lake.

Over the roar of the flames, some passengers heard what they thought were gunshots or explosions. The source of these noises was never determined, but it was later surmised that the sounds originated in the hold, where the flammable goods were burning and possibly exploding.

In many a shipwreck, cowardice will walk in the shadow of heroism. While the *Niagara*'s captain remained at the wheel, braving the flames surrounding him, others thought only of themselves. Near the height of the tragedy John Macy, a former Wisconsin congressman, offered $100,000 to anyone who would save his life. Finding no takers, Macy spied a lifeboat filled with women and children. While the small boat was being lowered, Macy leaped into the craft. As he landed in the boat the lines snapped. The boat dropped like a stone, depositing all of its occupants into the lake. Everyone drowned. It was the capsizing of both lifeboats that is blamed for the large loss of life.

Rushing to the rescue were two steamers, the *Traveler* and the *Illinois*. They were joined by several schooners. Many of those who perished did so in sight of shore. Fortunately for the survivors, there were a number of vessels in the area, which were quick to respond. The loss of life due to drowning could have been higher.

A boat was lowered from the *Traveler*. No sooner had the wooden hull struck water than the crew made for the *Niagara*. The captain of the ship's boat was Frederick Pabst, who was later to become famous as one of Wisconsin's premier brewers. This small boat was responsible for saving Captain Miller and a handful of others.

The *Niagara* came to rest in 52 to 55 feet of water a heartbreaking one-and-a-half miles from Port Washington and safety. At least 70 crew members and passengers perished in the incident. Some accounts state that the death toll is more than 100. In only 20 minutes, perhaps less, the boat was abandoned.

Over the next several days, bodies, carried by the waves, washed up on shore a full seven miles north of Port Washington. As Dave Swayze points out in his excellent book, *Shipwreck!*, the wreck of the *Niagara* "caused an uproar in the Cleveland papers about the shipping of contraband flammable goods."

Despite the possibility that the conflagration was the result of the *Niagara*'s cargo, the reason for the disaster has never been satisfactorily determined. On the trip prior to the *Niagara*'s fated last journey, a note threatening arson was discovered on board. It was considered a hoax. Another theory regarding the origins of the fire has the conflagration starting in the engine room. This possibility was ruled out by Captain Miller, who pointed out that the engine room was fireproof. The most likely cause is linked to the sounds of explosions and "gunshots" heard by some of the passengers. These sharp sounds were probably the burning cargo.

The *Niagara* stands as a lonely monument to an era when steam was new and accidents common. The *Niagara*'s burned remains and aging steam engine offer mute testimony to one of the worst disasters ever to strike on Lake Michigan.

The Rouse Simmons.—*Courtesy of the Wisconsin Maritime Museum*

III THE ROUSE SIMMONS:
THE "CHRISTMAS TREE SHIP"

Despite the tragic nature of shipwrecks, many nevertheless possess a romantic allure. Parents may relate the story of a given wreck to their children. No child is ever able to view any of the Great Lakes in quite the same way again once they understand the mortal struggles that have taken place on these waters. The history of a particular wreck, the possibility of treasure or simple fascination holds the imagination of children and adults.

The story of the *Rouse Simmons* shows the power over the imagination that a wreck can provide. The *Rouse Simmons* was one of many vessels employed in the Christmas tree trade and it is from this simple business that the aging schooner derived its nickname, the Christmas Tree Ship.

The *Rouse Simmons* was built in 1868 by the firm of Allen, McClelland & Company of Milwaukee. The *Simmons'* keel was laid to support a schooner 123 feet in length, with a beam of 28 feet, and a draft of 8 feet. The schooner's displacement was 195 net tons and 205 gross tons. Due to the amount of financing Rouse Simmons of Kenosha gave toward the construction of the new schooner, it was given his name. Simmons hoped that this new schooner would allow Kenosha to play a role in the lumber trade.

The construction of the *Rouse Simmons* in 1868 came well after the early beginnings of the lake Christmas tree trade. For that matter, the *Simmons'* early occupation was spent hauling lumber and various other items of value, not holiday trees for Chicago homes.

According to the *Milwaukee Sentinel*, the trading of Christmas trees began roughly around the end of the Civil War. As pioneers and enterprising businessmen and women moved north, timber operations and settlements were established. Near the villages of Ahnapee and others, land cleared for lumbering gave way to farms. In order for those who worked the land to pay their bills, a system of barter gradually developed between farmers and merchants. Cutting down evergreens on their property, the farmers would give them to storekeepers as a means of settling debts. It was the task of the storekeeper to cut and shape the trees prior to shipping. During this era, the most efficient means of transportation was either rail or lake.

The larger vessels, those unable to enter some of the smaller harbors, were not always able to participate in the tree trade. Filling this need were the shallow-drafted schooners that relied on centerboards to prevent them from capsizing. These schooners were generally captained by men who learned their trade the hard way, by rising from seaman to skipper of their own boat. Such men were quick to make a profit and would capitalize on any current or potential boom. While summer might witness cargoes of wheat and corn, early fall would find the same captain ferrying timber, hardware, or supplies for the winter from port to port. Profit margins could be negligible. To earn as much money as possible in a given season, many captains sailed late into the year. Willing to take on any cargo for a few extra dollars, some of these captains began to haul Christmas trees to lakefront communities.

October and November account for approximately 46 percent of all the shipwrecks on Lake Michigan. Captains who sailed during this storm-prone season did so with the knowledge that they might come back rich or not at all.

The captains who risked everything were a unique breed of entrepreneur. In their ranks were the Schuenemann brothers, August and Herman. Like their contemporaries, the Schuenemanns learned the lake trade by working for other captains and saving their money until they could afford a boat of their own.

August bought his first share in a vessel in 1875. It was the *W.H. Hinsdale*. Since profits could be hard to come by, expenses were cut by purchasing schooners that had seen better days. In 1898, August headed to northern Wisconsin to buy trees. His boat on this trip was the *S. Thal*, a vessel that should have been consigned to a ship graveyard. Sailing south, the *S. Thal* entered Illinois waters, where the schooner went down in a storm with all hands.

Undaunted by his brother's fate, Herman entered the trade. Herman arguably was a gifted sailor and businessman. He could brave any sort of weather in vessels better suited to the scrap heap. Herman established the Northern Michigan Evergreen Nursery at Chicago's Clark Street Bridge, where he would tie his boats following each trip north. It was Herman's idea to bring lumberjacks along to cut his trees. In addition, he sold trees off the decks of his boats while his two daughters used cut boughs to make decorative wreaths. Chicagoans stopped to purchase trees. The smell of freshly cut pine filled the brisk winter air. Unlike other captains who only dabbled in the tree trade, Herman avoided selling to stores or other businesses, preferring to manage the operation under his own authority.

In 1910, Captain Schuenemann bought the *Rouse Simmons*, a boat that was no stranger to the type of work that quickly aged a schooner. The following year, Herman saw to it that the *Simmons* was caulked and made seaworthy. Unfortunately, this job was not repeated in 1912.

Able to manage his affairs with an uncanny sense of what was vital to his interests, Herman's sixth sense seems to have failed him in 1912. On November

25, the *Rouse Simmons* departed Thompson Harbor between Point Aux Barques and Manistique in Michigan's Upper Peninsula.

The barometer was falling as Captain Schuenemann entered the open water. The crew and ten lumberjacks brought on board to fell Christmas trees watched from inside the cabin as snow danced through the rigging. Those on duty pulled their collars up against a wind that blew with increasing strength. The spray of the rising seas lashed the Christmas trees on deck. There was nothing the crew could do as their cargo froze beneath a layer of ice. There was concern because any shifting of the frozen cargo could spell disaster.

Struggling along the eastern shore of the Door Peninsula, the *Rouse Simmons* was spotted by a tug and the brig *Dutch Boy*. Sometime between November 25 and 26, Captain Schuenemann raised the distress flags. The following day, the Sturgeon Bay Coast Guard Station observed the *Rouse Simmons*. The *Simmons* was spotted once again, this final time by the United States Lifesaving Station at Two Rivers.

Fighting the lake and a driving blizzard, the *Simmons* continued on. The distress flags still visible and tattered sails whipping in the wind, the *Rouse Simmons* refused to surrender without a battle of epic proportions.

The Revenue Marine boat *Tuscarora* was sent from the Two Rivers Lifesaving Station to aid the *Rouse Simmons*. The little powerboat and its crew fought the raging seas. Steering the *Tuscarora* directly for the *Simmons*, the crew of the small craft tried to keep the stricken schooner in sight.

The snow closed in a final time and the *Rouse Simmons* vanished from view. Unable to forge on, the *Tuscarora* returned to its dock. It was a valiant effort doomed to failure. Lost from sight of land, the *Rouse Simmons* slipped beneath the waves. Both the *Simmons* and the *S. Thal*, each with a load of Christmas trees, were at the bottom of the lake. August and his brother Herman were reunited.

Later, after the storm had ravaged Lake Michigan, a bottle washed up on shore near Sheboygan. Inside was a simple message, penned in Captain Herman Schuenemann's own hand. The message read:

> *Friday. Everybody good-bye. I guess we are all thru. Sea washed over our deck load Thursday. During the night the small boat was washed over. Ingvald and Steve fell overboard Thursday. God help us. Herman Schuenemann.*

The story of the *Rouse Simmons* refuses to end. When it sank, the ice-covered schooner went down with 17 crew members and a load of 5,000 or more trees. The following year, fishermen from Two Rivers brought up numerous trees from the bottom of the lake in their nets. This problem continued for the next 25 years following each storm strong enough to stir the lake bottom. In 1925, 13 years after the sinking of the *Rouse Simmons*, Captain Schuenemann's oilskin wallet washed up at Two Rivers.

In 1934, the three daughters of Captain Herman Schuenemann opened a store on the north side of Chicago where they sold Christmas trees and wreaths. The store's name was Captain and Mrs. Schuenemann's Daughters. For older Chicagoans, the name brought back fond memories.

The Christmas Tree Ship remained lost until 1971, when the *Rouse Simmons* was discovered by a diver. Two evergreens were removed from a hold still of Christmas trees meant for the Chicago market 59 years previously. One of the trees was placed in the Marine National Exchange Bank. The *Rouse Simmons'* anchor has found a permanent mooring outside the Milwaukee Yacht Club. In addition to these two trees, a china bowl and hand-cranked foghorn were recovered.

The *Rouse Simmons* rests in 180 feet of water off Rawley Point. The schooner's tale is one of many Lake Michigan stories that conjure images of a simpler time and continues to fascinate.

OTHER SIGNIFICANT WRECKS

As we saw, the *Phoenix* was the victim of one of the first documented shipwrecks along the central Wisconsin coast. The only other major incident during the decade in which the *Phoenix* was lost came two years later, in 1849, with the capsizing of the schooner *W. G. Buckner* off Ozaukee. When it sank during a gale, the *Buckner* went down with at least five crew members and a load of lumber.

Possibly the first wreck of the 1850s occurred on July 7, 1851. This was the 145-ton schooner *Gallinipper*, which capsized in a squall off Sheboygan. With the hull turned toward a cloud-covered sky, the *Gallinipper* gradually drifted northward before sinking south of Manitowoc.

A lull of three years followed without major incidents. This grace period lasted until 1854, when three schooners wrecked. All three were destroyed as a consequence of foul weather. The following year witnessed the sinking of the propeller steamer *Delaware* near Sheboygan. The *Delaware* was bound for Chicago from Buffalo when it beached during a gale. Ten or eleven of a complement of 18 did not survive the stranding. This tragedy was overshadowed in 1856 by the sinking of two large steamers, the *Niagara* and the *Toledo*.

There was little, if any, loss of life until 1860. This changed on September 7. Bound for Cedar River, Michigan, the schooner *St. Mary* was loaded with pig iron when it departed Kewaunee. In addition to the cargo, the *St. Mary* carried a crew of nine and two passengers. The schooner's position when it foundered has never been determined, but the vessel was claimed by the storm in which the *Lady Elgin* was destroyed.

It was on the same day that the *St. Mary* disappeared that the side-wheel steamer *Lady Elgin* sank following a collision with the schooner *Augusta*. The *Lady Elgin* was the second worst accident on Lake Michigan in terms of lives lost. It would be another 55 years before this dubious honor went to the excursion boat *Eastland*.

The remainder of the 1860s through the 1880s continued to see bodies and cargo wash up along the sandy beaches of the states bordering Lake Michigan. The waters near Two Rivers are littered with china, wheat, lumber, and ore from this period. Off Manitowoc, Lake Michigan hides cargoes of wood, corn, and iron ore beneath its waves, while Sheboygan has a wealth of leather, telegraph poles, lumber, railroad ties, coal, and brick in its cold waters.

TWO OCTOBER SINKINGS

The Great Lakes are well known for providing tense and often tragic drama. Exposure to the elements, lack of sleep, hunger, and physical and mental exertion can lead to exhaustion and surrender to the forces of nature.

On October 23, 1887, the crews of the steamer *Raleigh* and its consort, the schooner barge *Polynesia*, faced such an epic struggle against nature. Laboring in heavy seas produced by a storm bearing down from the northwest, the crews of the two vessels struggled to reach the safety of land. A triple-masted schooner barge, the *Polynesia* lost part of its mainmast and mizzenmast in the wind. Adding to the crew's problems was the fact that the barge was taking on water.

The steamer towing the *Polynesia* was also flooding. By the time night fell, the *Polynesia* was partly submerged and the waves enjoyed free reign over the deck. Fighting to keep the pumps ahead of water entering the hold, the crew of the *Raleigh* tried to convince Captain A.H. Reed to cut the tow line, thereby saving the *Raleigh* but abandoning the *Polynesia* and its crew of eight. Faced with the possibility of losing both vessels, Captain Reed refused to cut the line, a measure that would most likely have condemned the men of the *Polynesia* to death.

As the crew of the *Raleigh* fought the storm, the crew of the *Polynesia* shivered in the cold dark night. Unable to eat or sleep, the men of the *Polynesia* clung to life and prayed for morning's light.

In the morning, Captain John Kerr of the *Polynesia* ordered his crew into the lifeboats. As they attempted to close the 200 yards between the *Polynesia* and *Raleigh*, Captain Kerr's daring escape was observed by Captain Reed, who brought the *Raleigh* around.

The crew of the schooner barge was taken on board the *Raleigh*. While this rescue was taking place, the *Polynesia*, having fought all night to stay afloat, began to founder. The towline attaching the two vessels was cut with an ax before damage could be done to the *Raleigh*'s stern. The *Polynesia* sank beneath the waves, but its crew, as well as the crew of the *Raleigh*, survived.

Two days later, the propeller steamer *Vernon* was en route from the northern reaches of Lake Michigan to Chicago. The *Vernon* was only a year old at the time, having been launched the prior year by James Parker Smith of Chicago for Alfred Booth of the Booth Fish Company of Chicago. At the time, Alfred Booth owned a fishing enterprise that included the largest fish-processing facility in the country. This plant was in Escanaba and was part of a fishing empire that included a fleet of boats.

The *Vernon* was 177 feet in length, with a 26-foot beam and an 18-foot depth. The vessel was built with two Scotch boilers and amenities in the 18 state rooms and cabin lounge that included a wealth of brass fittings and other luxury items.

When the *Vernon* was first launched, there were many who claimed that the high upperworks and narrow beam would make it difficult to manage in rough seas. Despite the warnings, the *Vernon* was used to ferry passengers and freight around the lake.

The *Vernon* was still well north of Chicago when the crew encountered a gale on October 28. The steamer was eight days out of Chicago on a trip to Cheboygan, Michigan, and was completing the return leg of its voyage. By the time the steamer was off Two Rivers, Wisconsin, it was in serious trouble. Loaded with more general freight than it could safely haul, the vessel went down with between 36 and 41 doomed souls on board. A number of passengers took what refuge they could in the water. Exposure gradually took all but one person, who was found adrift on a raft two days after the incident.

Similar to other wrecks of this era, the passenger list was kept on board the *Vernon*. It is for this reason that an accurate accounting of passengers and crew is impossible to obtain. Although several vessels passed through the area of the debris field and saw the living and the dead, no help was rendered. According to reports made at the time, at least a few of these boats were dealing with storm damage and in no position to provide assistance.

The sole survivor of the *Vernon* disaster was Axel Stone, a Swedish immigrant and watchman on board the steamer. According to Stone, the *Vernon* was heavily overloaded and, after completing his shift, he observed that the engine room was flooding. Informing Captain Thorpe of the situation, Stone recommended that some of the cargo be dumped overboard in order to lighten the *Vernon*'s load. After being told by Captain Thorpe to "Go to hell," Stone retired to his cabin, only to be tossed from his bunk at about three o'clock that Saturday morning.

Escaping the dying ship by crawling through the cabin window, Stone found the safety of a raft. On board, he was told by two of the surviving firemen that the flooding engine room had put out the fires in the boilers, denying the *Vernon* power. The steamer was at the mercy of the wind and waves, which made short work of the *Vernon*.

After his rescue, Axel Stone reported that of the vessels that passed by, he was able to discern facial features of passengers and crew. This indicates how close some of the boats came, but not a single vessel attempted a rescue. The life-saving service at Two Rivers was not informed of the incident until Sunday and even then it was by a reporter from the *Milwaukee Sentinel*. The failure of anyone to come to the immediate aid of the *Vernon* contributed to the loss of life and is one of the inexplicable tales of the Great Lakes.

A QUIET END OF THE CENTURY

There were at least 17 more wrecks before the century came to a close, but these occurred with remarkably little loss of life. Three died when the schooner *Silver Cloud* capsized near Port Washington during the summer of 1891. The schooner *Lottie Cooper* capsized three years later, in 1894, taking a Norwegian immigrant to a watery grave. It is possible that these are the only incidents involving fatalities for the decade prior to 1900.

The tale of the *Lottie Cooper* is sad but also fascinating: It is one of the few wrecks ever recovered from Lake Michigan and placed on display. In this respect the *Lottie Cooper* is similar to the *Alvin Clark*, which was used as part of a museum following its raising in the 1980s. Unlike the *Clark*, which gradually fell apart until paved over for a parking lot, the *Lottie Cooper* is visited by tourists at its home in Sheboygan.

Launched on March 30, 1876, the three-masted schooner was a product of the Rand and Burger ship building company of Manitowoc, one of many schooners built by this firm for the lake trade. Sold to Cooper and Jones, the *Lottie Cooper* was named after the wife of George Cooper, one of the owners. Originally given a rating of A1 and valued at $11,000, the vessel aged quickly. Following a stranding at Sherman Bay in 1880, another stranding at Port Sanilac, four owners, and 18 years of service, the *Lottie Cooper* received a rating of B1.

On its final voyage, in the twilight of a Saturday evening in April 1894, the *Lottie Cooper* departed Pine Lake, Michigan, en route to Sheboygan with a load of 230,000 board feet of lumber. By Monday morning the captain, Fred Lorenz, was facing a gale blowing from the southeast. Reaching Sheboygan about

11 p.m. Monday, the *Cooper* was unable to enter the harbor and dropped anchor just shy of the piers. Flashing a signal light to request a tug, the six members of the crew were unable to raise assistance and were forced to spend an anxious night on board the stricken schooner. Unknown to the crew, a nearby tug and the local lifesaving service were aware of their plight, but a signal lamp could not be found to reply to the *Cooper*'s pleas.

By sunrise, the *Lottie Cooper* could be seen from land falling apart under the assault of the sea. The schooner filled with water and capsized. The crew was thrown into the lake, where all but one man clung to the rigging. It was a precarious situation. The cargo of lumber was caught in the rigging and the constant shifting of wood was a threat.

At this point, crewman Edward Olson, who had been in the United States for three years trying to save enough money to bring his wife and two children from Norway, attempted to swim for shore. Had he waited for the lifesaving service with the rest of the crew he would most likely have been saved. His body was never found.

The tug *Sheboygan* and the lifesaving service reached the doomed schooner and rescued the survivors just five minutes before the lumber broke free of the rigging. If the rescue crew had been any later, the crew would have perished.

A hole was later torn into the side of the *Lottie Cooper* so that the cargo could be salvaged. The ruined hulk was towed a short distance into the lake, where it was forgotten. The *Lottie Cooper* remained lost for nearly 100 years until it was raised in 1992.

THE TWENTIETH CENTURY

At least twenty-two vessels were lost along the coast in the twentieth century, with the most recent wrecks being the oil screw *Humko*, destroyed by a fire on July 22, 1956 near Twin Rivers Point, and the fishing tug *Linda E.*, which went missing in 1998. While it is possible that there were more wrecks along the central Wisconsin coast during the twentieth century, the number remains substantially lower than the previous century.

The *Linda E.* was a gas-powered fishing tug originally built as the *Le Clair Bros.* by the Burger Boat yards in 1937. Forty feet in length, the sturdy little tug was built 13 feet in beam with a depth of 6 feet. In addition, the tug was 20 net tons and 29 gross tons. At the time of its construction, the *Linda E.* was built as an oil screw, but that engine was eventually replaced with a diesel.

It was on December 11, 1998, that the *Linda E.* and its crew of three set off to examine their nets and unload half a ton of chub at the Smith Brothers Fisheries in Port Washington. The day was perfect for such work, with calm seas, and the tug was outfitted with modern communications equipment. It was a routine job and there was no reason for concern. On board were Captain Leif Weborg, Warren Olson, and Scott Matta, the son-in-law of Captain Weborg. All were experienced commercial fishermen.

After setting 14 nets, the *Linda E.* vanished, leaving no wreckage and no trace of its passing. Despite repeated searches, it was not located until June 18, 2000, when the Navy minesweeper *Defender* found the remains.

As evidence pertaining to the destruction of the *Linda E.* was collected, it became apparent that an Indiana barge, 400 times larger than the fishing tug, had collided with the vessel. Despite the fact that both craft were equipped with radar, no evasive action was taken to prevent the accident. It is believed that the crew of the *Linda E.* was below decks cleaning fish at the time and were unaware of the barge bearing down on them.

As the *Linda E.* proves, even with better technology and safety such as the widespread use of life preservers and steel hulls, no boat is immune from peril. Another such wreck was the steel freighter *Senator*.

The *Senator*'s origins were rooted in the bulk carrier trade, but the vessel was converted so that it could haul automobiles from port to port. On the last day of October 1929, the *Senator* was en route to Milwaukee with a load of 241 automobiles. These were Nash cars, made in Kenosha, Wisconsin, and destined for the Milwaukee docks.

Captain George Kinch, in charge of the *Senator*, had no way of knowing that his course was about to cross that of the steamer *Marquette*, under the command of Captain W. F. Amesbury and bound for Milwaukee with a load of iron ore. At 10:40 a.m. and 20 miles from Port Washington, in one of those famously thick fogs, the *Marquette* struck the *Senator* amidships. Within five minutes, the *Senator* turned on its port side and went under. Most of the crew of 31 was rescued, but seven perished in the incident, including Captain Kinch.

The *Senator* had sunk before, in the St. Mary's River in 1909. Despite being salvaged and returned to service, the *Senator* was an ill-fated vessel. Today, at the bottom of Lake Michigan lie 241 automobiles from a bygone era, ghostly relics whose only visitors are fish and the occasional diver.

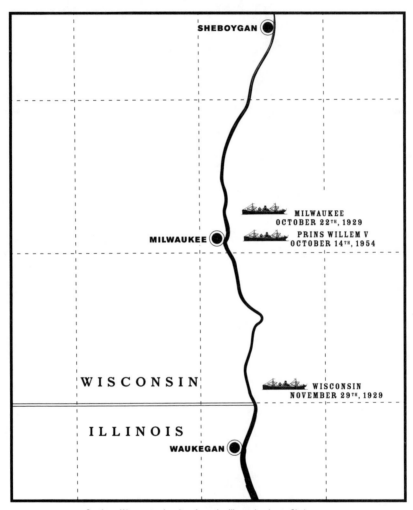

Southern Wisconsin shoreline from the Illinois border to Sheboygan.
—*Courtesy of the National Oceanographic and Atmospheric Administration*

SOUTHERN
WISCONSIN

The Black Hawk War of 1832 can generally be credited with opening the lands of Illinois and Wisconsin to European settlement and, consequently, to a tremendous increase in ship traffic on Lake Michigan. This short and tragic war had its origins in the efforts of the Sauk Indians to unite neighboring tribes in an attempt to prevent the forcible movement of their people further west. The Black Hawk War involved a great leader and one who had yet to make a name for himself, the Sauk chief Black Hawk and Abraham Lincoln. Although Lincoln was only a militia captain and was never involved in any engagements, his first-hand views of the sufferings of war would lead to his understanding of, and sympathy for, the trials of Union troops during the Civil War. The Black Hawk War was a defeat for the Indian tribes of the region and a victory for the settlers seeking to move beyond the Ohio Valley.

With the way west open, families poured into the Midwest. European immigrants in search of a new life and cheap land gradually established communities throughout the region, including the important port cities of Milwaukee, Racine, and Kenosha in southern Wisconsin.

Of the three, Milwaukee emerged as the most active port and commercial center, rivaling Chicago. It was especially noted for its leather-tanning operations, meatpacking, heavy machinery, wheat milling, and, of course, beer.

To ship its products, Milwaukee depended on a well-developed system of rail and lake commerce, a situation that was repeated in the smaller ports of southern Wisconsin. More heavily populated than the northern reaches of the state, and with a greater diversity of industry, the southern ports managed a booming trade. It was therefore inevitable that boats would eventually wreck with some frequency along Wisconsin's southern coast.

I THE CAR FERRY MILWAUKEE

Lake Michigan has its share of vessels that sail and disappear without a trace. As in the case of the *Rouse Simmons*, recreational divers occasionally stumble across a wreck that has been lost for years. It is rare, however, that a boat of any size goes missing. Nevertheless, this is precisely what happened for 43 years to the car ferry *Milwaukee*, which "sailed through a crack in the lake."

There are quite a few vessels named *Milwaukee* lying in the thick silt at the bottom of Lake Michigan. The first of these boats was the side-wheel steamer *Milwaukie*, which sank in the Kalamazoo River near the lake in 1842. Others include a passenger and freight steamer that sank following a collision in the

The car ferry Milwaukee.—*Courtesy of the Wisconsin Maritime Museum*

Straits of Mackinac in 1859. This boat was followed by a passenger and freight side-wheeler in 1868, which stranded at Grand Haven Bar. Grand Haven witnessed yet another collision of a boat named *Milwaukee* early in 1886. The *Milwaukee Belle* foundered during a storm in the Straits of Mackinac the same year as the collision at Grand Haven. The worst wreck of a boat named *Milwaukee* happened in the fall of 1929 and it is the history of this vessel that is examined here.

Built in 1903 by the American Ship Building Company of Cleveland, Ohio, the *Milwaukee* was known as hull *Number 413* until being christening as the *Manistique, Marquette & Northern Number One*. The name reflected its new owners, the Milwaukee-based Manistique, Marquette, and Northern Railroad Company. When built, the *Milwaukee* was 338 feet long, 56 feet at the beam, had a depth of 19 feet, and displaced 2,933 gross tons. The *Milwaukee* was built as a steam ferry at a time when such craft were common.[1]

The ferry was sold to the Grand Trunk Milwaukee Car Ferry Company in 1908 and renamed the *Milwaukee* the following year. In its new role, the ferry

---

[1] By the close of the 20th century, the only steam ferry remaining in service on the Great Lakes was the car ferry Badger, which sails between Manitowoc, Wisconsin and Ludington, Michigan.

shared the Milwaukee to Grand Haven route with the steamer *Grand Haven*.

On October 22, 1929, the ferry was docked at Milwaukee. The *Milwaukee's* skipper was Captain Robert McKay, also known as "Heavy Weather" McKay. In this day and age, many considered a huge, steel-hulled boat such as the *Milwaukee* to be invincible. This overconfidence continued throughout the 1920s, despite the fact that the wreck of the *Titanic* was a recent memory.

The day began with an overcast sky coupled with rapidly deteriorating weather conditions. The *City Of Grand Rapids* was also in port that day, but its captain wisely opted to keep his boat at dock rather than deal with an increasingly angry lake. Captain McKay had other plans, and since he intended to set out that day, the *Grand Rapid's* cargo was loaded on board the *Milwaukee* prior to getting under way.

When the *Milwaukee* left port bound for Muskegon, it was riding low in rough water, carrying 27 rail cars. Although the ferry was capable of hauling 30 cars, the ones the *Milwaukee* took on that day appear to have been substantially loaded. Some of the freight included lumber, perishable foods, bathtubs, and Nash automobiles.

Witnesses in the bar at the top level of Milwaukee's Schroeder Hotel reported that, as soon as it reached open water, the *Milwaukee* "came right up out of the water." Overladen and steaming into the sharp teeth of a fierce gale, the *Milwaukee* appeared to be a plaything in the lake.

But "Heavy Weather" McKay pressed on. Early in the evening, some of the cars in the *Milwaukee's* hold jumped their rails and hammered away at the boat's steel hull like battering rams. Unable to withstand the relentless assault, the sea gate broke.[2] As water poured into his boat, Captain McKay ordered the *Milwaukee* turned around. It was an act of desperation. When the captain and crew realized that all was lost, some of the lifeboats were lowered. In its death throes, the *Milwaukee* lost part of its superstructure as changing air pressure blew the upper cabins free of the deck.

Aircraft were sent to search the route the *Milwaukee* had taken, but no evidence of the boat was discovered. The only wreckage, and the few bodies that were recovered, were later found by several freighters in the area.

Two days after the ferry foundered, the steamer *Colonel* located some of the *Milwaukee's* wreckage near Racine. Farther south, off Kenosha, the steamer *Steel Chemist* discovered two bodies wearing life preservers stenciled with the legend, *SS Milwaukee*. Nine other bodies were found that same day. The watch on one

---

[2] Although a note discovered after the incident indicated that water gained access to the Milwaukee's hold through the sea gate, it wasn't until the ferry's discovery in 1972 that the role played by the freight cars in the Milwaukee's destruction was learned.

of the crew members was stopped at 9:35. On the other side of the lake, a lifeboat was discovered near South Haven. In the boat were four bodies and a waterproof case. Inside the case was a letter written by the purser. It read: "S.S. MILWAUKEE, October 22, 29, 6:30 PM. The ship is taking on water fast. We have turned around and headed for Milwaukee. Pumps are working but the sea gate is bent and won't keep water out. Flicker [crew's quarters] is flooded. Seas are tremendous. Things look bad. Crew roll is about the same as last payday. A.R. Sadon, Purser."

Another note, presumably written by Captain McKay and found in a bottle states:

"This is the worst storm I have ever seen. Can't stay up much longer. Hole in side of boat."

The *Milwaukee* was discovered in 1972 in 125 feet of water northeast of Milwaukee in Whitefish Bay. When it sank, the *Milwaukee* went down with a cargo valued at $163,500, including the cost of the rail cars. Far more valuable were the lives of the 52 men who, with their boat, never returned.

II THE SS WISCONSIN

The SS *Wisconsin* was built in 1881 at Wyandotte, Michigan. Designed to serve as a passenger freighter, the *Wisconsin* was over 204 feet in length, 35 feet in the beam, had a depth of 12 feet, and displaced nearly 2,000 gross tons when launched in October of 1881. Built with an iron hull, the freighter was a sound vessel, able to withstand nearly anything the lakes could throw at it. Designed by Frank Kirby and built at the Detroit Dry Dock in Wyandotte, Michigan, the *Wisconsin* was known simply as *Hull 49*. Eventually, it was assigned an official number, 80861. In addition to the *Wisconsin*, a sister ship was built, the steamer *Michigan*.

While many Great Lakes boats undergo name changes, few do so with the regularity and frequency of the *Wisconsin*. Christened the SS *Wisconsin*, the freighter was named the *Naomi* in 1899. By 1910, the vessel was known as the *E. G. Crosby*. This name was followed by the *General Robert M. O'Reilly* in 1919 and the *Pilgrim* in 1920 until it was reassigned its original name of *Wisconsin* in 1924. Built for the Goodrich Transportation Line, the SS *Wisconsin* was sold to four more owners before the *Wisconsin* was repurchased by the original owners at Goodrich. In addition to multiple names and owners, the *Wisconsin* was rebuilt in 1899 and then again in 1920. In 1885, the *Wisconsin* burned off Grand

Haven, Michigan, in an incident that nearly destroyed the vessel. On May 27, 1907, as the *Naomi,* the ship once again caught fire off Grand Haven. In the second incident, crewmen aboard the steamer *Kansas* spotted the fire at 1:30 a.m. The *Kansas* and two additional steamers, the *D. G. Kerr* and *Saxona,* arrived and began transferring the roughly 50 passengers and 30 crew members on board the *Wisconsin.* The *Kerr* had taken up station near the stricken steamer's stern and many of the survivors fled to the steamer. Others from the *Wisconsin,* by now in lifeboats, were picked up by the *Saxona.*

The action displayed by the crews of the *Kerr, Saxona,* and *Kansas* is credited with saving most of those on board the *Wisconsin.* Tragically, not everyone was able to safely abandon the doomed vessel. A passenger and four coal passers were caught below decks. The passenger, J.M. Rhoades, an employee of the Diamond Match Company, was taken off the burning *Wisconsin* but did not survive his injuries. The coal passers were lost in the fire. Desperately, they took turns taking fresh air from open portholes. The rescuers could hear their cries for help, but the temperature in the forecastle continued to climb until there were no more shouts for help. As though to redeem itself for those who perished in the 1907 fire, the vessel, now known as the *E. G. Crosby* served as a hospital ship in New York during the First World War.

The ship continued its Great Lakes service well into the 1920s, undergoing several more name changes along the way, including the readoption of the ship's original name. On October 29, 1929, the *Wisconsin,* under the command of Captain H. Dougal Morrison, was bringing a cargo of passengers, automobiles, and machine tools from Chicago to Milwaukee. Included among the automobiles were an Essex, a Ford, and a Packard.

A storm was blowing and the deck hatches were being secured when the crew learned that the *Wisconsin* was flooding aft. Captain Morrison ordered the craft to drop anchor in the waters about six-and-a-half miles from Kenosha. It was to be the vessel's final anchorage. As the flooding continued, Captain Morrison instructed the radio operator, Kenneth Carlson, to issue an SOS.

Cutters were sent from the Coast Guard stations at Kenosha and Racine. In addition to the Coast Guard a fishing boat, the *Chambers Brothers,* also responded. The rescue craft arrived around 7:30, twenty minutes after the *Wisconsin* foundered. Personnel were taken from the lifeboats and water, but 18 of 26 passengers and crew were lost.[3] Included in this number was Captain

[3] Sources differ as to the number of crew and passengers, as well as casualties. At least one source claims that there were 75 people on board with 16 casualties, whereas another source states that 76 were on board the *Wisconsin* with 18 fatalities. One other source indicates that the *Wisconsin* was 215 feet long and 44 feet in the beam, which is 6 feet longer and 3 feet wider than reported here.

Morrison. One of the survivors was 21-year-old Kenneth Carlson, who found the safety of a lifeboat minutes before the ship went under.

The *Wisconsin* rests in 130 feet of water at a site often visited by divers.

III THE PRINS WILLEM V

Not all the boats that have been lost in Lake Michigan have been lake boats. One ocean-going vessel that met a fateful end in this inland sea was the Dutch freighter *Prins Willem V. Willi,* as it was affectionately known, was built in 1940 by N.V. Scheepswerf en Machinefabreik of Rotterdam in the Netherlands. As the armies of Nazi Germany swept across Holland, the *Willi* was scuttled in order to prevent the Germans from impressing the vessel into the service of the *Kriegsmarine,* as well as to block the Rotterdam waterway.

After the war, the still-unfinished ship was raised from the canal, and construction on it was completed in 1949. The *Willi,* 258 feet long and 2,800 gross tons, was owned by the Dutch Oranje Line and was a smart-looking ship. The superstructure was built amidships, giving the *Willi* a distinct outline in waters where the superstructures of most freighters are near the bow or stern.

Leaving Milwaukee for Holland during the evening of October 14, 1954, the *Willi* headed into Lake Michigan with a cargo of car parts, musical instruments, printing equipment, pork fat and hides, lawn mowers, film projectors, outboard motors, jukeboxes, kitchen supplies, and 230 boxes of television vacuum tubes. The cargo was worth about $750,000, and the ship was estimated to be worth about double that. Also on board was a crew of 30.

Not far north of the Milwaukee Harbor Light, the *Willi* sighted the tug *Sinclair Chicago.* What no one in the *Willi*'s wheelhouse noticed was the 800-foot line attached to the unmanned barge *Sinclair XII,* which was being towed by the tug. At 7:16 p.m. the barge, with its load of oil, swung around, striking the *Willi* a hard blow on the starboard side and tearing an 8-by-20-foot hole in the hull.

As the *Willi* filled with water, the freighter's skipper ordered the boat abandoned and the lifeboats lowered. The stricken vessel continued its course an additional two miles after the collision, sinking at 8:30 p.m. nearly four miles north of the Milwaukee Harbor lighthouse and in 80 feet of water. The 180-foot buoy tender *Hollyhock* was prompt in rescuing the crew of 30 who had taken to the lifeboats. They were offered lodging at the Pfister Hotel in Milwaukee.

The parties involved, the Oranje Line and Sinclair Refining Company, sought to place blame for the accident on the other. The *Willi*'s captain insisted that the barge did not have any lights and that there was no warning whistle from the tug, charges refuted by the captain of the *Sinclair Chicago*. For his part, the tug's captain reported that the captain of the *Willi* did not signal his intentions. A Coast Guard board of inquiry faulted both captains in the accident.

The following month, Lloyds of London and the ship's owners gave the wreck to the Army Corps of Engineers, which appears to have been less than flattered by the gift. It was, after all, a navigational hazard. In order to remove any part of the boat that might pose a threat to shipping, the Army Corps of Engineers offered the *Willi* to a Milwaukee diver, Max Gene Nohl. Nohl agreed to clear the wreck for $50,000.

In September 1958, Max Nohl and Seaboard Excavators, Inc. were given 180 days to raise the ship by using a system of pontoons that would enable the salvagers to bring it into shallower water. Once accomplished, the plan was to patch the *Willi* and pump out the water. While Nohl was able to clear the vessel, raising it for salvage proved impossible. Due to treacherous weather, the attempt was abandoned for the remainder of the year.

The following year, Seaboard Excavators, Inc., went bankrupt. Although Max Nohl intended to raise the *Willi*, he and his wife were killed in an automobile accident in 1960. Another effort to raise the *Willi* followed in 1961. This attempt was headed by Robert Meissmer, who had previously worked with Nohl; it, too, met with failure. The final push to bring the *Willi* to the surface occurred in 1965 and was led by Charles Huthsing, who purchased the vessel at an auction. Once again, the salvage venture proved fruitless.

Today, the *Prins Willem V* is a favorite site for recreational divers, but this activity has not been without cost. Although the entire crew of the *Willi* was rescued, the wreck has claimed the lives of four divers between 1985 and 1997, reminders that Lake Michigan is full of unexpected dangers and indiscriminate in its choice of victims.

OTHER SIGNIFICANT WRECKS

1840 TO 1870

Because of Milwaukee's role as a center of maritime activity in the mid-nineteenth century, it is no surprise that southern Wisconsin saw more than its share of wrecks. Three of the earliest in the area involved side-wheelers. The first of these was the small steamer *C. C. Trowbridge*, which stranded near Milwaukee in a December storm in 1842. The *Trowbridge* was followed four years later by the loss of the brand new passenger and freight steamer *Boston,* and by the destruction of the *Nile* in 1850.

The *Boston*, less than a year old at the time of its demise, made an emergency run for the relative safety of the open lake. A winter storm was raging and this was the *Boston*'s only chance to avoid being damaged while at dock. The *Boston* quickly lost its stacks and, as a consequence, the draft to the engines. Steam pressure was lost and the *Boston* was at the mercy of the lake. The steamer ran up on the beach, where it was destroyed by wave action. Despite wrecking, the entire crew was able to safely abandon the *Boston*.

The first fire to destroy a steamer near Milwaukee occurred in 1850 when the 642-ton side-wheeler *Nile* went up in flames, along with a nearby warehouse. Arson was suspected, but concrete evidence of wrongdoing was never established.

Two years later, on November 5, the bark *Buckeye State* stranded during a storm off Milwaukee Point and was abandoned after being considered a total loss. The wreck occurred less than three months after the ship's baptism in the waters of the Great Lakes.

There were at least eight shipwrecks during the 1840s and these were followed by 19 during the subsequent decade. The first of these was the schooner *Howard*, which preceded the *Nile* by only one month. It wasn't until the 1860s that shipping losses in the area declined, to perhaps no more than ten for the entire decade. During the 1850s, nearly all of the shipwrecks in the southern Wisconsin region were, in all probability, the result of storms. There were few exceptions. There appears to have been relatively little loss of life for this decade, but not every vessel was so fortunate.

Built in 1855 at the Luther Moses boat yards in Cleveland, the wooden steamer *Sebastopol* was a beautiful vessel. The *Sebastopol* was 230 feet in length and built with a beam of 26 feet. The side-wheels of the 863-ton craft were a grand 50 feet in diameter. A good-sized vessel, the steamer was a sight to behold. Wherever it traveled, the *Sebastopol* left a long, wide wake to mark the steamer's passage as the power of its gigantic wheels churned the lake to a white froth.

In September of the year it was built, the *Sebastopol* was en route to Milwaukee, having departed the Lake Erie port of Buffalo. Heading across Erie, the steamer next drove northward the length of Huron before sailing through the Straits of Mackinac into Lake Michigan. The *Sebastopol*'s skipper, Captain Webb, had on board approximately 60 passengers and 600 tons of general merchandise such as sewing equipment, copper, tin, lead, iron, and tobacco pipes.

As the *Sebastopol* approached Milwaukee, a crewman discovered a leak in the hold. Exacerbating the situation was the fact that the *Sebastopol* was caught in the grip of a powerful storm. Captain Webb, desperately trying to read the harbor lights, approached the port entrance on several occasions but the high winds and rain-lashed night made it impossible to identify the lights. The *Sebastopol* ran aground three miles south of the harbor and 200 feet from shore.

Four crew members made a desperate bid for shore but drowned as they tried to swim the distance between the wrecked steamer and safety. They were the only victims.[4] The rest of the crew spent an anxious night on board the *Sebastopol*. The vessel's side was perpendicular to the surf, which meant that the steamer was under constant assault. Subjected to such stresses, the *Sebastopol* was rapidly falling apart. To make matters worse, help was not forthcoming. A rescue attempt was launched the following morning by the local life-saving service in the shape of a small boat. After a tricky and dangerous rescue operation, those passengers and crew who had stayed on board the disintegrating steamer were saved.

TWO DISASTER-FILLED DECADES

Although the 1860s were relatively uneventful on Lake Michigan, the following two were the worst the region would ever face. In the 1870s, at least 22 boats of all classes were wrecked. Their numbers include steamers, a tug, schooners, a barge, and three barks. A variety of wreckage such as pig iron, coal, grain, and lumber eventually washed ashore between Port Washington and the Illinois border.

One of the more well-known boats of the period, famous for being the first iron-hulled cargo ship built on the Great Lakes, was the propeller steamer *Merchant*. In a twist of irony, the *Merchant* also became famous for being the first iron-hulled vessel wreck on the lakes.

The *Merchant* was built by David Bell of Buffalo in 1862 and was 200 feet in length with a displacement of 750 gross tons. On October 6, 1872, the vessel was carrying a cargo of passengers and lumber when the steamer blew onto a reef near Racine. This particular reef was well known to the *Merchant*—it had been stranded there twice before. Various reports state that the *Merchant* was destroyed by either a fire or by a storm and wave action soon after grounding on the reef. Whatever the actual reason for the *Merchant*'s ruin, crew and passengers were able to reach shore safely.

One week later, the steamer *Lac La Belle* was lost during a storm 20 miles from Racine. The victim of an autumn gale, the *Lac La Belle* foundered with a cargo of grain. Eight crew members drowned when their lifeboat capsized. September of the following year would witness a similar voyage by the *Lac La Belle*'s sister ship, the *Ironsides*. Both vessels were making the run from

---

[4] Other sources state that six or seven people perished in the accident.

A typical nineteenth-century advertisement for a Lake Michigan passenger steamer.
—Courtesy of the Library of Congress

Milwaukee to Grand Haven, only to be lost to Lake Michigan during foul weather.

Fire is not a common cause of destruction on Lake Michigan, but it is certainly not a rare occurrence. One such example of the dangers posed by fire was the schooner *St. Lawrence*. Owned by its skipper, Captain Martin Larkins, the *St. Lawrence* was carrying a cargo of timber when a kettle of pitch on the galley stove boiled over and caught fire. Used as a sealant to protect a vessel, the pitch now served to destroy the *St. Lawrence*. Captain Larkins and a passenger attempted to launch the schooner's lifeboat but the vessel was still traveling about six miles an hour. Captain Larkins and the passenger fell overboard with the lifeboat, which immediately capsized. Both men drowned. Sailing in the same waters off Milwaukee, the schooner *Granada* came across the scene and rendered assistance. Despite the danger posed to the *Granada*, her crew braved the flames to save the four remaining members of the *St. Lawrence*'s crew.

While the seventies witnessed numerous wrecks up and down the coast, the 1880s were by far the worst decade ever for southern Wisconsin. Although shipping losses for this ten-year period exceed the prior decade by only a handful, the loss of life was much higher. Accurate counts are not available, but at least 17 died during the 1870s. By the following decade this number climbed to as much as 46 in seven different wrecks, four of which went down with all hands.

Ice is a factor in many wrecks on Lake Michigan. The steamer *St. Albans* was one of many boats destroyed by this floating menace. The *St. Albans* had just departed Milwaukee for Ludington on January 30, 1881, when the steamer struck a large piece of ice and took on water.

These tiny and seemingly insignificant icebergs, common in the months leading to the spring thaw, can punch a hole in the hull of a wooden ship. A captain may force his boat into an ice field, back up and ram the ice sheet again and again until a passage has been cleared, only to sink days later following a collision with a seemingly insignificant ice chunk.

The captain of the *St. Albans* ordered his boat to shore, but the steamer sank eight miles from Milwaukee. All 27 on board successfully abandoned the *St. Albans,* but the cargo of flour and cattle was lost.

Nearly half the loss of life during the 1880s can be traced to just three separate incidents. Twenty-one sailors perished during a single 34-day period between late October and early December 1882. The first boat was the tug *Rudolph Wetzel,* which was destroyed when its boiler exploded on October 28. All on board perished. The *Wetzel* was followed on November 25 by the *Collingwood.* A schooner, the *Collingwood* capsized during a storm, taking four or five of a crew of eight with it. Less than a week later, on December 1, the steam barge

R. G. Peters caught fire well out on Lake Michigan. The *Peters* and the crew of 17 were lost.

The 1890s were not much kinder to the boats sailing to and from the southern ports than the previous decade, but the toll on human lives was not as great. The schooner *Lumberman* is indicative of the typical shipwreck for this period.

Built in 1862 in Grand Haven, Michigan, the *Lumberman* started its career as a bark. Like many such vessels, the sails and rigging were adapted to those of the more practical schooner. The *Lumberman* was making the trip from Chicago to Kewaunee when a gale caught the schooner off Oak Creek, just south of Milwaukee. Capsizing, the *Lumberman* dumped its crew. Captain Voss barely managed to escape. He was caught underwater in the rigging but was able to free himself and reach the surface. The crew was forced to wait for three hours before the steamer *Menominee* happened by and rescued them.

As is true with many lake wrecks, the *Lumberman* was a navigation hazard. The masts stuck above the surface where they could tear into the bottom of an unsuspecting vessel making its way through a blinding lake fog or howling snowstorm. For this reason, the masts were removed.

A NEW CENTURY AND NEW WRECKS

The double-masted schooner *John V. Jones* was a product of the Rand and Burger Company in Manitowoc. Built in 1876, the *Jones* was originally used to haul general freight, then coal and iron, prior to carrying a cargo of wood. On October 18, 1905, the *John V. Jones* was loaded with a cargo of hardwood for the Milwaukee market.

All but one of the crew was from Scandinavia, including Captain Fredreksen. Departing Beaver Island for Milwaukee on a Wednesday morning, Captain Fredreksen was able to pick up a good northeast wind by afternoon. By midnight, the wind was strengthening and by the following morning the crew of the *Jones* was fighting a storm.

All Thursday the crew battled the wind and waves. By Friday morning they were busy manning the pumps. Outside, the snow continued to tear at the *Jones*. Waterlogged, battling a snowstorm, and unable to compete with the elements, the ship capsized at 3 a.m.

Desperately, the crew hung onto the hull and waited for help. Although they could see an occasional boat pass by, they were never spotted. Two of the crew members succumbed to exposure and slipped from the hull into the freezing water. Still waiting for rescue, the remaining members of the crew watched as darkness descended over the lake. A short while later the *Jones* began to roll and everyone aboard was tossed into the water. Fortunately, the ship rolled back onto its hull, leaving the half-submerged deck facing the sky. It took the crew a while to realize the good fortune, but after about an hour the survivors were back on board the waterlogged schooner.

On Saturday morning, the car ferry *Pere Marquette 18* was on a course with the remains of the *John V. Jones.* The *Pere Marquette 18,* commanded by Captain Peter Kilty, had left Ludington the night before, bound for Milwaukee. Spying the wreckage of the *Jones,* Captain Kilty had the *Pere Marquette 18* brought on a course that took the large ferry to where the survivors huddled on board the wrecked schooner. After assisting the barely living crew on board the *Pere Marquette 18,* Captain Kilty brought the four survivors to Milwaukee.

Kept afloat by its cargo of lumber, the *Jones* was salvaged and returned to service. Captain Kilty and the crew of the *Pere Marquette 18* were not so fortunate. Seven years later, crew and boat were lost in a September storm (see chapter 10 for the account).

On land as well as at sea, safety and living standards were improving as the country moved into the twentieth century. Still, this was the age of smoke belching factories, when little was known about industrial pollution and the impact of coal produced smoke on the environment. Smog, finally reduced in the latter half of the twentieth century, has its origins in the early industrial era. Large cities, such as Chicago and Milwaukee, with their industrial infrastructure, were known for their pollution.

On November 2, 1905, the wood-hulled steamer *Appomattox* and two other vessels were blinded by heavy smoke blowing across the lake from Milwaukee. Unable to find their way, all three boats stranded. Although two of the boats were eventually worked off, the *Appomattox* remains in 20 feet of water.

Occasionally, some wrecks border on the humorous. The bulk freighter *E.M. Ford* sank at its dock in Milwaukee during a storm on Christmas Eve 1979. At the time the *Ford* was in service as a cement freighter. To refloat the freighter, thousands of tons of hardened cement had to be removed. The ship was recovered and celebrated its 100th birthday in 1998, still with a coal-fired quadruple expansion steam engine.

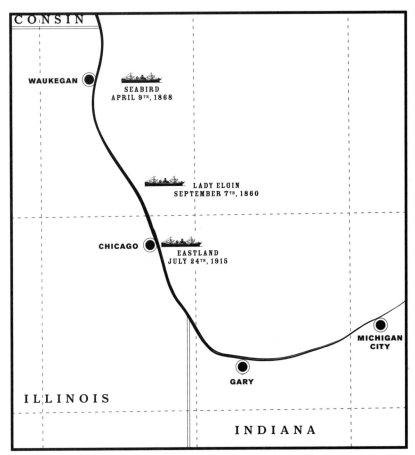

The Illinois shoreline.
—Courtesy of the National Oceanographic and Atmospheric Administration

CHAPTER

7

ILLINOIS

An early view of the Rush Street Bridge over the Chicago River.
—*Courtesy of the Library of Congress*

In 1673, European explorers on Lake Michigan first visited the shoreline of what was to become Illinois. Their venture was part of the French effort to explore the course of the Mississippi River in search of a route from the Atlantic Ocean to the Pacific. Father Jacques Marquette, a Jesuit priest, and Louis Joliet, a Canadian explorer and cartographer, led this early expedition.

It would be more than 100 years before the first permanent settlement would be established on the shoreline. In 1779, Jean Baptiste Point du Sable, an African American born in Santo Domingo, established the first community in the area that would one day be the city of Chicago. A man of refinement, du Sable's talents included carpentry, milling, animal husbandry, and other enterprises. Shortly after settling along Lake Michigan, du Sable married an American Indian woman. It was the area's first wedding involving a non-native.

Coastal Illinois flourished with the construction of Fort Dearborn in 1803. Following that, a relatively brief period of prosperity lasted until the War of 1812. On August 15, 1812, a large force of Potawatomi and Winnebago Indians, allies of the British, attacked Fort Dearborn and burnt it to the ground. It would not be until 1816 that the fort would be rebuilt and security once again offered to settlers moving into the region. With this guarantee, boats returned to the area and commerce resumed. At the time, the area was part of the Indiana Territory, and it wasn't until 1818 that Illinois was granted statehood.

Chicago became a town in 1833, four years prior to being incorporated as a city. The name Chicago is based on an Indian word for "great" or "strong." This name was prophetic, since the city's subsequent growth was nothing less than spectacular. In 1833, the first year official status was given to the metropolitan area of Chicago, the population was a mere 350. By the end of the decade it was more than 4,500.

The area's early growth was closely linked to Lake Michigan, which provided easy access for new settlers and the transportation of goods. In 1848, completion of the Illinois and Michigan Canal created a passage between the Great Lakes and the Mississippi River. Fifteen years prior to this, soldiers from Fort Dearborn dug an opening through the sandbar at the mouth of the Chicago River. These engineering feats allowed lake traffic into the interior of Illinois and to the Gulf of Mexico via the Mississippi River, creating opportunities for transporting goods and the growth of commerce. They also ensured Chicago's development as the preeminent port on Lake Michigan and one of the world's major commercial hubs.

By 1850, the population of Chicago had risen to 30,000. This was the same year that the state's first railroad commenced operations. As a result, increasing numbers of settlers poured into Chicago. Ten years later, the city's population passed 109,000.

The burgeoning rail system also contributed to an increase in overland shipping, allowing goods and people faster and more convenient passage westward. The railroads sparked the growth of the meatpacking industry, steel mills, foundries, and hundreds of manufacturing plants. The city's location and access to cheap labor provided an ideal climate for growth.

As a consequence of the increase in maritime commerce, an inland distribution network, and the development of the city's manufacturing infrastructure, Chicago assumed the mantle of "Queen of the Lakes." As an inevitable consequence of the heavy ship traffic that accompanied the city's growth, the Illinois shoreline has borne witness to a parade of shipwrecks. In addition, Illinois lays claim to the two most deadly disasters, the capsizing of the *Eastland* in 1915 and the sinking of the *Lady Elgin* in 1860. All this occurred despite the fact that Illinois's land exposure to Lake Michigan is limited—only Indiana's shoreline is smaller.

I THE LADY ELGIN

Lake Michigan holds the dubious honor of being the scene of three of the four worst disasters, in terms of lives lost, on the Great Lakes: the *Eastland,* the *Lady Elgin,* and the *Phoenix,* which burned to the waterline in 1847 off Sheboygan, Wisconsin. Besides the *Eastland* and the *Lady Elgin,* the only other Great Lakes shipwreck with a greater loss of life than the *Phoenix* involved the *G. P. Griffith,* which was lost to fire on Lake Erie, a tragedy that followed the *Phoenix* by three years.

The story of the *Lady Elgin* is a compelling one. With long, sleek lines, the passenger steamer was one of the most beautiful boats ever to dip its paddles into the Great Lakes. It was built in 1851 by Bidwell & Banta of Buffalo, New York, for $96,000 and was named after the wife of a former governor general of Canada. The ship was 231 feet long, 33 feet at the beam, and had a draft of 12 feet. Built of white oak, the double-decked vessel displaced 1,037 gross tons. The pair of side-wheels were 32 feet in diameter.

In 1857, Jack Wilson became captain of the *Lady Elgin,* possibly as a reward for his earlier maritime accomplishments. One of them was his role in helping build the Soo Canal, a navigable link between Lake Superior and the lower lakes that was completed in 1855. Prior to this, lake travelers had to portage their cargo or carry it in wagons to avoid the inhospitable rapids of the Saint Mary's River, which was the only water link between Superior.

As a gesture of appreciation for his assistance in building the canal, the Fairbanks Scale Company gave Captain Wilson the honor of bringing the first boat through the canal's locks. Wilson's command at the time was the 927-ton side-wheel steamer *Illinois*. Two years later, he was given command of the *Lady Elgin*, a darling of the Great Lakes community.

Each year, Captain Wilson and the *Lady Elgin* opened the shipping season by being first through the Straits of Mackinac and the Soo Canal. Despite its grandeur and seaworthiness, the *Elgin* had several accidents prior to its fatal voyage in 1860. Four years earlier, the *Elgin* caught fire while on Lake Superior. Two years after that it stranded at Copper Harbor in Michigan's Upper Peninsula. As a consequence of these incidents, the vessel's insurance rating was lowered. Nevertheless, the *Lady Elgin* was a well-built craft, strong enough to handle nearly anything the lakes could throw at it.

By 1860, political, economic, and social divisions were slowly tearing the country apart. There was strong abolitionist sentiment in Wisconsin. The governor, Alexander Randall, so despised the institution of slavery that he suggested Wisconsin secede from the Union.

One of the state's militias, the Irish Union Guard of Milwaukee's Third Ward, led by Captain Garrett Barry, backed Randall's abolitionist views but stated that it would remain loyal to the United States. Since the Union Guard supported the state but was independent of any government, they were able to hold to such views. For this act of defiance the Union Guard was ordered to disband. Instead, it turned to private sources for financing and support.

The two chief rivals at the time for the office of the presidency were Stephen A. Douglas and Abraham Lincoln. One of the chief sources of funding for the Union Guard was to come from an excursion on board the *Lady Elgin* from Milwaukee to Chicago, where Douglas was scheduled to speak on Friday, September 7, 1860. After spending the day in Chicago and listening to Douglas, the Irish Union Guard and their families returned to the *Lady Elgin*.

A stiff breeze picked up as the *Lady Elgin* left port a little before midnight. It was in the grip of gale-force winds spawned by a heavy thunderstorm. Despite the poor weather, many of the passengers were dancing to the music of a German band.

Closing distance with the *Lady Elgin* that night was the schooner *Augusta*. Loaded with lumber, the *Augusta* was carrying nearly full sail despite the weather. Skippered by Captain Darius M. Malott, the ship was taking a beating in the storm. On deck, the lumber shifted, threatening to capsize the *Augusta*, which by now was almost on its side. It seemed doubtful that the vessel would reach port. Reports differ as to whether the *Augusta* was sailing without running lights, but regardless the ship was invisible to the *Lady Elgin,* even though the schooner's lookout spotted the steamer 20 minutes before the collision. Only when they were nearly upon the *Elgin* did Captain Malott issue orders to avoid an accident. By then it was too late.

The *Augusta* tore into the port side of the *Lady Elgin,* just behind the paddlewheel and near the gangway. The *Augusta*'s jib boom ripped into the steamer's hull and cabins. The two vessels were carried a short way together before separating. In addition to the storm damage, the *Augusta* was leaking badly as a consequence of the collision.

At 2:30 a.m., those who had already retired for the night, as well as the dancers still enjoying the comforts afforded by the *Elgin*'s salons, felt a jolt at the moment of collision. Moments later, the dance floor canted at a sharp angle.

One of the best insights into what took place at that instant comes from a survivor who was in the dance hall at the time. He states:

> *At the moment of the collision there was music and dancing in the forward cabin. In an instant after the crash all was still, and in half an hour the steamer sunk. I passed through the cabin; the ladies were pale but silent. There was not a cry nor a shriek; no sound but a rush of steam and surge of heavy seas; whether they were not fully aware of the danger, or whether their appalling situation made them speechless, I cannot tell.*

Captain Wilson, asleep seconds before the impact, rushed to the engine room, where he found water pouring through the gash the *Augusta* had torn in the hull. Heading to the pilothouse from the engine room, he ordered the helmsman to set a course for shore. Realizing that they would never reach the coast in time, Captain Wilson ordered a lifeboat lowered over the side. Inside were a handful of men who were to determine the extent of the damage. One of the men in the boat was the first mate, George Davis. Unfortunately, the boat was lowered without oars and the vessels quickly separated.

Captain Malott grabbed a speaking trumpet and hailed the *Lady Elgin* to find out if any assistance was required. What happened at that moment is uncertain. Conflicting accounts exist that obscure clear understanding of Captain Wilson's response. One account states that Wilson shouted back, "No, proceed on your course," while another claims that Wilson did not reply. In either case, Captain Malott assumed that he could continue to Chicago.

One of the most amazing things about the wreck of the *Lady Elgin* was the remarkable calm with which passengers and crew confronted the circumstance. There was neither panic nor cries of fear. Part of the reason for this was the calm and deliberate manner in which Captain Wilson and the crew handled the situation.

The *Lady Elgin* was carrying approximately 400 passengers, fifty head of cattle, and iron stoves. The cattle were forced overboard to lighten the load. The stoves were taken to the starboard side in order to shift the weight, bringing the hole in the *Elgin*'s side out of the water. While this was being done, crewmen were trying to stem the flow of water by stuffing mattresses into the large gash. It was apparent that none of these efforts would be sufficient. The *Lady Elgin* settled lower in the water.

The crew began to rip apart the superstructure to use for rafts. Doors were smashed with axes in order to free trapped passengers. Apart from the splintering wood, the only other noises were the surf and the hiss of escaping steam.

Captain Wilson, who had been assisting trapped passengers escape, handed out life preservers. Roughly 20 minutes after being rammed by the *Augusta*, the *Elgin*'s engines tore through the bottom. The seas battered the stricken steamer, which broke into three large sections. Of these, one sank immediately. The pressure inside blew the cabins free of the deck as this portion of the steamer disappeared beneath the surface of Lake Michigan. The remaining two sections floated for a while before breaking apart.

Shouting encouragement to the survivors, Captain Wilson saw to it that as many as possible clung to the largest section of wreckage still afloat. Taking a child from the arms of an exhausted woman, Wilson gave it to another while he attempted to rig a sail. A wave washed over the wreckage and the infant was lost.

It was a heart-rending scene. Clinging to whatever flotsam they could find, scattered groups of people or lone survivors waited for the waves to wash them nine miles to shore. Lightning split an angry sky as rain lashed the passengers and crew.

The first survivors to reach shore were in the lifeboat that had floated away from the *Lady Elgin* early on. The first mate, Davis, climbed a cliff and discovered a house owned by the Gage family. The Gages saw to it that Chicago and the neighboring areas were alerted to the plight of the ship and its passengers.

By 8 a.m., students from Northwestern University and others were on hand to help the survivors of the *Lady Elgin*. Approximately 100 people perished in the nine-mile stretch between the *Elgin*'s resting place. Approximately 150 more died within 50 yards of shore as their makeshift rafts hit shallow waters and were torn apart. At least half of these came close to safety, only to drown in the coastal surf. An estimated 297 people perished in the accident.[1]

---

[1] Due to the lack of passenger lists, the count of passengers on board the Lady Elgin at the time of the incident may have been as high as 500, with 380 lost.

Reaching shore safely, Captain Wilson noticed two women struggling in the surf. He returned to the lake in an attempt to save them. His body was found several days later at Michigan City, Indiana, on the opposite side of the lake.

Edward Spencer, a divinity student at Northwestern University, entered Lake Michigan 15 times before exhaustion and the cold forced him to build a small fire with driftwood. Seated at his fire, he spied a couple desperately trying to reach safety. Already pushed to the edge of endurance, Spencer went out a final time and helped bring the couple, a husband and wife, safely in. Eighteen years later, the Evanston, Illinois, U.S. lifesaving station was established due to the number of wrecks in the area. As a result of Edward Spencer's efforts, a bronze plaque at the university commemorates his actions. Captain Garrett Barry of the Union Guard also distinguished himself in the rescue operations and survived the ordeal.

The *Augusta* entered Chicago that morning unaware of the tragedy in its wake. On hearing of the incident, Captain Malott was horrified. Despite the fact that he did not realize the damage he had caused the *Lady Elgin,* and regardless of the fact that a board of inquiry later found both captains innocent of any wrongdoing, the public was outraged.

No other crew wanted to serve on the *Augusta.* That winter the *Augusta* was painted black and renamed the *Colonel Cook.* While in Milwaukee the following May, a group of Irish protesters marched on the *Augusta* with the intention of destroying the boat and possibly the crew. The renamed *Augusta* took flight immediately for the Atlantic seaboard. Years later, the ill-fated schooner returned to the lakes. In 1894, the *Augusta* wrecked on the south shore of Lake Erie between Lorain and Cleveland.

Darius Malott was destined to die on Lake Michigan. The son of a lake skipper, he was with his family on board the double-masted schooner *Experiment* when it capsized during a storm off St. Joseph, Michigan, around 1840. The only survivors were young Darius Malott, a child at the time, his mother, and another sibling.

Four years after the *Lady Elgin* disaster, Captain Malott and his crew from the *Augusta* were working a new boat, the three-masted bark *Mojave,* when it met disaster.[2] A year old, the *Mojave* and its crew set sail in fine weather, only to disappear on September 8, 1864. The fact that this was the anniversary of the collision with the *Lady Elgin* may be more than mere coincidence. While

---

[2] At least one other account claims that Captain Malott and his crew were lost on the schooner Mohare and not the Mojave. Most reports indicate that it was the Mojave.

The schooner Augusta.—*Courtesy of the Library of Congress*

it is possible that the *Mojave* disappeared with the full crew of ten due to a sudden squall, a shifting of the cargo, a collision with some sort of debris, or for some other reason, there are those who suspect that the *Mojave*'s crew were murdered for retribution. There were also those who suspected Captain Malott of being a Confederate sympathizer. There were even far-fetched claims that Malott rammed the *Lady Elgin* to destroy the political clout of the Irish Union Guard.

The fate of the *Augusta*, the captain, and crew are not the only footnotes to the story of the *Lady Elgin*. When the *Elgin* went down, it did so with between 297 and 380 people and left behind more than 1,000 orphans. Among the lost were Colonel Landsden and his family and Herbert Ingraham, a member of the British Parliament, and his son. Landsden and Ingraham were important figures in the newspaper industry. This fact could hardly have helped the image of the *Augusta*'s crew painted by the press.

In a case heard before the U.S. Supreme Court in 1860, the destruction of the *Lady Elgin* on Lake Michigan and the *Erie* on Lake Erie, both with large loss of life, prompted this opinion:

The appalling destruction of life in the loss of the Erie *upon Lake Erie, and of the* Superior *and* Lady Elgin *upon Michigan, are still fresh in the recollections of the country. The policy and justice of the limitation of the liability of the owners, under this act of 1851, are as applicable to this navigation as to that of the ocean. The act was designed to promote the building of ships, and to encourage persons engaged in the business of navigation, and to place that of this country upon a footing with England and on the continent of Europe.*

The accident had political repercussions as well. Several groups blamed Governor Randall for the disaster because they claimed it would never have happened were it not for his disbanding of the Milwaukee Irish Union Guard.

As the shadows of war gradually lengthened, the wreck of the *Lady Elgin*, receded from everyone's attention. But the *Elgin* has never been totally forgotten. A memorial mass at St. John the Evangelist Roman Catholic Church is said annually for those who perished that storm-driven night. In 1989, the large sections that broke up while the *Lady Elgin* was in its death throes were discovered in 60 feet of water off Winnetka, Illinois. The remains are a favorite attraction for divers and have been contested by a salver and the state of Illinois in the courts. By the close of the twentieth century, this legal battle had yet to be settled.

II THE SEABIRD

The *Seabird* is best remembered for three notable facts: the ease with which the accident could have been avoided, the large loss of life involved, and the impact the wreck had on regulations governing design and construction of lake boats.

Built by the R.C. Conwell firm in 1859, the *Seabird* was a handsome side-wheel steamer carrying passengers and freight. It received its baptism in the waters of Lake Erie at Newport, Michigan. Its only significant accident occurred in 1863, when it went ashore at Whitefish Bay, Wisconsin. The *Seabird* was freed a year later by its owners, Ward and Blodgett, who sold the steamer off. By 1868, the *Seabird* was in the hands of the relatively new Goodrich Line.

Established in 1856 by Captain A.E. Goodrich, the Goodrich Transportation Company grew to become the premier shipping line on the Great Lakes. It was a shipping empire that would last until the competing interests of rail and highway strained the firm's resources to the breaking point. The Great Depression proved to be the final blow and the Goodrich Transportation Company, after 77 years of service, closed its doors in 1933.

Known for providing passengers with plush surroundings, the Goodrich boats were called "floating palaces." The first vessels owned by Goodrich were primarily side-wheel steamers, although these gave way to the new propeller steamers.

On April 9, 1868, the *Seabird* was steaming south toward Chicago, having departed Manitowoc where the boat had spent the winter. This was the *Seabird's* first run of the season, and it was carrying from 50 to more than 100 passengers.

Off Waukegan, Illinois, before dawn on this bitterly cold spring morning, the boat's porter was cleaning the stove in the aft cabin on the top deck. Taking his scuttle, by now loaded with ash and glowing embers, he opened the door and stepped outside. Although he undoubtedly knew better, the porter threw the contents of the scuttle over the side and into the wind, then quickly returned to the warmth of the aft cabin. The wind, blowing from the northeast, caught hold of the embers and threw them onto the lower deck. Landing on freshly varnished tubs filled with hay, the embers burst into flame.

Two men, the porter and an unidentified man in the aft section, noticed the blaze and raised the alarm. By the time assistance arrived it was too late to save the *Seabird*. The flames spread quickly. Desperately, the captain headed for the Illinois shoreline, but the fire was whipped into a frenzy by the wind.

An explosion made the four lifeboats useless. Passengers poured from their staterooms in various stages of undress. In their panic and confusion, men and women leapt overboard. Those who could swim quickly succumbed to the numbing effects of the water.

The *Seabird*, by now a funeral pyre, continued in a clockwise circle through the debris-strewn water until the engines quit. One of the few survivors held to a piece of wreckage for twelve hours.

In the waters off Waukegan, the schooner *Cordelia* saw the inferno on the horizon. In the predawn hours, such an enormous blaze on the open lake was impossible to miss and could mean only one thing—a ship was in peril. The *Cordelia* reached the disaster scene as soon as possible but was able to locate only two survivors. Counts as to the number of survivors and those who perished disagree. One, two, or three survivors are generally regarded as the handful who lived to tell their stories. Three is the most probable number, with one surviving on a raft and the remaining two picked up by the *Cordelia*.

Either no passenger manifest existed, as was common in those days, or it went down with the vessel. As a result, the number of dead has never been determined. Estimates range at anywhere from 102 to 250, with the death toll most likely in the lower range.

III THE EASTLAND

It is perhaps fitting that Chicago, the largest city on the Great Lakes, was the scene of the greatest maritime catastrophe in their history. The nature of the tragedy also reflects something about the city's multicultural makeup and its role as one of the nation's leading manufacturing centers. Many of the passengers who perished worked in the huge Hawthorne manufacturing plant of the Western Electric Company—a predecessor of AT&T (now Lucent Technologies). They were either immigrants from Central Europe or the sons and daughters of these immigrants. Many lived in the close-knit ethnic neighborhoods that marked Chicago. In the end, the 1915 disaster was a tragedy for the city and for the Great Lakes.

The *Eastland* was built by the Jenks Ship Building Company for the Michigan Steamship Company. Prior to its launching at Port Huron, Michigan, the boat was known as *Hull Number 25*. In April of 1903, Mrs. David Reid of South Haven won a contest to name the new excursion steamer. For her efforts, Mrs. Reid received the sum of ten dollars and a free season pass on board the *Eastland.* The following month, the 1,218-ton steel steamer was launched.

A propeller steamer, the *Eastland* was a handsome craft. With four decks, the passenger boat was something radical for the Jenks Company, which typically built only freighters. The *Eastland* was the sole exception in the firm's history. At the time of its construction, the vessel was 265 feet in length, 38 feet at the beam, and 19 feet in depth. Able to cruise at speeds of up to 22 miles an hour, the *Eastland* was dubbed the "Speed Queen of the Lakes."[3]

But the *Eastland* was not without flaws, one of which led to tragic consequences. The length and beam were designed for speed rather than stability. Furthermore, the metacentric height was questionable from the very beginning.[4] From drawing board to construction, unplanned changes occurred. Sixty feet were removed from the design and an additional deck was added. In the years after the *Eastland*'s christening, additional alterations were made.

In 1904, equipment was added to improve engine performance and speed and to provide the *Eastland*'s passengers with the comfort of air conditioning. Five years later, the cabins on the cabin deck were removed and this open deck where passengers could congregate became known as the "'tween deck." As a

---

[3] Speed on the Lakes is measured in terms of miles per hour rather than knots per hour.
[4] The metacentric height is a measure of a ship's stability in water.

The Eastland in her glory days.
—Courtesy of the Michigan Maritime Museum

consequence, the upper deck, where most passengers would be expected to enjoy an excursion, became the promenade deck. In 1912, the twin stacks were reduced by a third of their height. This was also the year of the *Titanic* disaster. By 1915, La Follette's Seaman's Act was signed into law.[5] From this point forward, passenger capacity rather than gross tonnage was the determining factor in establishing lifeboat accommodations. Three lifeboats and six rafts, an additional ten tons, were added to the promenade deck. That same year, tons of concrete were added to the main and 'tween decks to cover wooden planking weakened by age and rot. These improvements served to further reduce the *Eastland*'s metacentric height, making it less stable.

Passengers and crew could attest to problems with the boat's equilibrium. In fact, there were enough events in the *Eastland*'s history to suggest trouble in its ability to handle. In 1903, the *Eastland* struck the tug *George W. Gardner*. The captain was removed from command as a result of the incident. The following year, more than 3,000 passengers were sailing on board the *Eastland* on the open lake when the vessel listed an estimated 20 to 25 degrees, first to port, then to starboard. As a result of this incident, the carrying capacity was lowered from 3,300 to 2,800 passengers. In 1906, another instance of severe listing reduced the

[5] Referred to as the Boats for All law.

Postcard of the Eastland leaving port. Note the schooners off to the side.
—Courtesy of the Eastland Memorial Society

number of passengers the *Eastland* could carry to 2,400. By now, the *Eastland* was sailing under the colors of the Chicago-South Haven Line.

Starting in 1907, the *Eastland* ventured onto Lake Erie for the Lake Shore Navigation Company. Two years later the boat was purchased by the Eastland Navigation Company, but rumors continued to persist about *Eastland*'s seaworthiness. To counteract these rumors, in 1910 the Eastland Company placed this half-page advertisement in the *Cleveland Plain Dealer*:

FIVE THOUSAND DOLLAR REWARD

The steamer Eastland *was built in 1903. She is built of steel and is of ocean type in construction. Her water compartments when filled carry 800 tons of ballast. She is 269 feet long, beam 36 feet, and draws 14 feet of water. She has twin screws driven by two powerful triple expansion engines supplied with steam from four Scotch boilers.*

The material she is built of, the type of her construction, together with the power in her hold, makes her the staunchest, fastest, and safest boat devoted to pleasure on the Great Lakes.

All this is well known to people acquainted with marine matters. But there are thousands of people who know absolutely nothing about boats, the rules and regulations for their running, and the inspection and licensing of the same by the United States Government. In the hope of influ-

encing this class of people there have been put into circulation, stories to the effect the steamer Eastland is not safe.

Unfortunately, we do not know who the persons are that have caused to be put into circulation these scandalous stories. Their motives however, are easily guessed. Therefore, in justice to ourselves and in fairness to the 400,000 people that have enjoyed themselves during the past four years in this palatial craft (and that without a single mishap), we offer the above reward to any person that will bring forth a naval engineer, marine architect, a shipbuilder, or anyone qualified to pass on the merits of a ship, who will say that the steamer Eastland is not a seaworthy ship or that she would not ride out any storm or weather any condition that can arise on either lake or ocean.

—The Eastland Navigation Company

No one accepted the offer. Nevertheless, two years later, it was reported that the *Eastland* again experienced stability difficulties.

Sold in 1914 to the St. Joseph-Chicago Steamship Company, the ship returned to Lake Michigan and received a new skipper, Harry Pedersen. Later that same year, the *Eastland*'s carrying capacity was reduced to 2,183.

In 1915, the St. Joseph-Chicago Steamship Company requested that the *Eastland* be reinspected. On the basis of the number of life jackets, the inspector raised the passenger capacity from 2,183 to 2,500. The inspector's son-in-law, Joseph M. Erickson, was hired as the *Eastland*'s chief engineer shortly thereafter. Joining him was Peter Erickson, Joseph's 19-year-old brother, who signed on as oiler.

In July 1914, the Western Electric Company contracted with the Indiana Transportation Company to charter the firm's annual picnic. The outing was a daylong excursion to Washington Park in Michigan City, Indiana. Apparently, Western Electric was pleased with the contract, for they hired the services of the Indiana Transportation Company again for 1915. The contract for 1915 stipulated that six boats would be used to ferry the employees to Michigan City and back. It further specified that the *Eastland* would be the first vessel to leave the downtown dock, on the Chicago River near the Clark Street bridge.

Saturday, July 24, 1915, was an overcast and drizzly day. Despite the weather, nothing could dampen the high spirits of the approximately 5,000 Western Electric employees who turned out to participate. The price per ticket for passage on board the *Eastland*, the *Maywood*, the *Petoskey*, the *Racine*, the *Rochester,* and the *Theodore Roosevelt* was 75 cents per person. Children were free of charge.[6]

This was a working-class crowd of families and single men and women hoping to meet the right person with whom to start families. The ladies arrived in dresses and bonnets, while the men wore straw hats. Although the air temperature is generally cooler over the lake in summer, the passengers were dressed for an inland picnic. With children in tow, parents waited patiently for boarding to commence. The favorites were the *Eastland* and the *Theodore Roosevelt,* and those who arrived first received seating on board these liners. A steam calliope added to the festive air.

Standing in line was Borghild Aanstad, who was only a few days shy of her 14th birthday. The daughter of Norwegian immigrants, she was caught up in the excitement of the moment. Wearing her Sunday best and a wide brimmed Easter bonnet, Borghild was with her widowed mother, her nine-year-old sister and her uncle, Olaf Ness, who was employed by Western Electric. Soon, they would be on board the *Eastland* and on their way to Michigan City.

Boarding began at 6:40 a.m. Despite the gray skies, a pale light penetrated the layer of clouds. Chief Engineer Joseph Erickson, having just finished breakfast, was seeing to it that the *Eastland* was loaded with coal.

As the passengers walked up the gangway onto the main deck, the ship listed slightly to starboard. Given the sudden extra weight this was not surprising, but it made the task of boarding more difficult. Joseph Erickson ordered the port ballast tanks partially filled. By 6:51 a.m., the list had disappeared. The *Eastland* was taking on about 50 passengers per minute. Despite the extra weight on the starboard side, the boat began a ten-degree list to port. Erickson promptly filled the starboard tanks to correct this new imbalance.

The steady, dull throb of the engines starting up was felt by the passengers and crew on the main deck at 7:05 a.m. More than 1,000 passengers were now crowding one another on board the *Eastland*. At 7:10 a.m., Erickson instructed his crew to empty the port ballast tanks. Despite this measure, the *Eastland* began listing back toward port.

In an effort to offset this new list, Radio Officer Charles M. Dibbell tried to encourage passengers to cross the deck toward the starboard side, overlooking the dock. Such a temporary relocation of the passengers and control of the *Eastland's* equilibrium by filling and emptying the ballast tanks was standard procedure. No one had yet begun to worry and the passengers, enjoying the music of Bradfield's Orchestra, displayed little inclination to walk across the promenade deck to starboard.

---

[6] Accounts regarding the actual cost of passage differ. At least one other source states that the cost was one dollar for adults, with children admitted two for a dollar.

At least 2,500 passengers were now on board, in addition to a crew of 38. The number may have been higher. Given the pace at which the passengers were being boarded, it was difficult for the crew to accurately count the number of Western Electric employees and others who were on board.

By 7:16 a.m., bystanders noticed a 15-degree list to port. The starboard ballast tanks were opened to compensate. At this point one of the fundamental flaws of the *Eastland*, present since the boat's construction, displayed itself.

The *Eastland* was fitted with twelve ballast tanks. This system was designed so that it was impossible for the crew to fill tanks on one side of the boat while simultaneously draining tanks on the opposite side. Further, there was no gauge indicating how full the tanks were, although this could be ascertained with a dipstick. Still, it was difficult for Chief Engineer Joseph Erickson to have a clear idea of how much water the *Eastland* had taken on. Had there been a faster means of verifying the water level in the ballast tanks, Erickson might have realized that the most recent attempt to fill the tanks had been delayed a full seven minutes. As it stood, this error went undetected.

Unaware of events taking place below, the passengers were enjoying the fresh air of the upper decks and dancing to the music being played by the band. Others, including Borghild Aanstad, were inside the *Eastland* waiting for the children's dance music to begin. The Aanstads had a picnic lunch, which was safely stored in a basket beneath a seat. Having a strong knowledge of ships, Mrs. Aanstad remarked to her daughters that she didn't like the way the vessel felt. This comment was something Borghild would remember for the rest of her life.

The *Eastland* soon returned to an even, but unsteady, keel. The gangway was taken in and the stern line cast off. Minutes later the vessel listed to port. Beer bottles crashed to the deck, sending shards of glass underfoot. By this time, water was pouring through the scuppers and the *Eastland* began its inevitable descent into history. People in neighboring office buildings noticed the problem. Curiously, no one on board the *Eastland*, save a few of the crew, was aware that the boat was in mortal peril.

By 7:23 a.m., water streamed through the gangways. The crew attempted a second and final time to lead the passengers to starboard. A warning whistle was sounded, but Captain Pedersen, apparently unaware of what was happening to his boat, signaled the operator of the Clark Street bridge to raise the drawbridge.

By now the list was an alarming twenty degrees. Despite the fact that the *Eastland* was moving away from the dock with its cargo of picnickers, not all of the mooring lines had yet been released.

Numerous explanations have been presented for what was seconds away from occurring. One source states that a fireboat blew its whistle, much to the delight of the passengers, who rushed to port to watch the smaller craft glide past. Some observers said it was a speedboat or even a vessel with a motion picture camera mounted. Whatever it was, at about this time the bilge pumps were ordered into operation. This action was necessary given the amount of water entering the ship.

Many insisted that there was a mass movement to port, but certain facts make this assertion questionable. Given the number of people crowding the decks, it was difficult if not impossible to even dance. This casts doubt on the possibility that a substantial body of passengers were able to move from one side of the *Eastland* to the other.

Despite the best efforts of the crew, the list worsened, reaching 25 and then 30 degrees. Crew members fled the engine room. The port list soon reached 35, then 40 degrees. Still, there was no sense of disaster among the passengers, who were enjoying the lively strains of ragtime.

As the ship's clocks reached 7:28 a.m., the list touched 45 degrees. The list was severe enough that china and other items were spilling from shelves. As the piano slid across the rain-slick surface of the promenade deck, passengers fought to get out of its way. The refrigerator behind the bar fell over with a loud crash, injuring several women in the process. By now it was obvious to all on board that the *Eastland* was a doomed ship. Many of those who survived raced to the starboard side, where they leapt to the safety of the wooden dock below.

The *Eastland* hung, as if suspended in time, for the briefest of moments. Then, the boat tipped over, spilling those on deck into 20 feet of water. Many managed to crawl onto the starboard side, where they were rescued. Others swam across the Chicago River to safety. Sadly, many in the water could not swim.

Aggravating the situation was the fact that many passengers were trapped inside the craft and drowned. As the boat capsized, people were thrown across staterooms and salons. Desperate men and women crawled across the walls, but the filthy Chicago River water entered faster than they could flee. A young man freed himself from a tangle of furniture and people. He rushed to the side of his girlfriend, but he was too late. She disappeared overboard before he could reach her.

The Aanstads were fighting for their lives. Borghild, with the assistance of Uncle Olaf, held onto a life preserver. Nearby, floating in the water, were the bodies of two women. Olaf Ness was doing what he could to help others, but when Borghild's mother and sister vanished beneath the water, he returned to their side and rescued them. One of many heroes that day, Olaf Ness was cred-

Rescue efforts for the capsized Eastland.
—Courtesy of the Eastland Memorial Society

ited with saving the lives of 27 people.

Fearing an explosion once the river water reached his boilers, Chief Engineer Erickson filled the boilers with water. He escaped through a porthole.

Bystanders immediately did whatever they could to help. Some dove into the water while others threw wood crates or anything that might float into the river. Panicking, passengers grabbed at one another. In the process, they pulled others under with them. Three tugs pulled alongside passengers thrashing in the water to render what assistance they could.

Peter Boyle, a sailor on the *Petoskey*, dove into the water to rescue a woman, but his efforts were in vain. He was the only one not on board the *Eastland* to perish. A truck driver for a nearby laundry, William Corbett, stopped his vehicle and entered the water, where he helped as many as he could. He was joined by Morris Gault, a Russian immigrant and tailor at Hart, Shaffner & Marx, and John Quinlan of the *Chicago Daily News*.

One of the survivors and an employee of Western Electric, Mary Vrba was thrown a life preserver by a man who had run out of a nearby office. Once safely on dock, soaked and possibly a bit dazed, she walked to the nearest set of tracks, stepped onto a streetcar, and went home.

There were others who selflessly offered whatever assistance they could. Included in their number were the police, firemen, the Red Cross, employees at the Department of Health, bystanders, bridge tenders, and more. These rescuers stood on the starboard side of the *Eastland,* where they tried to help those in the water. More often than not, people pulled from the river slid back once they reached the slippery side of the *Eastland*'s steel hull.

Captain William Bright, who had just brought in the steamer *Missouri,* took a taxi to the scene of the disaster after hearing the news. Unable to work his way through the throngs crowding the accident site, Bright went to the second floor of a nearby building. From his vantage point, he could see everything. Shouting orders from the window, he instructed the rescuers to take the ashes from the fireboxes of the three tugs and scatter them on the *Eastland* so that survivors and rescuers could grip the slick hull. He telephoned the Marshall Field department store several blocks away and instructed the company to send blankets.

The hiss and red glow of cutting torches soon indicated that a rescue attempt was underway to free those trapped inside. Holes were burned into the steel hull, through which survivors were pulled out to freedom by rope.

For most of the day, the Aanstads were trapped in an upside-down cabin. The entire family had survived. They were fortunate. There were only a handful of families that survived without losing a member. Perhaps 22 families disappeared completely in the disaster.

Eventually, the survivors and the dead were plucked from the water. The death toll stood at 835, although at least one other account places the number at 844. The bodies were taken to the Second Regiment Armory on Washington Boulevard. The armory served as one of three temporary morgues, even though it took days for all of the victims to be identified. In cases where entire families had been wiped out, it was necessary to wait for extended family to claim the dead.

Only three of the victims were crew members. Some 832, possibly more, were passengers. When the *Titanic* sank, 1,523 lives were lost. Of those lost on the *Titanic,* 694 were crew and 829 were passengers. More passengers were lost

A view of the Eastland from the opposite bank of the Chicago River.
—Courtesy of the Eastland Memorial Society

in the *Eastland* disaster than the *Titanic*. But the *Titanic* was a famous vessel carrying many wealthy passengers from as far away as Japan when it went down in the Atlantic Ocean. The *Eastland* was filled with working people from Chicago who never left the dock on the Chicago River.

The crew was arrested but acquitted of wrongdoing, although the chief engineer's filling and emptying the ballast tanks was strongly criticized. It was determined that the construction of the *Eastland* and the design of the ballast system were at fault. Approximately 20 years later, the final lawsuit was settled.

The *Eastland* was raised by the Great Lakes Towing Company and eventually sold to the federal government. Following modifications that improved its metacentric height, the ship was renamed the USS *Wilmette* and served as a Great Lakes naval training vessel during World War II. It was decommissioned in 1945 and two years later was sold for whatever the metal was worth.

Borghild Aanstad, the 13-year-old girl who survived the worst maritime disaster in Great Lakes history, lived to be 90.

OTHER SIGNIFICANT WRECKS

The first wreck on record in Illinois waters was the schooner *Hercules* in 1818. On October 3, the double-masted ship, carrying a load of whiskey, five

Salvaging the Eastland.
—Courtesy of the Michigan Maritime Museum

crewmen, and a single passenger, stranded near the Calumet River, south of Chicago, during a storm. The *Hercules* played an important role in the history of the Lake Michigan region. It appears to have been the first decked vessel to operate on a regular basis on the lake. Although LaSalle's *Griffon* may have been the first vessel to wreck in Lake Michigan, the *Hercules* is the first documented vessel to be destroyed on the lake. Furthermore, when the *Hercules* wrecked, it did so with all hands on board. In grim testimony to the nature of the western lakes of the time, wild animals consumed the bodies.

As immigrants and settlers filtered into Illinois, they established towns and cities that were quick to grow, giving rise to increasing lake trade. Despite the growing number of vessels docking at Illinois ports, it would be six years until the loss of another boat. In 1824, the schooner *Heartless* stranded near Chicago. The *Heartless* was followed ten years later by the side-wheel steamer *Newburyport*, which stranded at Chicago during a storm. Another wreck of the 1830s was the schooner *Owanungah*. This vessel stranded a short distance from the Chicago in June of 1836, but was salvaged and returned to service.

At least four more wrecks followed during the 1840s, the last of which occurred in 1849 when the steamer *Oregon* was consumed by fire. Fortunately, the *Oregon* was destroyed without injury to the crew.

MORE LAKE TRAFFIC...AND MORE WRECKS

The large number of wrecks in the 1850s provides an indication of how fast Illinois, and especially Chicago. At least 38 wrecks occurred in this decade, though most were unremarkable. Some of the more interesting include the schooner *Citizen* built by J. Edwards of Manitowoc. When launched in 1847, the *Citizen* was the first of many boats built in the Manitowoc shipyards. There is also the tale of the steam tug *Seneca*, destroyed by a boiler explosion that took the captain and a crew member.

On October 16, 1855, the double-masted brig *Tuscarora* was sailing from Buffalo to Chicago when it stranded on Harrison Island during a storm. Two attempts were made to reach the stranded vessel. The last effort, comprising nine lake captains and four seamen, used two Francis boats to rescue the *Tuscarora*'s entire crew of eleven. While the crew was saved, the vessel lasted only five days before breaking apart by wave action.

Two of the three worst disasters in Illinois history occurred during the 1860s. The death toll from these accidents would not be surpassed until the capsizing of the *Eastland* in 1915. This terrible chapter in the maritime history of Illinois began with the *Lady Elgin* disaster in 1860 and concluded with the *Seabird* in 1868. Between them, the shipwrecks may have accounted for as many

The Eastland reincarnated as the USS Wilmette.
—*Courtesy of the Michigan Maritime Museum*

as 399 lives.

With the heavy flow of ship traffic along the Chicago River, it was not long before pedestrian and vehicular traffic met with long delays. Drawbridges were raised on such a regular basis that serious traffic jams resulted. This problem was dealt with in 1869 with the construction of the Washington Street Tunnel, which went under the Chicago River. That tunnel was followed in 1871 by the LaSalle Street Tunnel. The construction of these tunnels allowed carriages easy access from one side of the river to the other. Three months after the grand opening of the LaSalle Street Tunnel, the Great Chicago Fire gutted the business district.

The fire claimed five lake boats. The most remarkable fact about these wrecks is that they happened without loss of life. The schooner *Alnwick* was lost to the flames, as were the barks *Valetta* and *Fontanella*, the propeller steamer *Navarino,* and the side-wheel steamer *Philo Parsons*. The *Navarino* made an attempt for the open lake but was forced back to its dock by the wind anf destroyed.

One of the ships destroyed by the Chicago Fire was *Philo Parsons,* which had an interesting and somewhat checkered past; it involved a Confederate scheme to capture a Union vessel during the Civil War. In 1864, Captain John Y. Beall of the Confederate Navy traveled to Toronto, where he met with Colonel Thompson, another Confederate officer. It was Thompson's plan to seize the USS *Michigan,* a 14-gun Union iron-paddle frigate. This was part of a greater scheme to free Confederate officers held prisoner on Johnson's Island in Lake Erie and at Camp Douglas in Chicago. Attacks would also be made throughout the Great Lakes.

The idea was not as far-fetched as it may seem. Due to an international treaty between the United States and Canada, both countries were allowed to keep only one gunboat on the Great Lakes. By depriving the Union of its only gunboat, the Confederates would be able to wreak havoc on lake commerce and the surrounding communities.

Assisting Beall and Thompson was Charles Cole. In August of 1864 in Sandusky, Ohio, Cole and his wife, Annie, met Captain Jack Carter. Carter was in command of the *Michigan,* Charles Cole was a Confederate spy, and Annie was a Buffalo prostitute. Introducing himself as an oilman from Pennsylvania, Cole convinced Captain Carter to invite him on board the *Michigan.* It was Cole's intention to treat the crew of the *Michigan* to champagne. At least this is what the Southern spy led Captain Carter to believe. His real goal was to drug the champagne and incapacitate the crew of the *Michigan* so that Captain Beall could seize the vessel. Cole was to signal Beall with a flare once the *Michigan*'s crew was disabled.

Captain Beall's part of the plan was to capture a boat in Detroit and travel to Sandusky, where he and his crew would capture the *Michigan.* It was a daring plan. With 20 men, Captain Beall captured the *Philo Parsons* off Kelley's Island. Shortly thereafter the *Philo Parsons* was discovered to be low on fuel. Steaming to Middle Bass Island for wood with which to fuel the *Philo Parsons,* the crew seized the *Island Queen* and its passengers, including 25 vacationing Union troops and their families.

The prisoners were sent ashore while the *Island Queen* was towed into Lake Erie and scuttled. Captain Beall then undertook an operation against the *Michigan.* Coming within sight of the vessel, the crew of the *Philo Parsons* waited for Charles Cole to give a signal. But Captain Carter had been informed of a plot against the *Michigan* and had taken actions to prevent it. This quick thinking prevented Charles Cole from boarding the *Michigan,* where he was to have used a flare to signal Captain Beall. Without a signal, the crew of the *Philo Parsons* democratically voted on whether to continue the venture. Although Captain Beall and one other conspirator, Bennett G. Burleigh of Scotland, were in favor of attacking the *Michigan*, the remaining 17 crewmen were considerably less than enthused.

When all but three of his men mutinied, Captain Beall was forced to turn back to Ontario. Beall was captured at Niagara Falls and hanged on February 24, 1865. Charles Cole was also captured and went to prison. Similar to his coconspirators, Bennet G. Burleigh was captured, but he escaped and returned to Scotland.

This daring attempt to liberate Confederate prisoners of war and take possession of a Union frigate failed. It was the only engagement between Union and Confederate forces on the Great Lakes during the Civil War. Seventeen years later, the *Philo Parson* was destroyed in the Great Chicago Fire.

1875–1900

At the end of the 18th century, Chicago's landscape was little changed from that seen by the original Native Americans and by French explorers when they set foot on its shores. As the 19th century ended, coastal Illinois bore scant resemblance to the sparsely populated land crafted thousands of years ago by the glaciers.

Skyscrapers dominated Chicago's downtown, and department stores and office buildings sprouted everywhere. The city's industrial might was reflected in hundreds of area factories, many of them casting a thick pall of smoke for miles. The city had become one of the world's major transportation and commercial hubs.

Despite the progress and activity, the maritime history of Illinois during the last two decades of the 1800s is remarkable for the fact that only one wreck occurred with a significant loss of life.

One of the more interesting wrecks involved heroic rescue efforts by the U.S. lifesaving service and by private citizens. In November 1889, the propeller steamer *Calumet* stranded north of Chicago at Fort Sheridan with 18 crew members and a load of coal. The crew was rescued by the Evanston lifeboat station and students from Northwestern University. Keeper Lawrence O. Lawson of the lifeboat station was singled out for his bravery during the rescue. His actions were so noteworthy that he became a recipient of the Gold Lifesaving Medal, an award for valor that was created 15 years before. According to an article in a 1995 issue of the *Virginian Pilot,* this was one of the first of 656 gold lifesaving medals awarded to individuals between 1874 and 1995. Of the recipients, the Great Lakes account for about 80.

Occasionally, disaster struck while a boat was docked. This can be especially true while loading or unloading flammable or explosive goods. On July 10, 1890, the steamship *Tioga* lay at its berth in Chicago, having just completed a trip from Buffalo. On board the *Tioga* was a cargo of general merchandise and barrels of oil. The night crew, all African Americans, were working in the light cast by kerosene lamps. At 7:32 p.m. an explosion and flash fire killed 27 men, injured many others, and damaged the dock and surrounding buildings.

Despite the heavy damage, the *Tioga* was raised from the depths, the bodies removed, and the boat repaired. During the recovery, two men, Hans Christiansen and Thomas Johnson, entered the vessel, only to have the lantern they were carrying set off another explosion. Both men were seriously injured survived.

During the World's Fair of 1893, the U.S. lifesaving service rescued all ten crewmen from the three-masted schooner *F.L. Danforth*. Visitors to the fair were treated to the unexpected spectacle and broke into applause once the *Danforth*'s crew was safe.

On May 18, 1894, the schooner *J. Loomis McLaren* foundered during a violent storm off 27th Street in Chicago. The first mate was the only casualty and was lost when the towline snapped and recoiled, killing him. Police and passersby saved the rest of the crew.

The *McLaren* was not the only vessel lost on that storm-plagued day. Chicago and the neighboring ports saw more boats wrecked than on any other day in Illinois history. The cause was one of the massive storms that occasionally sweeps the lake with an unforgiving fury. Fourteen vessels were destroyed that spring day. Thirteen occurred in the southern end of the lake. Eight took place in Illinois water.

One of the tragic victims of the storm was the schooner *Myrtle.* The schooner *Evening Star* was entering the port of Chicago when winds out of the northeast forced the waterlogged *Myrtle* into it. The crew of the *Myrtle* tried to get the schooner's anchor to grab onto something on the bottom, but the anchor dragged, causing the collision with the *Evening Star* and then with the schooner *Clifford.* The *Clifford* survived. The crew of the *Evening Star* reached land, but all on board the *Myrtle* drowned as a waves swept the crew of six from the deck before taking the *Myrtle* under. People lining the beach watched helplessly. Another ship lost that day off the Illinois coast with all hands was the *Lem Ellsworth,* going down with a crew of six.

Other vessels wrecked include the *Mercury, Rainbow, C.G. Mixer,* and the *Jack Thompson.* Each boat destroyed in Chicago or off the Illinois coast that day was a schooner. In the case of the *Mercury,* the *McLaren,* and the *Thompson,* civilians and the police played an important role in aiding the crews out of the surf.

On board the *Rainbow,* the crew of seven faced a bleak situation. What was left of the schooner's sails was nothing more than a tattered mess. The tugboat *Spencer* pulled alongside the *Rainbow* and removed four of the crew, but the schooner was approaching the breakwater. The *Spencer* backed away, leaving three men on board the imperiled vessel. An electrical engineer, William H. Havill, swam 80 feet from shore to the wreck with a rope and small raft. This rescue enabled Captain John Pew and a crew member to safely reach shore. Braving the surf again, William Havill swam back to the *Rainbow* and rescued the final member of the schooner's crew.

Two years later, on May 17, 1896, the schooner *Mary D. Ayer* suffered a fatal blow following a collision with the first iron-built freighter in service on the Great Lakes, the *Onoko.* This incident occurred in a heavy fog off Evanston, Illinois, and the *Ayer* went down with its crew.

The *Ayer* is indicative of the changes that were gradually taking place on the lakes. Originally constructed as a barkentine, the *Ayer* was rebuilt as a schooner. At the time of the *Ayer*'s destruction there were few, if any, barkentines still working the lake. The days of the schooner were also numbered. In the collision between the *Ayer* and the *Onoko,* sail lost to steam.

THE TWENTIETH CENTURY

The years between 1900 and 1915 were generally peaceful, despite the great increase in commercial traffic and in the number of pleasure cruises between Chicago and resort towns in lower Michigan. Only nine boats were wrecked, with little loss of life. The record changed in 1915, when the *Eastland* capsized, taking with it 835 men, women, and children. It remains the worst disaster in the history of the Great Lakes.

One of the more interesting shipwrecks lies beneath 200 feet of water off the Illinois coast. It involves a German *Unterseeboot,* or U-boat, built by Blohm und Voss of Hamburg in 1918, that served as *UC-97* in the Imperial Kriegsmarine when Germany was at war with the United States and its allies in World War I.

One of the UC-III class of mine-laying submarines, the *UC-97* displaced 491 tons on the surface and 571 submerged. This underwater craft was 184 feet in length and 19 at the beam. The *UC-97* was one of five U-boats brought to America for study after the war. The *UC-97* also toured the United States as part of a Victory Bond drive. In 1921, in accordance with the Treaty of Versailles, which required the dismantling of Germany's military capabilities, the *UC-97* was towed out into Lake Michigan by the USS *Hawk.* There it was destroyed by gunfire by the salvaged *Eastland* in its new role as the gunboat USS *Wilmette.*

The UC-97 in Toronto Harbor, 1919.
—*Courtesy of the Mike Filey Collection, Toronto*

Illinois has seen its share of shipwrecks, which were due to many different causes. Fogs and blizzards, white squalls and gales, collisions, fires and explosions, piracy, ice, and gunfire have contributed to the wrecks that occurred along the coast and in port. Many of these boats were salvaged prior to their ultimate destruction, broken apart by wind and wave, or returned to service. Others lie at the bottom of Lake Michigan, sometimes remembered, but more often forgotten.

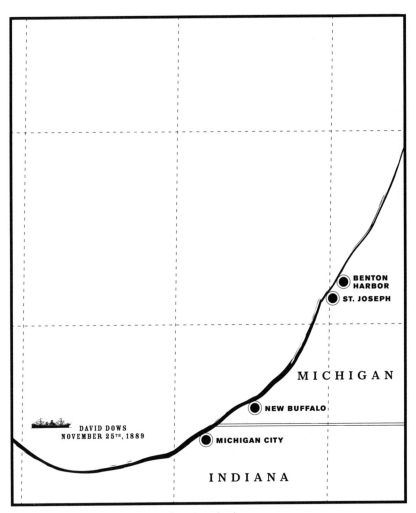

The Indiana shoreline.
—Courtesy of the National Oceanographic and Atmospheric Administration

CHAPTER

8

INDIANA

Although primarily known as an agricultural state, Indiana can also lay claim to a rich maritime history. As commercial lake traffic increased in the nineteenth century and port cities sprang up and down the Lake Michigan coast, Indiana kept pace with the growth of its neighbors. Ports such as Gary and Michigan City became major shipping centers for grain, ore, lumber, machinery, and other goods. In the later part of the century, Gary's favorable location gave rise to enormous steel mills that depended on iron ore shipped from Minnesota's Mesabi Range. It did not hurt that Chicago, the busiest port on the lake, was nearby and in need of extra space to relieve its crowded docks.

Other parts of Indiana's shoreline had been desirable locations for holiday and vacation travel ever since Chicago developed into a major metropolis. For more than a century, throngs of Chicago residents made the short lake crossing eastward to enjoy the natural beauty of the Indiana Dunes. Stretching 60 miles along the lake from Gary to Michigan City, "the Dunes" has been designated a national lakeshore and is the largest park bordering Lake Michigan. With a history of commercial and recreational traffic, it is no wonder that the waters off Indiana conceal a graveyard of broken and battered ships.

THE DAVID DOWS

When the *David Dows* was launched in the mid-afternoon hours of April 21, 1881, this schooner entered service under the gaze of hundreds of well-wishers and special guests. The largest sailing vessel ever built on the Great Lakes, the *Dows*'s christening at Toledo was a major event, with visitors arriving from various parts of the country to watch the grand display. Constructed by Bailey Brothers of Toledo for Carrington & Casey, the *David Dows* was built for speed. Construction was a valiant effort by the proponents of sail to stave off the eventual demise of wind in favor of steam, oil, and diesel.

The *David Dows* was 278 feet in length, with a 37-foot beam, and a draft of 18 feet, with a net tonnage of 1,481 tons.[1] With the possible exception of the *Golden Age*, the *David Dows* was the only five-masted vessel ever to grace the waters of the Great Lakes. Built as a barkentine, the ship's five masts varied in diameter from 21 to 36 inches and stood between 88 and 97 feet. To each of these was added a 65-foot topmast. Total height of the largest masts was 162 feet.

---

[1] Sources vary as to the length of the David Dows. One source states that it measured 265 feet. This may be a reference to the keel, which was 260 feet. According to another source, the Dows' overall length was 278 feet.

The foremast was square-rigged, while the remaining masts were all fore-and-aft rigged. The masts carried 70,000 yards of Mount Vernon duck canvas that required eight hours of hard labor by a donkey engine to raise. Because of the schooner's massive size and unique rigging, the *David Dows* carried an easily identifiable silhouette on the lakes. Its black hull was solid oak banded with ten tons of 8-inch strapping for additional support. The anchors were raised and lowered by 540 feet of chain, and the main anchor weighed a full two tons, while the smaller anchor was 3,600 pounds.

The forecastle and cabin were designed with comfort in mind. The forecastle included eight berths and sitting room for playing cards or swapping stories. The cabin included a dining room with hand-carved ceiling panels.

Built not just for speed but for cargo capacity as well, the *David Dows* could carry more than 2,500 tons of coal or 90,000 bushels of wheat. Due to its size, beauty, and cargo capacity, the vessel was dubbed the *Queen of the Lakes* and was considered the largest schooner in the world at the time.

Despite the fanfare and promise, the *David Dows* was a cursed vessel. During its construction, the *Dows* was scuttled to prevent destruction at the hands of ice-choked floodwaters. The firm of Bailey Brothers, builders of the *David Dows*, soon went out of business while the company responsible for outfitting the famous schooner burnt to a total loss. As if this weren't enough, the second mate suffered a fatal heart attack during construction. All of this happened before the *David Dows* was launched.

As Captain Joseph Skeldon took his new charge into Lake Erie for the first time, he had to wait to leave Toledo harbor until the two massive 25- and 27-foot retractable centerboards were put in place. In some ports, the ship's immense size and deep draft continued to cause problems, as the *Dows* was unable to take on a full load, even after both centerboards had been raised.

Troubles continued for the *Dows*, even in relatively benign circumstances. In 1881, it was challenged to a race on Lake Erie by the owners of the 514-ton schooner *Charles K. Nims*. Joining the two was the 189-foot-long schooner *John B. Merrill*.[2] During the race, the *Nims* pulled ahead of the *Dows*. Unexpectedly, the *Nims* then shot directly in front of the *Dows* and was rammed. The Nims sunk in the vicinity of Pelee Island, but the crew was saved.

Another collision involving the *Dows* occurred with the schooner *Richard Mott*. Four men on board the *Mott* drowned as a result of the accident. Immediately following this incident the *Dows'* topmasts were removed as a safety measure.

---

[2] The John B. Merrill survived the race with the David Dows to break up after stranding on Holdridge Shoal, near Drummond Island on Lake Huron twelve years later during a storm. The crew managed to reach shore safely.

The David Dows.
—Courtesy of the Wisconsin Maritime Museum

Despite these misfortunes, the *David Dows* was a magnificent sight and could still perform its duties at record levels. Bets were often placed as to whether the *Dows* or the *Adams*, both boats owned by Carrington & Casey, could haul more cargo. The *Dows* also set several records, including a run from Buffalo to Toledo in just 18 hours carrying a record cargo of 2,400 tons of coal.

As the *Dows'* fortunes declined in the 1880s, Captain Skeldon left for a new posting. Several strandings followed, including one that led to trouble with Canadian customs officials. On another occasion, going through the Soo Locks at Sault Ste. Marie, the huge vessel damaged a wharf. By now, the once proud ship was little more than a barge without means of self-propulsion. As if to prove that the age of sail was slowly fading, the *Dows'* sister ship, the *Adams,* was also reduced to this sorry state.

On Wednesday, November 29, 1889, the day before Thanksgiving, the steamer *Aurora* was towing the *Adams* and the *Dows* to Chicago. Each barge was loaded with a cargo of coal, which caused them to ride more heavily in the water. All three vessels were caught in the grip of a winter storm. With high seas and gusting winds, the *Aurora* and its two charges braved the elements. It was a lonely battle, fought out on the lake away from sight of land and other boats.

By 8 p.m., Wednesday, the *Dows* was taking on water. The steam and hand pumps were not up to the task of emptying the water streaming in. The donkey engine was started and the steam pump went into operation. At about 3 a.m. on Thanksgiving Day, the engine quit. Unable to be of any use to the two barges, Captain Kelly of the *Aurora* cut the cables to the *Adams* and *Dows*.

Alone and adrift, the crews of the *Dows* and *Adams* spent the night battling the elements. The *Adams* survived, but the *David Dows* was taking on water fast. Eventually, the crew of the *David Dows* climbed high into the rigging, where they hoped to catch sight of a rescue ship.

Captain Kelly urged the *Aurora* on to Chicago. Reaching the Windy City, he informed the lifesaving service of the plight of the barges. The lifesaving service dispatched the tug *Crowell* under the command of Captain Peters. The *Dows*'s crew, by now suffering from frostbite and exposure after spending the night and part of the morning in the rigging, were taken on board the *Crowell*. The *Dows* was abandoned.

By mid-afternoon, the barge slipped beneath the surface of Lake Michigan in 40 feet of water. The ship's towering masts, however, remained above the water, posing a navigational hazard. They disappeared as the ravages of wind and wave and ice took their toll. By spring, the masts were gone. An attempt was made to salvage the cargo of coal and raise the *Dows,* but the efforts were abandoned.

The *David Dows* remains at the bottom of Lake Michigan in shallow waters off Whiting, Indiana, near Chicago. This once proud boat recalls an era when sailing vessels were more than a source of recreation, they were a means of livelihood and commerce. In a bygone age, the *David Dows* was truly the Queen of the Lakes.

OTHER SIGNIFICANT WRECKS

THE NINETEENTH CENTURY

In September 1838, the side-wheel steamer *William F. P. Taylor* beached near Michigan City during a storm. The steamer was only three years old, having been built at Silver Creek, New York, in 1835. The *Taylor* was a relatively small vessel, being 88 feet long and displacing only 95 tons. The *Taylor* was one of the first shipwrecks in Lake Michigan but was not the first in Indiana waters. That honor went to the schooner *Sea Serpent*, which stranded near Michigan City during a storm in the summer of 1836.

Another incident involved the twin-masted schooner *Post Boy*. Carrying a load of gunpowder, the *Post Boy* disintegrated after an explosion at Buffington Harbor in 1841. The event claimed the lives of ten men.

Two years after the loss of the *Post Boy*, the side-wheel steamer *Superior* was taking on a load of wheat at a dock in Michigan City during an fierce October storm. The gale-force winds and rough seas drew the *Superior* away from its dock. As the lines snapped, the *Superior* found herself at the mercy of wind and waves. The steamer was beached and destroyed by wave action. The *Superior* was equipped with the original steam engine from the *Walk-In-The-Water*, one of the two earliest steamers on the lakes. It is possible that the engine was recovered from the *Superior* and found final use at a sawmill in Saginaw, Michigan.

The experiences of the *Superior* and its crew illustrate one of the major problems faced by vessels throughout the Great Lakes: the lack of an adequate harbor. Michigan City is as an excellent example of how the requirements of lake trade led to the development of suitable harbors.

Although the early residents of Michigan City built piers into the lake to accommodate lake traffic, work on a harbor did not begin until 1836 and continued up to 1870. Trail Creek, which flowed into the lake, was widened, deepened, and protected with revetments. Additional piers were added but, with the lack of a decent breakwater, vessels such as the *Superior* were dependent on the whims of nature and Lake Michigan. This situation changed as the demands of a shipping and commercial center led to better harbor facilities. Beginning in 1870, the harbor was expanded and a breakwater added to protect boats.

Roughly three-quarters of all the wrecks in Indiana waters occurred near Michigan City. The schooner *Flying Cloud* was an exception. Built in 1851, the *Flying Cloud* was sailing the waters of southern Lake Michigan in November 1857 when it stranded north of Gary during an autumn storm. The crew of seven died of exposure.

This was not the first disaster to befall the *Flying Cloud*. In 1853, the vessel capsized during a gale near Racine, Wisconsin, floating in Lake Michigan for three weeks before being towed to port. As with the schooner's previous brush with disaster, the *Flying Cloud* was returned to service, although it took three years. This may be the same *Flying Cloud* that stranded in 1890 at Glen Arbor, Michigan, near Sleeping Bear Dunes. The 1890 stranding witnessed the end of the *Flying Cloud,* although this final incident happened without any loss of life.

The early half of the nineteenth century is remarkable for the modest number of wrecks off the Indiana coast. Although the number increased with the passing of the century, there appear to have been few, if any, incidents until the 1870s. This remarkable record ended with the wreck of the *J. Barber* in 1871.

When it sank 14 miles from Michigan City, the *J. Barber* may have been only the second disaster since the wreck of the *Flying Cloud* 14 years earlier. A propeller steamer, the *J. Barber* was traveling across the lake from St. Joseph, Michigan, to Chicago with a load of fruit when the boat caught fire on July 19, 1871. The *J. Barber* was followed two years later by the propeller steamer *Eureka*. These were the only wrecks of the decade. The final 20 years of the century were not to prove so kind: nearly half of Indiana's Lake Michigan wrecks occurred in the years between 1882 and 1898, a string of misfortunes that began with the stranding of the schooner *Beloit* in 1882.

Four years later, the schooner *Ray S. Farr*, named the *Dan Newhall* when it was christened in 1864, foundered in a December storm off Michigan City. The crew managed to safely launch the boat's yawl, but in order to reach shore crew members were forced to traverse an ice field. These fields of ice begin with the shorter days of winter in shallow waters and can cover large portions of the lakes, creating hazards for navigation. It was one such field that the crew of the *Ray S. Farr* walked to reach the safety of land. Although the crew survived, frostbite cost several of the men heavily.

As noted earlier in the chapter, the *David Dows,* the largest sailing ship ever to grace the waters of the Great Lakes, foundered off the port of Whiting in 1889. That same year the schooner *Michigan City* sank just off the shores of its namesake city.

Of the 15 vessels wrecked in Indiana waters during this 16-year period, three were powered by steam. The rest relied on sail. Therefore it is no surprise to see that most of these wrecks were caused by bad weather. Only 11 of the estimated 39 shipwrecks in Indiana waters over the last two centuries may have been destroyed for reasons other than foul weather.[3] Typically, they were schooners that ended their days due to storms and a reliance on wind.

TWENTIETH-CENTURY PERILS

One example of a vessel fitted with an engine and lost for reasons other than weather is the propeller freighter *Muskegon*. On October 10, 1910, the *Muskegon* was unloading a cargo of sand at Michigan City when a fire started in the stern and spread throughout the vessel. Considered a total loss, the *Muskegon* was towed into the lake and abandoned, with the intention of having the freighter sink. Defying the wishes of its owners, the *Muskegon* drifted back toward shore and beached near Michigan City.

[3] Of these eleven wrecks, accurate descriptions of their last hours do not always exist. It is probable that at least half of these sank due to inclement weather. As noted previously, these numbers are an estimate and may grossly underestimate the actual number of shipwrecks off the coast of Indiana.

The year after the fire on board the *Muskegon,* the freighter *J.D. Marshall* was caught in a storm off Michigan City. Weathering the seas and nature, the *Marshall* fell prey to one of the worst fears of sailors—its cargo shifted. Carrying a freight of pig iron and machinery, the *Marshall* capsized, taking four of its crew beneath the waves.

The most recent of Indiana's shipwrecks involved small tugs. The first of these was the fishing tug *Martha,* which sank in 1933 with all four crew members near Michigan City. The *Martha* was followed in 1945 by the 13-ton tug *Charlotte.* As is common in the lake waters of Indiana, both tugs were lost during storms.

Approximately 32 vessels have gone down near Indiana, but this number may be deceiving. There are numerous wrecks half buried in the silt at the bottom of Lake Michigan waiting to be discovered. Some, suspected to lie in Illinois or Michigan waters, may be closer to Indiana. The opposite may hold true as well. As recreational diving and improvements in technology continue, a more accurate picture of the location of the wrecks that lie undiscovered in Lake Michigan will emerge.

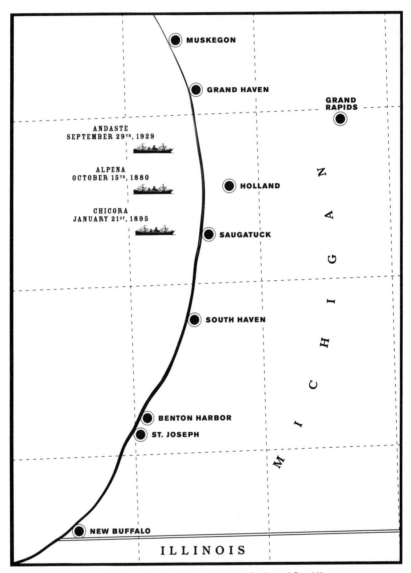

MUSKEGON

GRAND HAVEN

GRAND
RAPIDS

ANDASTE
SEPTEMBER 29TH, 1929

ALPENA
OCTOBER 15TH, 1880

HOLLAND

CHICORA
JANUARY 21ST, 1895

SAUGATUCK

M I C H I G A N

SOUTH HAVEN

BENTON HARBOR

ST. JOSEPH

NEW BUFFALO

I L L I N O I S

Southern Michigan shoreline between the Indiana border and Grand Haven.
—*Courtesy of the National Oceanographic and Atmospheric Administration*

Shipwrecks of Lake Michigan

CHAPTER

9

SOUTHERN MICHIGAN

The port cities of Grand Haven, South Haven, Saugatuck, St. Joseph, and smaller communities on the southern Michigan coast are no strangers to shipwrecks and tales of courage. Early in the 19ᵗʰ century, sailing craft and then steamers visited the small settlements in the area. As people populated this isolated region, the lake boats arrived with increasing frequency.

Long before the arrival of Europeans, this isolated region was home to the Potawatomi and Miami Indians. One of the first Europeans to visit the region was Father Jacques Marquette in 1675, who explored the coastline and inland passages in detail. Four years later, Sieur de La Salle built a small fort along the St. Joseph River. It was abandoned soon thereafter, but in 1785 a trading post was opened in the vicinity.

One of the region's major ports, St. Joseph, was incorporated in 1834. It was followed two decades later by the incorporation of the city of South Haven. Other new towns and cities sprang up, farmland was cleared, harbors were built, and a manufacturing base took solid hold. By the latter half of the nineteenth century, southern Michigan was also known as a tourist mecca. Charming and rustic buildings, seemingly endless miles of scenic coastline, and gaily decorated passenger steamers contributed to the influx of summer visitors. It did not take long before shipwrecks became commonplace along its shore.

I THE ALPENA

On Friday, October 15, 1880, Lake Michigan was enjoying an Indian summer day. The coastal communities bathed in the bright glow of the sun. All in all, it was a fine day to set sail.

Despite the pleasant weather, aboard the *Alpena,* Captain Nelson W. Napier was aware that conditions were about to worsen. The barometer was falling, but the captain, an experienced lake skipper, saw no reason to cancel the trip from Grand Haven to Chicago. On board the side-wheel steamer were between 80 and 101 passengers (no accurate records exist for numbers of passengers and crew). The ship was carrying general merchandise picked up at Muskegon and Grand Haven, including ten carloads of apples.

The *Alpena* was built in 1867 by the firm of Arnold & Gallagher of Marine City, Michigan. The vessel measured 170 feet in length, 35 feet at the beam, with a draft of 12 feet, and displaced 643 gross tons. The year after it was built, the *Alpena* was sold to the Goodrich Line, the largest shipping firm on the lakes

Alpena.—*Courtesy of the Wisconsin Maritime Museum*

at that time. Due to modifications, the *Alpena*'s final length was 175 feet, while gross tonnage was increased to 654 tons.

The ship was designed, like many of its contemporaries, as a passenger and package freight boat. Similar to other steamers of the era, the *Alpena* boasted two strengthening transverse arches on either side of the hull. These arches extended from the pilothouse near the bow to just behind the massive side-wheels, which were 48 feet in diameter. In addition, the *Alpena* was fitted with a "walking-beam" engine visible behind the single stack at the time of the steamer's construction.

On the evening of October 15, the *Alpena* pulled away from the Grand Haven dock and headed out into the lake. A stiff breeze turned into a strong wind. By 9 p.m., the *Alpena* was dealing with winds of gale-force intensity. The last vessels to sight the ship were the schooner *Irish* and a barge, the *City of Grand Haven*. At this point, the *Alpena* was approximately 35 miles from Kenosha, Wisconsin.

What happened to the *Alpena* in its final moments remains a mystery. What is known is that it was laboring in heavy seas. One possibility holds that the freight may have shifted during the storm. This would have caused the steamer to list, allowing water to enter the hull.

As the steamer became increasingly overdue at Chicago, people worried about loved ones aboard. After hours passed, it seemed certain that the *Alpena* had met an untimely end. This possibility was confirmed a few days later when wreckage washed up along the Michigan shore. Fire buckets, the ship's piano, doors, shingles, and other debris appeared near Holland and on Alpena Beach. Included with the remnants of the *Alpena* were the bodies of some of the crew and passengers. The death toll will never be known. The only passenger list was on board the *Alpena* when the passenger boat sank.

The Alpena Storm, as it came to be known, was the worst Lake Michigan storm on record up to 1880. Ninety boats wrecked during this two-day period. The lighthouse keeper on Pilot Island near the Door Peninsula, Emanuel Davidson, reported that the water around the island was white for a week after the storm. It was his belief that the severity of the storm had stirred the limestone on the lake bottom to such a degree that it mixed with the lake water.

Lake Michigan bore the brunt of the storm, although Lake Huron took a beating, too. While storms of greater intensity have occasionally swept across the entire Great Lakes basin, few have struck Lake Michigan with the fury of the Alpena Storm of 1880.

II THE CHICORA

Many lake steamers of the nineteenth century sported masts. Their use was a throwback to the early part of the century, when sails were relied on as a supplement to steam. As steam engines improved in reliability and power, the masts were gradually removed or simply excluded from a new vessel's construction, although many continued to be used as flag poles, antennas, and booms. Despite the fact that they were seldom necessary, by the later half of the 1800s a number of steamers continued to carry one or two masts.

One such boat was the propeller steamer *Chicora*, which was built for the cross-lake trade, carrying produce and passengers to Milwaukee and Chicago. It was designed with the harsh and unforgiving Midwestern winter in mind. Although the hull was made of wood, it was strengthened by an overlayment of iron sheets. The reinforced hull was an important feature—it gave the *Chicora* a limited ability to ram through the lake's thick winter ice. In all but severe ice conditions, the steamer could be relied on to maintain its schedule.

The steamer Chicora.—*Courtesy of the Michigan Maritime Museum*

The ship was built in 1892 in Detroit and was 217 feet in length, 40 feet in the beam, had a draft of 13 feet, 6 inches, and weighed 1,123 gross tons. A single black smokestack was located between the *Chicora*'s two masts. Beneath the masts and stack were staterooms capable of accommodating 200 passengers.

In early January 1895, three years after it first slid into the lake, the *Chicora* was wintering in its home port of St. Joseph when the opportunity presented itself to make a run to Milwaukee with a load of flour. The *Chicora* was under the command of Captain Edward C. Stines, also of St. Joseph.

Sunday, January 20, found the *Chicora* and a crew of 24 bound for Milwaukee. The voyage was uneventful, though the second mate was ill and Captain Stine's son, Benjamin, took his place. The vessel reached the big Wisconsin port and unloaded its cargo. At 5 a.m. the next day, while much of Milwaukee was still asleep, the *Chicora* sailed for St. Joseph.

About ten minutes after the *Chicora* had departed, a messenger arrived at the dock with a storm warning. The warning had been sent by telegram from John Graham of St. Joseph, part owner in the *Chicora*. Had the telegram arrived minutes before, the *Chicora* would most likely have waited out the storm at Milwaukee.

The new day dawned with one of those beautiful winter mornings for which Lake Michigan is renowned. Making good time, the *Chicora* churned the lake waters into frothy white foam. By the time the boat and crew were under way, a strong wind was blowing from the southwest, shifting to the northwest. Thermometer and barometer readings plummeted. The snow was blowing across the *Chicora*'s deck, limiting visibility.

Like the *Alpena* less than five years earlier, only speculation and theory can explain what may have happened to the *Chicora*. It is possible that the ship was near the Michigan shore, only to fall victim to the storm and waves just short of St. Joseph. Reports came in soon after the storm of a freighter in trouble off South Haven. Whether this was the *Chicora* will never be known.

Wreckage was discovered strewn between South Haven and Saugatuck, but no sizable piece of the *Chicora* was ever found. The only survivor was said to have been the ship's dog, found wandering on shore, although this story seems unlikely. The animal would have had to survive the wrecking of a large boat, freezing seas, a furious surf, and a raging blizzard.

Two messages may shed some light on the fate of the *Chicora* and its crew of 24. In mid-April, a message was found along the Michigan shore in a bottle:

> *All is lost, could see land if not snowed and blowed. Engine give out, drifting in shore in ice. Captain and clerk are swept off. We have a hard time of it. 10:15 o'clock.*

> *A second note, supposedly written by the chief engineer, was found in a jar the following week:*

> *Chicora engines broke. Drifted into trough of sea. We have lost all hope. She has gone to pieces. Good bye. McClure, Engineer.*

The ship's two masts were found on the offshore ice near Saugatuck and retrieved. One served as the flag pole for the village of Douglas from 1895 until well into the 1930s. The search for the *Chicora*'s resting place continued for five months. The ship and crew were abandoned to the shifting sands of history until a dive team from Michigan Shipwreck Research Associates discovered the remains of the steamer in May 2001.

III THE ANDASTE

Whalebacks were an unusual breed of boat, unique to the Great Lakes in the late 19th and early 20th centuries. The first whaleback, launched in 1888, was built as a barge. Most of its descendants served in this function, although 14 were steamers. The whalebacks, or pig boats, as they were known by lake men, were designed with efficiency in mind. They were long, iron-hulled vessels that bore a striking resemblance to the shape of a cigar. While some were less than 200 feet long, others were well in excess of 300. Loaded, they sat low enough in the water that waves could easily wash over the decks in foul weather.

The whaleback was originally designed by Alexander McDougall, a native of Scotland who emigrated to America as a boy, eventually becoming a Great Lakes captain. The first whaleboat was built by the American Steel Barge Company of Duluth. In the following decade, up to the launching of the last of the breed in 1898, 42 of these strange-looking vessels were launched at Duluth, Minnesota, and Superior, Wisconsin.

The *Andaste* and its sister ship, the *Choctaw,* were constructed by Cleveland Ship Building in Cleveland, Ohio. These were not authentic whalebacks, but shared enough features with the pig boats to qualify as "semi-whalebacks." In standard maritime parlance, the *Andaste* and *Choctaw* were known as straight-back steel freighters.

The two ships were built for the Lake Superior Iron Company in 1892. Four years later, the company folded and the ships were sold to the Cleveland Cliffs Iron Company. The *Andaste* was 267 feet long, with 1,574 tons gross burden. In addition, it was 38 feet at the beam and had a depth of 18 feet. Prior to the official christening, the freighter was known as *Cleveland Hull Number 16.*

On July 12, 1915, the *Choctaw* was steaming off Presque Isle in Lake Erie in fog when it collided with the steamer *Wahcondah.* This was the second collision and sinking of the *Choctaw*'s career and it proved to be the finale. Although the *Choctaw* was lost, the crew was rescued.

In the early 1920s the *Andaste* was still going strong, but it was shortened to 242 feet so that it could navigate the Welland Canal connecting Lake Erie and Lake Ontario.[1] In 1925, the freighter's new owners, the Cliffs-L.D. Smith Steamship Company, outfitted the *Andaste* with all the equipment the boat

---

[1] Reports differ as to the overall length of the Andaste and the amount by which it was shortened. The true figure regarding how much was removed is either 20 or 24 feet.

would need to be a self-unloader. It was hoped that these modifications would extend the freighter's life by increasing the *Andaste*'s ability at docks without adequate facilities. In fact, adding the new machinery may have been a grave error because it increased the vessel's metacentric height.

In 1928 the *Andaste* received a new skipper, Captain Albert L. Anderson of Sturgeon Bay, Wisconsin. One may easily wonder what Captain Anderson thought of his new command. While his ship was now equipped with self-unloading machinery, it lacked ship-to-shore communications, which most other vessels at the time possessed. Moreover, the *Andaste* lacked electric power, and the vessel's davits were so thoroughly rusted that the lifeboats could not be lowered into the water in an emergency.

On Monday evening, September 9, 1929, the *Andaste* departed Ferrysburg, Michigan, across the Grand River from Grand Haven, bound for Chicago with a load of gravel. On board the vessel were 25 crew members and Captain Anderson. By early morning, a gale was roaring across the lake, catching the *Andaste* in its grip. By Tuesday, the ship had not reached Chicago, and people began to fear for the freighter's safety. Several days later, wreckage washed ashore between Grand Haven and Holland, including the bodies of 14 crewmembers, leaving the other 11 missing.

Like the *Alpena* and *Chicora* before it, the *Andaste* simply disappeared. No one knows the fate of the freighter or where the wreck lies. Despite finality of the loss, several factors may have contributed to the *Andaste*'s disappearance. It is possible that the freighter was overloaded. Coupled with a high center of gravity, a result of the modifications, the storm appears to have been too much for the *Andaste* to bear.

Apparently, the *Andaste* did not suddenly disappear beneath the waves. Most of the crew members whose bodies washed ashore were wearing life preservers. They may have been aware of the *Andaste*'s plight and had sufficient time to put on life preservers and try to launch the life boats. Given the rusted state of the davits, the effort may have proven impossible in the stormy conditions.

Aircraft and Coast Guard search vessels were dispatched, but only bodies and some wreckage were discovered. One of the things recovered was a piece of wood from the *Andaste* on which Captain Anderson wrote a brief message in pencil about the last hours of the boat: "Worst storm I have ever been in. Can't stay up much longer. Hope to God we're saved— A.L.A."

Whatever the ultimate cause of the *Andaste*'s loss, the freighter lies somewhere at the bottom of Lake Michigan. Like many other vessels, the *Andaste* awaits discovery and the opportunity to tell its final tale.

OTHER SIGNIFICANT WRECKS

HEAVY TRAFFIC AND EARLY LOSSES

In 1834, the same year that the citizens of St. Joseph were celebrating the official birth of their city, the stern-wheeler *Davy Crockett* was stranded offshore near their community during a May 9 storm. Two months later to the day, the side-wheel steamer *Pioneer* was driven ashore near St. Joseph during a storm. The schooner *Marengo* rescued crew and passengers. These were the first two losses of steamers of appreciable size on Lake Michigan. Worse steamboat losses would follow.

The period prior to the Civil War witnessed 14 wrecks off the southern Michigan coast. Steamers such as the *Pioneer, Champlain,* and *Milwaukie,* and schooners with names such as *Experiment, Sylvanus Marvin, Hurricane,* and *Michigan* lie at the bottom of the lake in various stages of decay. Some have been obliterated by time and wave action.

Several vessels of note were wrecked during this period. One of these was the schooner *Caroline,* built on Presque Isle in Lake Erie in 1812. The *Caroline* was part of the original United States fleet under Commodore Oliver Hazzard Perry that saw action against British forces in Lake Erie during the War of 1812. Another boat, the *Experiment,* went down with the entire crew in 1840. Only the captain's wife and her two children survived. One child grew up to become the skipper of the *Augusta,* the lake schooner famous for dealing the steamer *Lady Elgin* the blow that cost an estimated 297 men, women, and children their lives 20 years later.

Southern Michigan's greatest loss of the mid-century was that of the propeller steamer *Hippocampus,* a 152-ton boat built in 1867 at St. Joseph. The following year, on September 8, the steamer was en route for Chicago from Benton Harbor when it was caught off St. Joseph in a heavy gale and was driven ashore. The vessel, brand new by lake standards, was a ruin. Worse, approximately 26 of those on board perished.

Two vessels named *Orion* were wrecked on Lake Michigan, and both wrecks occurred off southern Michigan. The first of these ill-fated vessels was a small to mid-size schooner that sank near St. Joseph in 1861. It was joined nine years later by a side-wheeler of the same name. On October 16, 1870, the 496-ton steamer *Orion* was outside Grand Haven Harbor during a heavy storm when a relentless series of waves forced the vessel onto a bar. It was beaten to pieces. Despite the storm raging around them and the lashing to which the *Orion* was subjected, those on board survived.

Grand Haven was the scene of two more wrecks that year, including the scow schooner *John Lillie,* which foundered in a storm. The loss of the wood side-wheel steamer *Daylight,* however, points up one of the worse fears of the nine-teenth-century lakeman—fire!

On October 7, the five-year-old *Daylight* was at a Ferrysburg dock across the river from Grand Haven. A nearby lumber mill caught fire. The ship was trapped by the blaze. The vessel and the dock where it was moored were destroyed, as was the mill. The boat was a total loss, but there appear to have been no fatalities.

THE IRONSIDES

The next major loss happened three years later, on September 15, 1873, when the propeller steamer *Ironsides* went aground on Grand Haven Bar. The *Ironsides* was built by Ira Lafrinier of Cleveland in 1865, and it was 233 feet long and weighed 1,123 tons.[2] Arches on either side of the boat, a common feature on steamers of the time, provided structural support. Painted white, the *Ironsides* sported twin screws and a pair of black stacks. A handsome boat, the steamer would become fodder for an autumn gale.

On September 15, the *Ironsides,* under the command of Captain H. Sweetman, was just off Grand Haven. On board were 19 passengers, approximately 30 crew members, and a cargo including wheat, flour, pork, and general merchandise. Based on contemporary reports, Sweetman tried on three occasions to enter the harbor at Grand Haven. It was while making the last attempt that the *Ironsides* most likely struck bottom.

Modern-day sport divers have reported that the ship's propellers were twisted and a hole ripped in the hull. Under those conditions, it must have been only a question of how long the steamer could stay afloat. Making matters worse was the fact that the rising water inside the steamer put out the boiler fires. Without power, there was nothing the crew could do to save their boat.

Captain Sweetman ordered the five lifeboats lowered. Three capsized in the surf, dumping the occupants. The remaining two small boats reached shore after a harrowing journey. Reports as to the number of dead vary between 18 and 28. In an irony, the *Ironsides* survived its sister ship, the *Lac La Belle,* by only eleven months. The *Lac La Belle* had gone down roughly 20 miles from Racine during a storm on October 13, 1872, with a cargo of grain. One more disaster of note occurred during the 1870s when the scow schooner *Spray* capsized during a storm off South Haven in 1875, taking its three-man crew with it.

---

[2] At least one other source states that its builder was possibly Quayle & Martin of Cleveland. Other sources state that the Ironsides was 218 to 231 feet in length.

In the last two decades of the century, there were 37 wrecks off the southern Michigan coast, but surprisingly few with any loss of life. Despite the generally safe nature of these years, 1880 was the year of the *Alpena* disaster (recounted earlier), the worst wreck ever to occur in the waters off southern Michigan.

One of the most harrowing incidents involved the *Arab, Protection,* and *H. C. Akeley* on the weekend of November 12, 1881. The *Arab* had stranded less than two weeks earlier on a shore near St. Joseph, where the crew had been rescued by members of St. Joseph lifesaving station. The *Arab* was a 29-year-old schooner with the official number of 311, indicating that it was one of the first lake vessels to use a new numbering system.

On November 11, the *Arab* was being towed by the steam tug *Protection*. Roughly 25 miles from Racine, Wisconsin, the towline became fouled in the *Protection*'s rudder. The line was severed, but not before all the men except one on board the *Arab* were able to get off before the schooner capsized. An engineer working below decks to get the pumps working was lost. Considering the conditions, the death toll could have been far worse.

But the crew of the *Arab*, now on board the *Protection*, and the crew of the steam tug were about to face an even greater ordeal. A storm was rapidly moving into the region. This was no usual lake storm, but something that had been described as a hurricane with an eye in the center.

Early Sunday morning, November 13, the wood bulk freighter *H. C. Akeley*, bound from Chicago for Buffalo spied the *Protection*, which was clearly in distress. Captain Stretch of the *Akeley* pulled alongside the *Protection* and brought the tug under tow. Soon, the two vessels were sailing into a full gale. The wind and the waves battered both boats unmercifully, but they fought the elements until the *Akeley*'s rudder broke, leaving the freighter helpless in the rough seas. The line to the *Protection* was cut and the boats quickly lost sight of one another in heavy snow.

The crew of the *Protection* attempted to rig a temporary rudder, but the cargo of corn shifted, producing a list. The port boiler sustained damage, and the strong possibility of an explosion became a concern. As the engineers worked frantically in the engine room, another event occurred that quickly rendered any fix useless. The guychains to the *Akeley*'s stack snapped. The stack went overboard, leaving the stricken freighter without a draft to stoke the fires in the boilers. Powerless and under the relentless beating of the elements, the *Akeley* fell apart.

By midday on Monday, the storm had abated. Captain Stretch ordered the anchor dropped offshore of Holland, Michigan, but this action exposed the freighter to the full fury of the seas and the waves pounded the vessel mercilessly. Fortunately, another vessel disabled by the storm, the schooner *Driver*, spied the *Akeley*. Captain David Miller of the *Driver* made for the *Akeley*, where crew members were divided on how to best abandon the freighter. Captain Stretch and five others stayed on board the *Akeley* while twelve crew members took to the ship's boat. The latter proved to be the wisest course of action. The crew still on board went down with their boat.

The ordeal for the *Akeley*'s remaining crew was not over. It was proving nearly impossible for the *Driver* to close with the small boat. Finally, two men, Daniel F. Miller, brother of Captain Miller, and First Mate Patrick H. Daly, launched the *Driver*'s boat. This act of courage on a storm-tossed lake ensured that the survivors of the *Akeley* were rescued. For their bravery, both men were later awarded the U.S. Lifesaving Service's gold medal.

The crews of the *Arab* and *Protection* fared substantially better. They were rescued by the crew of the St. Joseph lifesaving station, the second time in two weeks that the rescuers came to the aid of the *Arab*'s crew.

DANGERS IN ALL SEASONS

The perils of sailing Lake Michigan can manifest themselves at any time of the year, and some of the wrecks off Michigan's southern shore in the 1880s are a testament to that reality. One involved the bulk freighter *Michigan*, an iron-hulled propeller steamer built in 1881 in Detroit. A good-sized vessel, with a length of 209 feet, a beam of 35 feet, a depth of 14 feet, and 1,183 gross tons burden, the *Michigan* was one of the larger and sturdier boats steaming the lakes. On March 20, 1885, the *Michigan* went to help free the steamer *Oneida* from the grasp of lake ice when it became entrapped in an ice field. Efforts to free the *Oneida* were unsuccessful and the *Michigan*, by now trapped by the ice, was holed and sank. No records indicate that the *Oneida* fell victim to the same fate, suggesting that the steamer was recovered.

The night of July 8, 1886, found the wood bulk freighter *Milwaukee* several miles off Grand Haven, southbound for Chicago. The steam barge had departed Muskegon and was traveling light. The 18-year-old vessel was 137 feet in length and was fitted with a 75-horsepower engine. On board the *Milwaukee* was Captain "Black Bill" Alexander, Seaman Dennis Harrington, and additional crew. A fog had settled over the lake, cutting visibility but not enough to fully conceal the lights of the wood bulk freighter *C. Hickox*, sailing toward the *Milwaukee*.

The night fog was not the only problem facing the *Milwaukee*. According to the crew, its hull was warped, leaving the starboard side lower than the port by a matter of inches. For this reason, Captain Alexander usually turned to starboard when possible. This night, he did just that, though sources suggest that he should have turned to port. At the same time that Captain Alexander ordered a course change, Captain Simon O'Day on the *Hickox* gave a similar order, putting the two vessels on a collision course.

The *Hickox* struck the *Milwaukee*, then lost sight of the freighter in the fog. Captain Alexander ordered the crew of the *Milwaukee* to man the pumps and blew the ship's whistle in an attempt to provide the *Hickox* with its position. The *Hickox* and the *City of New York,* sailing in the area, came upon the stricken vessel. The only fatality was Dennis Harrington, who was assumed to have fallen overboard during the collision. Both captains temporarily lost their licenses as a result of the incident.

The *Hickox* lasted another 20 years until stranding and catching fire near Main Duck Island in Lake Ontario on December 2, 1906. Although the freighter was destroyed, there was no loss of life.

On October 3, 1887, a strong wind and heavy rain were blowing across Lake Michigan from the northwest. Vessels out that night were in for trouble. One of these was the two-masted schooner, *Havana*, which was laden with a cargo of iron ore.

Approaching St. Joseph, Captain John Curran decided that the best course of action was to drop anchor outside the breakwater rather than attempt to enter the harbor. During the night, the storm grew in intensity. Suffering under the relentless assault of wind and waves, the *Havana* took on water. Soon the pumps were in action, but the crew was unable to keep up with the water flooding the boat.

By dawn, the plight of the *Havana* was apparent to the people of St. Joseph. Captain Charles Mulhagen readied his tug, the *Hannah Sullivan,* for a rescue operation, but the proposed attempt did not promise to be an easy trip out to the schooner. The seas were rough and any rescue effort given the current weather conditions would be dangerous. Ignoring his safety, Captain Mulhagen got underway.

As St. Joseph was stirring, the *Havana* raised anchor and made a desperate bid for shore. At this point, Captain Curran apparently decided that the only hope for the crew and schooner was to make for the coast, but it wasn't to be. A wave washed over the *Havana*, which foundered.

Captain Mulhagen and a crew of six volunteers looked for the wreck. Only one mast was still visible above the waves and in the rigging clung five crew members. Captain Curran and two others had the misfortune of clambering up the main mast, which snapped and fell overboard, taking with it the three men. None who had sought safety in the main mast's rigging survived.

As the *Sullivan* reached the *Havana,* a small boat was lowered and the *Havana*'s survivors were helped to the tug. For its heroism, the crew of the *Sullivan* was awarded lifesaving medals. The wreck of the *Havana* was largely forgotten until rediscovered in 1895 by a boat looking for the propeller-driven *Chicora,* which sank the same year.

A QUIET CENTURY

The first significant maritime loss of the 20th century in the southern Michigan area occurred in 1892 when the steamer *Post Boy* caught fire while tied to a dock in Holland. The ship was completely destroyed. Thirteen years earlier the vessel had been more fortunate: it survived going ashore at Chicago during that city's Columbian Exposition, with no loss of life or major damage.

There were relatively few wrecks after the turn of the century. Most of these were minor, but there were exceptions. In 1907 the passenger freighter *Naomi* burned with the loss of seven lives. Despite the damage sustained by the *Naomi,* the passenger freighter was rebuilt and continued steaming under a variety of names before being assigned its final name. Known as the *Wisconsin,* the vessel sank off Kenosha on November 29, 1929, taking with it 18 of 76 souls on board. As recounted earlier, the *Andaste* went down near Holland just two months prior, with the loss of its 25-man crew, making it the worst wreck of the 20th century in the waters of southern Michigan. The final wreck of the century took place in 1982 when an unnamed crane barge foundered off Holland during a gale.

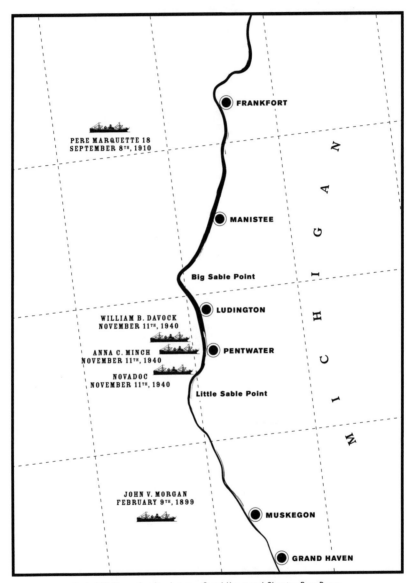

FRANKFORT

PERE MARQUETTE 18
SEPTEMBER 8ᵀᴴ, 1910

MANISTEE

Big Sable Point

LUDINGTON

WILLIAM B. DAVOCK
NOVEMBER 11ᵀᴴ, 1940

PENTWATER

ANNA C. MINCH
NOVEMBER 11ᵀᴴ, 1940

NOVADOC
NOVEMBER 11ᵀᴴ, 1940

Little Sable Point

M I C H I G A N

JOHN V. MORGAN
FEBRUARY 9ᵀᴴ, 1899

MUSKEGON

GRAND HAVEN

Central Michigan shoreline between Grand Haven and Sleeping Bear Dunes.

CENTRAL
MICHIGAN

Standard history teaches that the first people to settle in North America may have come from Asia via the Bering Land Bridge about 9,000 years ago, during the last ice age. They gradually spread across the continent. New research, however, is casting this theory in doubt.

Digging further beneath the sites of early known North American communities, archeologists have discovered artifacts indicating that these settlements may be more than twice as old as the traditionally accepted 9,000-year benchmark. Additional evidence in the form of tools and scientific dating suggests that the first North Americans migrated not only from northern Asia, but southern Asia and Western Europe, as well. Not only did the previous ice age provide possible routes of travel from Asia and Europe, it also carved out the region that would be known as the Great Lakes.

No matter how the region was populated, thriving American Indian cultures were established millennia before the first European explorers entered the Great Lakes in the 1600s. The first European to travel along the shores of eastern Lake Michigan may have been Father Jacques Marquette, who visited in 1675. Afterward, the French entered the region in increasing numbers, often marrying Indian women and raising families.

With the migration into the Great Lakes Basin following the War of 1812, French and Indian Metis society was supplanted by a new culture and new expectations of the land. The settlers were interested in farming, lumbering, and industry. The increasing movement of a large number of people into this sparsely inhabited region, coupled with thriving East Coast communities, created tremendous demand for the resources of the western lakes.

Cities sprang up almost overnight around Lake Michigan. The area of central Michigan between Grand Haven and Sleeping Bear Dunes was no exception. To carry agricultural goods to other Great Lakes ports and eventually to the East Coast, timber and general merchandise boats were built by the score.

South of Sleeping Bear, the small city of Manistee built such vessels for the lake trade by the middle of the 19th century. During this period, the city also served as a shipping port and timber center, with more than 100 lumber local companies. The number of Victorian buildings in Manistee earned this community the title of "The Victorian Port City."

South of Manistee lie other port cities, such as Pentwater and Ludington. Ludington grew from a single family that settled in the area around Pere Marquette Lake in 1847. They arrived on the schooner *Eagle* with a substantial amount of livestock. South of Ludington is the city known as "the Lumber Queen of the World"—Muskegon. The area around Muskegon was also known for trapping, an industry that gave way to lumbering and shipping. As the forests were depleted and shipping declined, Muskegon adapted by developing an industrial base that enhanced Muskegon's status as a major Great Lakes port. A region rich in history, central Michigan has been home to American Indians, explorers, East Coast settlers, and overseas immigrants. The region also has seen its share of significant and dramatic shipwrecks.

I THE JOHN V. MORAN

One of the most harrowing and mysterious wrecks in the central Michigan region, indeed, on the entire expanse of Lake Michigan, involved the steamer *John V. Moran*. A collision with another ship three years earlier was the basis of a well-documented court case.

The *Moran* was launched on August 16, 1888, at West Bay City, Michigan, by F.W. Wheeler. It was a handsome and well-built vessel. Constructed of wood, its hull was later reinforced with iron plates. The *Moran* and other craft were built in this manner to plow through winter ice, thereby enjoying a longer season of operation than was possible with woodhulled vessels.

The ship was 214 feet in length, 37 feet at the beam, with a draft of just over 22 feet.[1] It was built with a displacement of 1,035.26 net tons and 1,350.38 gross tons. The white superstructure was placed fore and aft, with the fore structure extending to a point amidships. The *Moran*'s superstructure rested on a black hull that was built to accommodate deck hatches and side ports. These features were advantageous in loading a package freighter because they allowed goods to be loaded from several different locations and using several different methods.

In 1897, the *Moran* was the subject of a law suit, brought before a New York State District Court, precipitated by a collision with another vessel a year earlier. In determining who was at fault, several confusing facts had to be sorted through. On May 7, 1896, the *Maurice B. Grover* was bound for Buffalo, the same port that the *Moran* had recently departed. The *Grover* was downbound on the St. Mary's River between Lake Superior and Lake Huron. Reaching a turn in the river, the crew blew the bend whistle to inform traffic of its presence. Unknown to the crew of the *Grover*, the *Moran* had stranded on a shoal at roughly 5 p.m.

Two hours later, the sunlight was fading and the *Moran* had on its running lights. In the dim glow of the setting sun, the *Grover* and *Moran* were clearly vis-

---

[1] At least two sources indicate that the John V. Moran was built with a beam of 32 feet, although two sources suggests that the Moran was as wide as 37 feet in the beam.

ible to one another and to other vessels. As the *Grover* got closer, the *Moran* apparently failed to inform the *Grover* that it was stranded. It was only when the *Grover* had closed the distance by a considerable amount that the *Moran* blew four whistle blasts. The crew of the *Grover* seems to have become confused as to the intentions of the *Moran*. The *Moran* was attempting to hail a tug with four long blasts as required in calling a tow, but four short blasts was the signal to hurry up. It is possible that with the *Grover* bearing down on them, the crew of the *Moran* panicked and gave a hurried, shorter signal. Although a tug answered the call, the crew of the *Grover* failed to hear the smaller vessel's reply and continued.

While the crew of the *Moran* claimed to have grounded at a specific shallow point within the channel, the crews of the *Grover* and several other vessels in the vicinity at the time of the collision suggest that the *Moran* was further out into the river.

In court it was argued that the *Grover* was at fault for not providing a signal to indicate a "meeting." However, since no "meeting" was intended, and since any signal by the *Grover* was considered useless as far as the crew of the *Moran* were concerned, this argument was rejected.

Two facts weigh against the *Moran*. The first was that it was grounded at a shallow part of the river and should have informed the crew of the *Grover* as to the stranded vessel's condition as soon as the *Grover* hove into view. The second argument held that the *Moran* should have signaled to the tug much sooner. In the end, it was these arguments that decided the case against the *Moran*.

Fortunately for the crews of both steamers there were no fatalities and damage was relatively light. The *Moran* would not be so lucky three years later. On February 8, 1899, the vessel departed Milwaukee with a cargo of barreled flour and packaged freight under the command of Captain John McLeod. The first mate was Robert McKay.

The winter of 1899 was one of the worst on the Great Lakes in a quarter century. Large sections were iced over, and whenever there was open water, the lake boats had to contend with drifting ice floes. It was into this dangerous mix that the *Moran* worked up a head of steam.

The *Moran* was now in the employ of the Crosby Transportation Company, owned and run by E.G. Crosby. In addition to the *Moran*, Crosby also owned the steamers *Boyce, Naomi,* and *Nyack;* all but one were fated to wreck. The *Naomi* went through a series of name changes, including *E. G. Crosby*, It is best known, however, by the name it was christened and died with—the SS *Wisconsin*. The *Nyack* caught fire at Muskegon on December 30, 1915, and, although declared a total loss, ended its days as a barge until being scuttled in 1925. Only the *Boyce* avoided an untimely end.

On what was a bitterly cold February morning, the *Moran,* having at last broken through the ice at its dock, was now on a course for the other side of Lake Michigan. Joining the ship was the *Naomi,* which had departed Manitowoc earlier that day. Both vessels were bound for Muskegon and the company was most likely welcome. Soon, it would make the difference between life and death.

That evening, with the lights of Muskegon shining in the distance, disaster struck the *Moran.* Throughout the day, the vessel had been driving through large fields of ice. Gradually, this action took its toll. At some point, the ice managed to work over the iron plating, tearing into the softer wood. Water poured in. As the pumps went into action, the crew tried to pinpoint the source of the leak. But the water continued to rise and it threatened the boilers. Sinking, and with the threat of an explosion as the cold water reached the boilers, Captain McLeod blew the ship's whistle to signal its plight to the *Naomi.*

The crew of the *Moran* abandoned the vessel and made their way across the ice to the *Naomi.* Planks and ladders were used to create a makeshift bridge that the *Moran's* crew used to escape the sinking steamer. The temperatures were nearly −30° F. Under these conditions, it was inevitable that the doomed steamer's crew would suffer frostbite but, one by one, they made it to the safety of the *Naomi.* While the *Moran's* crew was safe from the threat of going down with their ship, they and the crew of the *Naomi* feared a boiler explosion aboard the *Moran.* Prudently, the *Naomi* backed off.

Daybreak revealed a desolate scene. The *Naomi* found itself virtually trapped in a forbidding sea of snow and ice. Surprisingly, still rising defiantly above the ice was the wreck of the *Moran.* At this point, a decision was made to tow the *Moran* to Muskegon.

The *Naomi* closed once again with the *Moran* and a crewman clambered on board the stricken freighter to secure a towline. Together, with the *Naomi* in the lead, the freighters resumed the journey to Muskegon. But it was not to be. Attempting to tow the *Moran* and break a way through the unusually thick ice proved more difficult than the captain of the *Naomi* had reckoned.

A decision was made to transfer the *Moran's* cargo to the *Naomi.* Despite the danger, the crew removed as much of value as possible from the *Moran* and loaded it on board the *Naomi.* Well after the *Naomi* had departed, the steamer *Muskegon* came upon the abandoned wreck. The state of the *Moran* and the presence of the *Naomi* several miles away told the captain of the *Muskegon* all he needed to know. Confident that the *Moran's* crew was safe and unable to do more, the *Muskegan* continued on.

Even though the crew of the *Moran* was accounted for, the abandoned freighter was still held fast by Lake Michigan ice. The Crosby Transportation

Company was loathe to lose a valuable vessel, and so the *Boyce* and *Nyack* were sent from Milwaukee the following Monday to locate and, if possible, save the *Moran*. By that evening, the *Nyack* and *Boyce* were trapped by the ice. Tuesday morning saw the boats 40 miles north, transported there by the movement of the ice.

The following Sunday, the two steamers remained trapped by the vast sheets of Lake Michigan ice. Desperate, three crewmembers, First Mate E. J. Humphrey and Clerk William Hannrehan of the *Boyce,* and Wheelman Thomas O'Day of the *Nyack,* decided to make the six-mile walk to shore. The first attempt failed when the men broke through the ice and were forced to return to their respective freighters. To continue on, soaked through and with a howling wind and temperatures far below zero, would have been madness.

After recovering from their first attempt and putting on dry clothing, the trio set out. By evening and in the dark, suffering from frostbite, the three reached Muskegon, where the townspeople had lit a fire to help guide the men to shore. The men related news about the *Boyce* and *Nyack*, as well as the fact that they had been unable to find the *Moran*.

The fate of the *Moran* remains uncertain. After the *Naomi* and *Muskegon* abandoned the steamer, it was never seen again. Searchers were unable to locate the freighter and, in fact, found nothing but trouble for their efforts. Undoubtedly the *Moran* foundered, but where and when, no one knows. Claimed by the ice and Lake Michigan, the *John V. Moran* disappeared.

II THE PERE MARQUETTE NO. 18

The sinking of the *Pere Marquette* 18 in 1910 and that of the *Milwaukee* 19 years later (see chapter 6) are eerily similar. Both vessels were railroad car ferries lost in midlake after flooding during storms. In each case, water appears to have entered at or near the stern and in the vicinity of the crew's quarters. Each boat was carrying a cargo of rail cars for ports on the opposite side of Lake Michigan.

Ferrying rolling stock across the lake was an important business in the early part of the twentieth century. With the tremendous growth of rail services, shipping freight overland became the easiest way of transporting goods between the Midwest's cities and small towns. Chicago became the railroad crossroads of the Midwest.

Despite the amount of track in the Chicago area, there wasn't enough to satisfy the tremendous amount of rail trafffic. Shippers needing to transport between

The Pere Marquette 18.—*Courtesy of the Michigan Maritime Museum*

Wisconsin and Michigan grew frustrated at the long delays and numerous accidents, not to mention the long trip around the lake. The solution was to construct ships capable of carrying a good number of railcars across Lake Michigan.

Car ferries were built not only to move rolling stock but also to ship automobiles and passengers. A further benefit of the car ferries, which were meant to work the lakes year round, was that they served as excellent ice breakers, freeing up passages on the open lake and opening harbors for other lake vessels.

The *Pere Marquette 18* was a steel car ferry built by American Ship Building in Cleveland, Ohio. While under construction, the vessel was known as *Hull No. 412*. Launched in 1902, the vessel was christened with the name that it would one day die with. A large vessel for the time, the *Pere Marquette 18* was 338 feet in length, 56 feet at the beam, with a draft of 20 feet, and displacement of a total of 2,909 gross tons. The largest car ferry on the lakes, it boasted a black hull and gleaming white superstructure.

Shortly after midnight on September 8, 1910, the *Pere Marquette 18* left Ludington in a routine cruise to Milwaukee. The lake was a bit rough, and boat and crew felt the impact of each wave, but there was no cause for alarm. In the hold were twenty-nine railroad cars placed on four sets of tracks. These cars would have been secured with rail clamps placed to the front and rear of each wheel, a screw jack in the corners, and a chain and turnbuckle clamped beside each jack. Also on board were 62 passengers and crew. There were two stowaways.

Captain Peter Kilty was apparently unconcerned by the wind-tossed waves. The *Pere Marquette 18* was considered strong enough to handle foul weather and the elements that day, although far from friendly, were not unduly dangerous. Kilty's command had just been inspected by government officials in Ludington and found seaworthy. There was not a piece of evidence that might suggest anything other than a typical voyage.

All of that changed around three o'clock that morning. An oiler rushed into the engine room and informed the chief engineer, Ross Leedham, that a tremendous amount of water was entering the ferry in the compartment below the crew's quarters. The chief engineer promptly called the first mate who, at the time, was in the pilothouse. The first mate left went to locate the source of the flooding. On finding the area of the leak, he felt that it was nothing more than a damaged deadlight or porthole cover, but he reported the matter to the captain. An experienced lakeman, Captain Kilty investigated. Unable to find whatever was causing the ship to take on water, he ordered the pumps into action.

Despite the valiant efforts of the crew and the machinery they manned, flooding continued. Finally, Captain Kilty prudently decided to head for Sheboygan rather than continue toward Milwaukee. The water was rising fast and it was hoped both boat and crew could safely reach shore. In an attempt at staving off disaster, nine of the cars in the *Pere Marquette 18*'s hold were pushed overboard.

By five o'clock, just two hours after discovering that the vessel was in mortal danger, the first cries for help were sent forth over the wireless: "Carferry 18 sinking—help." The wheelman, who was having difficulty controlling the vessel, and the wireless operator remained at their posts.

One of the vessels to receive the Mayday was the *Pere Marquette 17*, which set course for the *18*. As a new day dawned, the *17* sighted the stricken ferry. The second car ferry was almost alongside when the dying boat lifted its bow in the air as if issuing a farewell and slipped stern first beneath the waves. Every officer on board the ship perished.

As the ferry sank, the wheelman leapt into the water, where he clung to a piece of wreckage until being picked up. The crew of the *Pere Marquette 17* launched a lifeboat, but it slammed against the ferry's hull, fatally dumping two rescuers. Two additional craft were launched and rescue operations were resumed.

The ferries *Pere Marquette 6* and *Pere Marquette 20*, plus two tugboats, also arrived on scene. Thirty-three crew and passengers survived. The cause of the *18*'s demise has never been determined. It appears that a broken deadlight or some other problem led ship *18* to rapidly fill with water. Prior to sinking, the ferry listed sharply to starboard. This may indicate that the cargo of rail-cars shifted.

Another factor that may have played a part in the ferry's destruction was the absence of a wave-resisting sea gate. This device is a steel gate that can be raised and lowered to prevent water from entering a boat. Such a gate might have prevented the loss of the *Pere Marquette 18*. The original car ferries were built with an open stern, a serious design flaw in the type of foul weather in which the *18* foundered. The first vessel to receive a wave-resisting sea gate was the *Ann Arbor 5*, which was built in the same year that the *Pere Marquette 18* went under.

Whatever the true reason for its loss, the *Pere Marquette 18* finally came to rest in 400 feet of water.[2] Nineteen years would pass before the ship would be joined by the car ferry *Milwaukee*. These two boats, which had so much in common, share a common grave.

III THE ARMISTICE DAY STORM

The annals of the Lake Michigan are filled with tales of great storms, epic battles against the elements, survival and tragedy. No storm has ever bested the Big Storm of 1913 in terms of fury and damage, but there have been a handful that came close.

One such storm occurred on Armistice Day, 1940. Had schooners and wood steamers been more common, as they were three decades earlier, the damage would have been worse. With general winds of more than 100 miles an hour, the gale lashed the Great Lakes with an intensity few could remember. Lake Michigan was especially hard hit, with the central and southern portions of the east coasts battered the worst. At the lighthouse at Lansing Shoals in the Upper Peninsula, winds were recorded at 126 miles an hour. Into this maelstrom ventured three of the largest lakers ever to wreck on Lake Michigan.

On Sunday, November 11, America was observing the allied victory 22 years earlier against Kaiser Wilhelm's Germany. Not everyone was celebrating. Out on Lake Michigan, a few brave souls were fighting for their lives with the kind of fortitude shown by the doughboys of World War I. A few old timers may even

---

[2] Although closer to the Wisconsin side of Lake Michigan, other sources indicate that the remains of the Pere Marquette 18 lie off Ludington in midlake. In fact, the Pere Marquette 18 rests in deep water roughly twenty miles off Sheboygan. Due to the fact that the history of the Pere Marquette 18 is tied to that of the Ludington Fleet and in keeping with several other sources, the wreck of this car ferry is mentioned under the section on central Michigan.

The Novadoc.—*Courtesy of the Wisconsin Maritime Museum*

have been reminiscing about the Big Storm of 1913, which occurred on this date 27 years earlier.

Running into the teeth of this monstrous gale was the wood bulk freighter *Novadoc,* carrying a load of powdered coke. A laker of Canadian registry, the *Novadoc* was returning to Fort Williams, Ontario, on Lake Superior, from South Chicago, Indiana, when it ran into trouble along the central Michigan coast.

Unable to maintain control of the vessel, the crew of the 235-foot vessel could not prevent the boat from going hard aground on a reef at Juniper Shore, south of Pentwater. There were 19 men on board the wreck, ten who huddled together for warmth in the forward cabin and nine in the aft cabin. Two in the aft section of the boat tried to make their way forward but were lost in the freezing surf that washed over the freighter.

Without power to provide heat, it was uncertain how long the survivors could stay alive. The seven remaining crew members in the aft cabin were forced to rely on a single oil lantern for warmth. The men on board the *Novadoc* had no way of knowing it, but the pale light cast from the forward and aft cabins would be their salvation.

Captain Clyde Cross was a member of a family known for its commercial fishing operations. On Monday evening he drove his truck along a road overlooking the beach and spotted the *Novadoc,* which was about a third of a mile offshore. Expecting everyone on board to be frozen, Cross was surprised to see light emanating from a porthole. Unable to do anything in the rough seas,

Captain Cross returned home.

The following morning the lake was somewhat calmer, although snow continued to fall. With two other men, Cross took his small fishing tug the *Three Brothers* into the lake. It was hard going. There was little heat inside the tug. Making matters worse, it was impossible to see over the mountainous waves. Only when the small tug and the intrepid rescuers crested a wave could they take their bearings.

The *Three Brothers* reached the *Novadoc*. The Canadian vessel was coated with ice. It was thought doubtful that anyone could have survived the freezing temperatures in the 36 hours since the freighter had gone ashore. It was with relief that the crew of the *Three Brothers* found the ten men in the forward cabin still alive. Informed of the plight of those in the aft cabin, Cross guided the *Three Brothers* toward the stern, where he was able to save seven additional crew members. In all, 17 men were rescued.

But it was not before the *Three Brothers* nearly became a victim of the storm-tossed seas. When it returned to Pentwater with the survivors, a sizable hole barely above the waterline was discovered. Had the hole been lower, the *Three Brothers* might have foundered. The tug was heavily damaged but survived.

After reaching shore, Captain Steip of the *Novadoc* offered Captain Cross an undisclosed sum of money for his heroic efforts. Having risked his life to save Captain Steip and the remaining crew of the *Novadoc*, Cross said, "Hell no, Captain. Glad to be of service." In the days to come, he received numerous letters and telegrams of thanks and appreciation; eventually he was awarded a medal from the Canadian government and was recommended by the press for the American Medal of Honor. A civilian, Cross could not receive the award, which is given only for military heroism.

Two other freighters were out on Lake Michigan that November 11, the *Anna C. Minch* and the *William B. Davock*. They were not as fortunate as the crew of the *Novadoc*.

The *Minch* was a steel freighter considerably larger than the wood *Novadoc*: 380 feet in length, 50 feet at the beam, with a draft of 28 feet. The *Minch* displaced 4,139 gross tons, substantially more than the *Novadoc*'s 1,934 gross tonnage. Built by American Ship Building in 1903, the *Minch* was an older craft but still in its prime. Like the *Novadoc*, it was Canadian registered, its home being Port Colburn, Ontario, along Lake Erie.

At approximately 4 p.m. on November 11, the *Minch,* loaded with coal and carrying a crew of 24, sailed through the Straits of Mackinac from Lake Huron into Lake Michigan. A few hours later, the *Minch* and its crew were at the bottom of the lake—yet another of its victims. No one is sure what happened, but its disappearance could be connected with another freighter fighting for its life in the same storm.

The *William B. Davock* cleared the Straits of Mackinac just four hours ahead of the *Minch*. Like the *Minch*, the vessel was carrying a cargo of coal and bound for Chicago when it encountered the storm. Like the *Novadoc*, the *Davock* was a wood freighter; it was 420 feet in length, with 4,468 gross tons burden.

Under the command of Captain Charles W. Allen and with a crew of 32, the *Davock* struggled through the storm, which tossed the ship as if it were a toy. With the wind shrieking and the snow obliterating visibility, the *Davock* disappeared off the central Michigan coast. The remains of the freighter, the largest laker lost during the storm, would stay hidden until its remains were discovered in 1982.

A few days after the *Minch*, *Novadoc,* and *Davock* wrecked, Captain Cross returned to Lake Michigan to search for wreckage. He discovered the remains of the *Minch* in 40 feet of water less than two miles south of Pentwater. All he could find was the forward portion of the boat. At some point the vessel had broken its back. The two halves appear to have floated far apart, because the stern section was never found. Wreckage and the remains of crewmen from the *Minch* and *Davock* washed up on the local beaches for days.

This section of Lake Michigan claimed two more boats before the Armistice Day storm blew out. A fishing tug, the *Indian,* went down off South Haven with five crew members. The *Richard H.*, another fishing tug, manned by three crewmen, vanished farther south without a trace.

Although Lake Michigan was hardest hit, none of the lakes was spared. The *City of Flint* struck the breakwater at Ludington while trying to enter the harbor. Stranded about 300 yards from shore, the freighter was scuttled by the relief captain, Jens Vevang, who ordered that the seacocks be opened to relieve the stress on the stricken vessel by the storm-driven waves. The *City of Flint* remained off shore until the storm ended.

Also wrecked along central Michigan was the freighter *Conneaut*, which ran aground on Lansing Shoal near Manistique. Similar to the *City of Flint*, the vessel could not be recovered until after the storm. Both vessels were recovered after stranding without a single casualty.

Three freighters either sank or beached and were never returned to service. Two tugs were lost. Four more freighters were beached. Numerous boats barely made it to safe harbor. Wearing thick coats of ice, the survivors limped back into port. The deck of the *New Haven Secony*, a vessel overdue at East Chicago, was only one and a half feet from the water when it finally entered that port. The vessel had been subjected to such a severe lashing on Lake Michigan that the roof of the pilothouse was ripped from the superstructure, only to be found on the beach at Grand Haven. This is an indication of how heavily the *New Haven Secony* was weighed down by ice. More than 70 lives and millions of dollars were lost.

OTHER SIGNIFICANT WRECKS

DISASTERS OF ALL TYPES

Central Michigan's first shipwreck was probably the double-masted schooner *Prince Eugene*, which sank north of present day Manistee in November 1834. The *Prince Eugene* was two years old, having been built in 1832 at Huron, Ohio. Forced ashore during a storm, the boat and cargo were worth a total of $70,000—a substantial fortune at that time.

The next loss was the brig *Neptune*. The *Neptune* boasted two masts and displaced approximately 166 tons. On November 25, 1839, the three-year old brig was bound for Chicago from Buffalo when it encountered a fierce gale. Going ashore at Little Sable Point, the *Neptune* mishap claimed 18 of the 21 souls and a cargo of general merchandise. Only the captain and two others survived.

The year after the *Neptune* disaster, the side-wheel steamer *Governor Mason* stranded during a storm in the Muskegon River. Eleven years would pass before the next significant wreck. There would not be a similar period of grace until the latter half of the 1940s, still more than a century away.

In 1855, the bark *L.M. Hubby* was in ballast when it capsized off Point Betsie. Only one of 11 crew members survived. That same year witnessed the foundering of the 84-foot schooner *Lester R. Rockwell* at Muskegon. A year later, the three-year-old bark *Arabian* was lost. On November 19, the *Arabian* stranded on Goose Island Shoal east by northeast of Mackinac Island. At the time, the 116-foot *Arabian* was only three years old. The *Arabian* was removed from the shoal by the steamer *Ogontz,* which towed it south along the Michigan coast until a storm blew up and the line snapped. As both vessels tried to make for shore they lost sight of one another. Although the *Arabian* sank off Point Betsie, the crew took to the ship's yawl and escaped. There were no casualties other than the *Arabian*.

Luck would take a turn for the worse during the 1857 shipping season. The side-wheel steamer *Commerce* was launched in 1848 at Portsmouth, Ontario, to carry passengers and freight. Two years later the steamer was renamed the *Reindeer*. Seven years were to pass before the *Reindeer* embarked on a voyage that would see the side-wheeler pass by Big Sable Point. It never made it. Foundering during a storm, the steamer went down with a loss of 23.

Many boats built on the Great Lakes could be found sailing ocean trade routes. One such vessel was the brig *Black Hawk.* In 1858, the *Black Hawk* made the voyage to Liverpool, England, and back. The brig was lost to a Lake Michigan storm four years later in November 1862. It went down with all hands on board and a cargo of stained glass.

The *Black Hawk* was not the only lake-built vessel to manage the transatlantic trade. Other examples include the schooner *C.B. Benson,* built by J. Duff of Port Clinton, Ohio, in 1873. The *C.B. Benson* is believed to be the first vessel to carry a load of corn from the United States to England. Prior to the *Benson* there was the *James McBride,* which hauled the first cargo from the West Indies to Chicago in 1848. The *C.B. Benson* and the *James McBride* both wrecked on the Great Lakes; the *McBride* in 1857 on Lake Michigan and the *Benson* on Lake Erie in 1893.

The shipwrecks of the 19th century include an assortment of ship types and cargoes, and they reflect the dreams and ambitions of the people who sailed them. Captains seeking to further their own fortunes or those of a ship's owners, crew members wanting to improve the financial position of their families, immigrants seeking a better life, or vacationers seeking respite from their jobs rest together at the bottom of Lake Michigan. Their bodies remain inside steamers and schooners along with cargoes of timber, agricultural produce, and ore.

THE LAST THREE DECADES OF THE CENTURY

There were some unforgettable wrecks during the last third of the 19th century. One of these was the schooner *Souvenir,* based in Pentwater, Michigan. On November 25, 1872, the 89-foot schooner departed Pentwater for Chicago. Carrying a load of shingles, the *Souvenir* set off on a night voyage in fine weather. But nature's capricious moods took a turn for the worse. A vicious gale blew in from the northwest, bringing with it a heavy snow.

The following day, the battered wreck washed up south of Ludington. People on the beach could see the mate alive at the wheel, but it was impossible to brave the surf and reach anyone on board. The lighthouse keeper, William Gerard, took a small boat out to the *Souvenir.* He was alone, the others having elected to stay on shore. Reaching the *Souvenir,* Gerard found a devastated vessel. The masts were gone except for a few pieces of rigging that littered the deck in heaps. Reaching the mate, Gerard gave assistance, but the man died in his arms. There was no sign of the other five crew members. Whether they were washed overboard or attempted to launch the ship's boat and were lost will never be known.

The next great loss involved the wood-propeller steamer *Equinox.* Serving as a bulk freighter, the *Equinox* was constructed by F. N. Jones of Buffalo in 1857. On September 10, 1875, the *Equinox* was carrying a cargo of salt and towing the schooner barge *Emma A. Mayes*. Both vessels were en route to Chicago from Sarnia when they encountered a heavy gale.

Shortly after midnight on the tenth, the *Equinox* signaled the crew of the *Emma A. Mayes* to release the towline. At 1 a.m., the *Equinox* foundered in heavy seas. Counted among the missing were the captain, his daughter, and his grand-daughter. The sole survivor, the helmsman, was found by the schooner *Havana* two days later. He was the only one of 26 to survive.

On October 19, 1878, in the vicinity of Ludington, the schooner *J.H. Rutter* went ashore. On board were 44 crewmen and grain trimmers, all of whom were saved. Captain Jerry Simpson apparently decided that the time had come for a career change and became a Kansas congressman.

In September 1881, the propeller freighter *Columbia* foundered in a storm, taking 16 lives and a cargo of corn. Three years later and in the autumn of 1884, the two-masted schooner *Kitty Grant* went down 20 miles from Little Sable Point with the entire crew of four. The following year, it was the turn of the three-masted schooner *Orphan Boy*. The *Orphan Boy* encountered a heavy gale on December 5. Unable to fight the winds and seas, the *Orphan Boy* was forced ashore. Twelve men lost their lives, presumably as the schooner was battered to pieces by waves.

The year 1886 was one of the worst of the decade. On November 17, the schooner *L.J. Conway* went ashore near Frankfort. The *Conway* was followed two days later by the schooner barge *Menekaunee*. Both ships were lost with all

The J.H. Rutter.—*Courtesy of the Library of Congress*

hands, a total of 12. The crew of the U.S. lifesaving service, stationed at Frankfurt, went to aid the crew of the *Menekaunee* but by the time they reached the site all they found were bodies and wreckage strewn across the beach, and the ship's badly injured dog, which died soon after the accident.

These were not the only serious incidents of the year. On November 18, the scow schooner *Helen* beached just north of Muskegon. In this single three-day period in November, Lake Michigan had claimed 19 lives.

A NEW CENTURY AND NEW WRECKS

Apart from the wreck of the schooner *Lydia* in 1905, the first few years of the twentieth century were a period of relative calm along the central Michigan coast. The first major incident in these waters involved the destruction of the *Arcadia* and its crew. The *Arcadia* was a wood bulk freighter built by the Milwaukee Shipyard in 1888, 119 feet in length, 26 feet at the beam, and with a 9-foot draft. Throughout its career, the *Arcadia* had been the property of Captain H. Mary of Arcadia, Michigan. On April 12, the ship steamed out of Manistee toward Two Rivers, Wisconsin, with a load of lumber when it encountered a storm. South of Manistee, just off Big Sable Point, the *Arcadia* and the crew of 14 disappeared. Speculation holds there may have been a boiler explosion, but the cause of the ship's demise has never been determined.

The same month that the *Arcadia* disappeared, the schooner barge *Argo* was driven ashore just north of Manistee. The number lost is uncertain, but it appears that 14 may have perished in the wreck.

The era of the side-wheel steamer as an open lake vessel had largely vanished before the 20th century. But the new century still saw an occasional side-wheeler gracing the lake its ancestors plied, and one of the vessels was involved in a tragic accident.

On September 22, 1919, the side-wheel steamer *Muskegon* was in the port city whose name it bears, when it experienced difficulty steaming into the face of a stiff gale blowing from the west. Built of iron, the *Muskegon* was a far cry from the sleek wooden steamers of the previous century. Even though its hull made the *Muskegon* better able to withstand damage, there was a limit to how much the steamer could suffer. At the height of the storm, the *Muskegon* sank after violently striking a pier. The vessel went down so quickly that 29 of 39 on board were lost, with most trapped below decks.

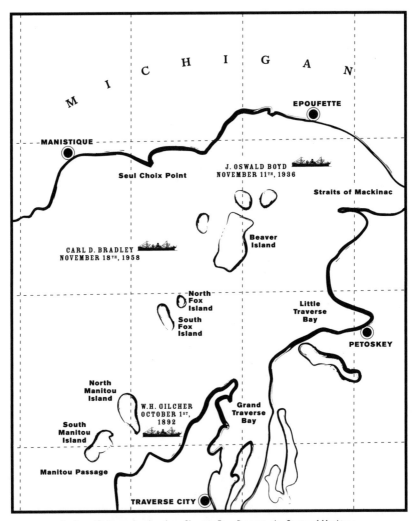

Northern Michigan shoreline from Sleeping Bear Dunes to the Straits of Mackinac.
—*Courtesy of the National Oceanographic and Atmospheric Administration*

CHAPTER

11

NORTHERN MICHIGAN

According to legend, a raging forest fire forced a mother bear and her two cubs to flee the western coast of Lake Michigan. Leaving behind the country that would be known as Wisconsin, the bears sought safety in the waters of the lake. The mother bear eventually reached the eastern shore of Lake Michigan. Glancing back, she discovered that the distance had been too great for her cubs, both of which drowned. Taking pity, the Great Spirit raised the cubs from the water and they became North and South Manitou Islands. As for the mother bear, the Great Spirit turned her into a massive sand dune so that she could watch over her children. This Chippewa tale provides one account of how Sleeping Bear Dunes National Lakeshore was created. Climatological and geologic history suggests less romantic but equally powerful forces at work.

The northern expanse of Michigan's Lower Peninsula, between Sleeping Bear Dunes and the Straits of Mackinac, has had more than its share of harsh weather and turbulent water. As a result, this cold, northern land is famous for its shipwrecks. From the Straits of Mackinac down through Traverse Bay and into Lake Michigan, the waters are littered with the skeletons of unfortunate vessels of all types and sizes.

Islands scattered across the northern reaches of Lake Michigan have caught many unwary and fog-blinded craft off guard. With colorful names such as Beaver, Squaw, Gull, Whiskey, and Fox, among others, the islands conjure up Native American lore. They also have been the scene of many wrecks that are near legendary in maritime circles. Farther south are mother bear's lost cubs, North Manitou Island and South Manitou Island. Between Manitous and Sleeping Bear is Manitou Passage, where an estimated 58 wrecks lie. Because this figure excludes any that are missing or have been recovered, the number may be much higher.

I THE W. H. GILCHER

Built by the Cleveland Ship Building Company in 1891, the steel bulk freighter *W. H. Gilcher* was the largest boat built in that city to that time. It measured 302 feet in length and 41 feet at the beam, with a 21-foot depth and a displacement of 1,987 net tons and 2,415 gross tons. In addition to its record size, the *Gilcher* carried a record cargo of grain from Chicago to Buffalo during the vessel's first, and what would prove to be its only, season working the Great Lakes.

The *Gilcher* was the sister ship of the *Western Reserve,* although there were slight differences in their construction. The first steel steamer built for use on the Great Lakes, the *Western Reserve* was a foot shorter than the *Gilcher,* with a depth of 25 fewer feet. Also, it was 22 fewer net tons less than the *Gilcher,* and displaced 2,392 gross tons.

On August 30, 1892, the *Western Reserve* broke in two off Deer Park, Michigan, during a storm on Lake Superior. The loss of the *Western Reserve* due to hull damage prompted laws that governed the testing of steel used in boat construction. Of the 27 on board, including the captain and most of his family, there was only one survivor.

Just 60 days after the loss of the *Western Reserve,* on October 1, 1892, the *W. H. Gilcher* was steaming through the Straits of Mackinac with a load of coal. On board was a crew of 21, including Captain Leeds H. Weeks. It was evening and the storm that had been blowing throughout the day was strengthening. As a new boat with a steel hull, the vessel was considered strong enough to weather the wind and waves and deliver its cargo, loaded in Buffalo, to Milwaukee.

The *Gilcher* was never heard from again, and the mystery of why it disappeared with all hands has never been solved. The scant evidence shed some, but insufficient, light on what may have happened. Wreckage was found in the vicinity of the Manitou Islands just north of Sleeping Bear Dunes National Lakeshore by the crew of the steamer *White and Friant,* under the command of Captain Jenks. A note scribbled on the handrail of the pilot house by a member of the *Gilcher's* crew stated simply, "James Rider – 9 PM." Further evidence suggests that whatever happened to the vessel occurred quickly. The fastenings to the lifeboats had been cut loose with axes, indicating that the ship's boats were launched in a hurry.

Speculation suggests that the *Gilcher* may have been the victim of a collision. Steaming through the same area at roughly the same time was the 36-year-old schooner *Ostrich,* which was traveling light. The *Ostrich* was under the command of Captain John McKay who also owned the vessel. On board the *Ostrich* was a crew of six, including a female cook. Captain McKay was headed for Torch Lake in Michigan's Keweenaw Peninsula along Lake Superior to pick up a cargo of lumber for delivery in Milwaukee. The *Ostrich* and its crew never made it. Sometime during the night of October 1, the *Ostrich* vanished.

Given the possible proximity of the two vessels and the discovery of wreckage from both boats in the same general area, it has been assumed that the *Gilcher* and the *Ostrich* collided in the darkness of a storm-driven night. Apart from the wreckage, the two vessels have never been found.

The *Gilcher* and its crew belong to a select and unfortunate club. The *Gilcher* is considered to be a Flying Dutchman, one of those lost vessels bound to sail or steam on for all eternity. Sightings of the *Gilcher* after the freighter's loss indicate that the steamer and its crew still haunt the area around Mackinac Island during periods of heavy fog.

II THE J. OSWALD BOYD

On November 11, 1936, the steel fuel tanker *J. Oswald Boyd* stranded on Simmons Reef north of Beaver Island with a cargo of between 800,000 and 900,000 gallons of high-test aviation gasoline valued at $180,000. The following day the crew of Beaver Island Coast Guard rescued the crew of 20 on board the stranded freighter. But this is only the beginning of the story.

When they departed the grounded vessel, the *Boyd*'s crew removed its compass, a simple act that signified two facts. One was the crew's acknowledgement that the *Boyd* was held too fast by Simmons Reef to be easily be worked off. The second was that the owners of the *Boyd*, the Gotham Marine Corporation, were quick to accept this state of affairs and abandoned the freighter. The *Boyd* was now open for salvage.

A number of Beaver Island residents took quick advantage of the situation. They used boats or drove motor vehicles across the ice to get as much free fuel as possible. The free fuel was a boon to ordinary people facing the prospect of heating their homes during the Great Depression.

Everett Cole of Beaver Island, however, was not considered ordinary. The Beaver Island Transit Company owned and managed the mail boat, the *Rambler*, which also brought groceries to the island. Controlling interest in the company belonged to Cole, who also owned a grocery on the island. Additionally, Cole rented cars, purchased a number of small houses to rent out, sold fuel, purchased a hotel, and owned a dance hall. He was widely seen by the citizens of Beaver Island as a person to build the island by means of increased tourism and a better, more modern infrastructure. At the time, the state of Michigan was interested in building new highways and Beaver Island was slated for some of this funding. Things were looking up and now, just north of the island, was the *J. Oswald Boyd* and nearly a million gallons of gasoline. For Cole the opportunity was a rare one.

Cole and his brother Raymond used the *Rambler* to remove gasoline from the tanker. They turned to the *Marold II*, which was a larger and safer boat. When the new vessel first came alongside the *J. Oswald Boyd* it did so with a fascinating history. Built as a yacht for Alexander Winton, an automobile magnate in the same mold as the steel multimillionaire Andrew Carnegie, the *Marold II* had

The J. Oswald Boyd.—*Courtesy of the Beaver Island Historical Society*

seen service in World War I as a sub chaser. Now the former luxury yacht was used to salvage the cargo of the *J. Oswald Boyd.*

Despite concerns they may have had with the safety of their small fleet in winter conditions, several members of the Beaver Island Transit Company appear to have been lax in following safety procedures while removing gas from the stranded tanker. Despite the high wages that Everett was willing to pay crewmen in salvaging the *Boyd*'s gasoline, at least several men worked for only one day or less and were never willing to even contemplate a return to the stricken vessel. This calls into question the transferring of gasoline between the vessels. On December 29, Nels LaFreniere of the Beaver Island Transit Company sold his share in the *Marold II*. His action was prophetic.

On New Year's Day, 1937, the *Marold II* ventured once again to the *Boyd* in weather that was more temperate than usual for that time of year, as a bright sun shone warm over a windless lake. On board were Everett and Raymond, Captain Hill with his son Leon, and Roland McDonough.

Late that afternoon, people on Beaver Island and in coastal towns such as Epoufette on the shoreline of the Upper Peninsula heard what sounded like thunder. The presence of smoke on the lake in the direction of Simmons Reef led people to realize that a boat was in trouble. Word of the suspected disaster spread. That evening, Captain Bill Ludwig and his crew of the Beaver Island Coast Guard approached the pair of burning wrecks. By 11:30 p.m., additional Coast Guard crews from Mackinac Island and Charlevoix had arrived.

The J. Oswald Boyd stranded on Beaver Island.—*Courtesy of the Beaver Island Historical Society*

The Marold II, a former luxury yacht.—*Courtesy of the Beaver Island Historical Society*

Due to the intense heat and additional explosions, the Coast Guard vessels kept their distance. The boat from Beaver Island was sent back around midnight with word of the disaster. By morning, the *Marold II* was still smoldering, but the only apparent flames were amidships on the *Boyd*.

Of the crew of the *Marold II*, the body of Everett Cole was found beneath the toppled stack. To remove the body it was necessary to cut off one of his arms. Raymond was identified by his pocket watch. Although an explosion destroyed the *Marold II* and badly damaged the *Boyd*, the gasoline in the *Boyd*'s hull was intact.

Soon afterward, a foolhardy soul drove a gas truck onto the ice in an attempt to reach the *Boyd,* despite having been warned about danger. Truck and driver broke through the ice to rest 100 feet beneath the surface of Lake Michigan. This raised the death toll to six. In early spring, parts of a third body and pieces of clothing were discovered on board the *Boyd* following the spring thaw. The remains of Captain Hill eventually washed up on the western shores of Beaver Island, while the body of his son, Leon, washed up in Green Bay on the opposite side of the lake in 1938.

This disaster produced a series of ripples that had an adverse effect on the people of Beaver Island. Five of their own, including the island's entrepreneur,

The J. Oswald Boyd after the explosion. *—Courtesy of the Beaver Island Historical Society*

were gone. Two boats and a truck were also lost. These events are credited with discouraging development on the island for 15 years.

The Beaver Island accident underscores the human impact of shipwrecks. In addition to the crews, boats, and cargoes that are lost, families and friends are left behind. As in the case of the *J. Oswald Boyd* and *Marold II,* some wrecks may hamper or prevent the economic growth of communities. These are some of the risks that the mariners of Lake Michigan and their loved ones face on a daily basis.

III THE CARL D. BRADLEY

From the time of its construction and well after its death, the bulk carrier *Carl D. Bradley* has been something of a legend. Built in 1927, the vessel was the largest laker sailing the Great Lakes. From the American Ship Building Company of Lorain, Ohio, the *Bradley* was an impressive 623 feet in length, 65 feet at the beam and constructed with a depth of 33 feet. It displaced a total of 7,706 net tons and 10,028 gross tons. Built as a self-unloader, the *Bradley* was intended to operate at ports where shore unloading services were negligible or nonexistent.

Like many boats built in the 1920s, the *Bradley* was powered by steam turbines, giving the ship some muscle. In 1929, the *Bradley* transported 18,114 tons of limestone on a single trip to Gary, Indiana. This put the freighter in the record books as hauling more cargo by weight than any other Great Lakes boat to that time.

The *Bradley* was owned of the Bradley Transportation Line. In fact, the freighter bore the name of the firm's president at the time of its construction, a testament to the confidence in the big ship. Bradley Transportation, a subsidiary of U.S. Steel, was well-established and respected, careful about command of their ships, especially the *Bradley.*

In 1954, that honor fell to Roland Bryan, a seaman with 38 years of experience to his credit. After beginning his sailing career in 1916 at the age of 14, he took a position as wheelman in 1929, and in 1947 was offered his first job as a captain. Seven years later, at age 52, Captain Bryan was responsible for the *Bradley* and its crew.

In November 1958, the *Bradley* was making its 46th and final run of the season. After unloading its cargo at Buffington, Indiana, near Gary, the vessel headed for Rogers City, Michigan, the origin of the first leg of the trip. The *Bradley* had damaged a plate on its hull after scraping the bottom earlier that month at

The Carl D. Bradley.—*Courtesy of the Wisconsin Maritime Museum*

Cedarville, Michigan, and was due for a new cargo hull during the 1958-59 winter layover. This overhaul was apparently much on Captain Bryan's mind. He confided to several friends that he was concerned about the safety of his boat and crew.

Still, there was little reason to expect that this trip would be different from any other. The Bradley Transportation Line had just been inspected by the National Safety Council and given the highest marks for safety. Furthermore, the *Bradley* had been inspected twice that year by the Coast Guard and was considered fit for service.

The crew was also glad when they departed Buffington for Rogers City. Twenty-six of the 33 crewmembers hailed from the Lake Huron port and they were looking forward to returning to family and friends for several months. At 6:30 p.m. Monday, November 17, the *Bradley* pointed its long nose north and set out for home.

Gale warnings were issued Tuesday morning, but big freighters can manage heavy winds and high seas without much concern. The *Bradley* was carrying 9,000 tons of water for ballast and was expected to reach Rogers City without difficulty. The *Bradley* stoically moved past the port cities dotting the Michigan shoreline.

Members of the crew had noticed increasingly disturbing signs as to the *Bradley*'s seaworthiness. The freighter was considered somewhat of a rust bucket. Several crewmen, including the first assistant engineer, stated that the rust holes were large enough in some of the bulkheads that it was possible to see from one compartment into the next. In addition, the ballast tanks leaked and the pumps were constantly working in order to remove water in the cargo tunnel. Furthermore, the steel plates were riveted, not welded. It was not uncommon for the rivets to pop during periods of high stress and they were certainly doing so now. Regardless, the *Bradley* was considered fit enough for this last run. As for popping rivets, this was so common on freighters constructed in this manner that no one seems to have taken serious notice.

The winds were at this point in excess of 60 miles per hour with waves upwards of 30 feet. Coupled with the damage sustained several weeks earlier, the *Bradley* was in peril. At 5:30 p.m. Tuesday, threats became reality. In the pilot-house were First Mate Elmer Fleming and Captain Bryan. It was at this point that the *Bradley* started to break in half.

A sudden, loud crack alerted Bryan and Fleming that something was wrong. From their positions in the pilothouse, the men watched as the hull broke apart amidships. Horrified as he realized what was happening, Bryan ordered the engines brought to a dead stop. The sound of the ship's alarm reverberated throughout the *Bradley*. Fleming issued a Mayday. Coast Guard stations around Lake Michigan picked up the distress calls.

The hull continued to sag in the middle with the bow and the stern of the *Bradley* slowly rising higher than the center. At this point, the crew of the *Bradley* was 12 miles south of Gull Island and not far from the Straits of Mackinac. First Mate Fleming sent his distress call for almost 15 minutes when the *Bradley* broke in half. The bow and stern slipped beneath the waves. The stern exploded as the cold water reached the freighter's boilers.

Nearly all of the men were thrown into the sea. They had time to don life preservers, but in the towering surf they lost sight of one another. There were a few fortunate souls who managed to reach an 8-by-10-foot life raft. The first of these were First Mate Fleming and Frank Mays, the deck watchman. Fleming and Mays took on two additional men, Gary Strzelecki, a deck watchman like Mays, and Dennis Meredith, a deck hand. Fleming fired off all but one of their flares. Waiting until they spotted a vessel, Fleming attempted to use the last flare but it was an impotent gesture. The only vessel near enough to see the flares was the German freighter *Sartori;* it was too far away to reach the men on the life raft before the wind and waves pushed the small craft away.

The *Sartori* was under the command of a former U-boat officer, Captain Muller, who directed his ship to the *Bradley*. Despite a distance of only four miles, it required a full two hours to reach the site in the violent seas. The crew of the *Sartori* could see the glow of red flares on the horizon, but they were powerless to aid the crew of the lost freighter. By the time they reached the location where the *Bradley* had been, there was no sign of the crew.

A 36-foot motor lifeboat was sent from the Coast Guard station at Charlevoix but was forced back by the elements after struggling for four miles. Nearly an hour after the *Bradley* began to break up, the 180-foot Coast Guard cutter *Sundew* left Charlevoix under Lieutenant Commander Harold Muth.

The *Sundew* reached the last known location of the *Bradley*, where it was joined by its sister ship, the 180-foot cutter *Hollyhock* from Sturgeon Bay. Aiding the two Coast Guard cutters in their search were the *Sartori* and an HU-16 Albatros seaplane from the Traverse City Coast Guard air station. Under the glare of flares dropped by the Albatros, the boats continued their desperate search.

By now there was the occasional gust of snow. The water was barely above freezing and it was doubtful that any survivors could last in the rolling seas.

A Coast Guard helicopter hailing from the same base as the Albatros finally spied a raft with two men on board the next morning. The two survivors were Fleming and Mays. They had been thrown from their raft repeatedly during the night by the high waves and were covered with ice, but they were still clinging to life. There was no sign of Strzelecki or Meredith. They had slipped from the raft during the night and disappeared.

The occupants of the raft were taken aboard the *Sundew* while the helicopter continued searching for survivors. Strzelecki was found floating in the water and taken on board the freighter *Transontario*. He was barely alive. A helicopter with a doctor was dispatched in an effort to save the young deck watchman. Strzelecki died minutes before help could reach him.

Fleming and Mays survived, but 33 friends and colleagues perished. Among the dead was Martin Enos, an oil stoker who was soon to be married. His body was never found.

The insurance companies and the Bradley Transportation Line insisted that the *Bradley* had not broken in half but had been overwhelmed by the elements. This argument was maintained for years despite the word of the two survivors who had witnessed the end of the *Bradley*. The following year the remains of the *Bradley* were discovered. Attempts to determine the cause of the ship's destruction commenced after the spring thaw but proved inconclusive. Not even remote television units, sent 360 feet to the bottom of Lake Michigan, could determine the cause of the accident.

The owners of the *Bradley* persisted in their belief that the freighter had not split in half. It seemed incredulous that a large, modern freighter could simply break apart. In 1997, 39 years after the *Bradley* sank, it was proven that the freighter had, in fact, broken in two. The stories of both survivors were accepted as the true version of events.

When it sank, the *Carl D. Bradley* was the largest vessel ever lost in the Great Lakes. The *Bradley* remains the largest wreck in Lake Michigan, but its Great Lakes record slipped to number two in 1975 with the loss of an even bigger freighter—the *Edmund Fitzgerald* in Lake Superior.

OTHER SIGNIFICANT WRECKS

ALWAYS A DANGEROUS REGION

Because of the treacherous weather, numerous islands and reefs waiting to smash unwary vessels, and frequent boat traffic, the northern region of lake Michigan was the scene of some very early wrecks. One of the victims was the war sloop *Welcome*. Constructed at Fort Michilimackinac in 1775, it was a single-masted craft, 60 feet in length, with 45 tons burden.[1] In the autumn of 1787, it was navigating the treacherous Straits of Mackinac when it fell victim to a late season storm. All hands on board the sloop disappeared when their boat was lost. The *Welcome's* final resting-place is either Lake Huron or Lake Michigan. The remains have never been found.

The next known wreck was the two-masted schooner *Free Trader*, which went ashore in 1835 after encountering a storm in Manitou Passage. The incident claimed the lives of two of its crew.

In the decade following the loss of the *Free Trader* no fewer than seven vessels wrecked between North Manitou Island and the Straits of Mackinac. Included in this number were two brigs—the *Albany* and the *Alert*; four schooners—the *Troy*, the *Champion*, the *Forester,* and the *Tribune*; and a steamer —the *Empire State*. The worst incident involved the *Tribune*.

The 104-foot *Tribune* appears to have been bound for points north when it disappeared while in southern waters. Traveling light, the *Tribune* went down in a gale on April 18, 1884, with all ten crew members. The wreck of the *Tribune* was discovered the following year by fishermen, who noticed the schooner's masts sticking above the surface. The masts serve as grave marker and as testimony to the violent death of a lake boat, its crew, and passengers.

Not only do captains have to set a course around navigational hazards such as islands, shoals, storm-veiled coasts, and shipwrecks, they also have to pay heed to lake currents. The wood side-wheel steamer *A.D. Patchin* was one such case. The *Patchin* was four years old when a strong current carried the steamer

---

[1] Fort Michilimackinac grew into a sizable settlement and was later renamed Mackinaw City.

several miles off course to deposit the vessel on Skillagalee Reef, a point south-west of Waugochance Point and due east of Beaver Island, in late September 1850. Attempts to remove the *Patchin* were abandoned. Within weeks, the relent-less beating the steamer received from wind and wave action proved too much and the *Patchin* broke apart.

The propeller steamer *Westmoreland*, built by Lafrenier & Stevenson of Cleveland, Ohio, found service hauling passengers and freight across the lakes. Despite the stout construction of the *Westmoreland*, the dangers posed by lake ice can never be underestimated. Ice has caused many Great Lakes accidents and the *Westmoreland* proved to be no exception.

Caught by a storm somewhere in Manitou Passage on December 7 and 8, 1854, the *Westmoreland* experienced ice freezing to its superstructure. Unable to maintain its balance in the large waves, the craft capsized. As it sank, the *Westmoreland* destroyed one of its lifeboats, killing 17 passengers and crew. The *Westmoreland* was reported to be carrying a small fortune in gold and liquor. This was in addition to supplies destined for Mackinac Island.

The year after the wrecking of the *Westmoreland*, the schooner *Energy* was completing its maiden voyage, which was from Kenosha, Wisconsin, to Buffalo, New York. The *Energy* was traveling back to Wisconsin when it encountered a stiff gale. Tossed about like a cork, the *Energy*'s cargo shifted. Unable to fight the wind and waves, the *Energy* was forced ashore in Little Traverse Bay, which is a trip of roughly 40 miles for a vessel southward bound from the Straits of Mackinac. All but one of the crew was rescued by nearby Indians, who braved the lake in rescue attempts.

In an era when the term right-of-way was either unknown by some captains or ignored, collisions were a common occurrence. On September 21, 1855, the 204-ton schooner *Asia* collided with the 515-ton propeller-steamer *Forest City*. The incident occurred at night and there are no reports to indicate that foul weather may have played a role in the accident. It is entirely possible that nei-ther vessel was keeping a sharp watch. The *Asia* sank in ten minutes, to be fol-lowed by the *Forest City* ten minutes later. Crews and passengers of both vessels waited in the ship's boats until the schooner *Hamlet* came upon the scene and took everyone on board. There were no fatalities.

The 1850s witnessed an assortment of vessels wrecked and cargo lost. Thirteen schooners met their end during this ten-year period, including a scow schooner. Added to this number were eight steamers, one of which was a side-wheeler, six brigs, and two barks. It was a diverse collection, indicative of the type of vessel in use at mid-century. The cargoes included pumps, general merchan-dise, grain, bricks, railroad ties, and scrap iron.

Little of consequence happened during the 1860s. Although approximately 20 vessels wrecked, few lives were lost. A fair amount of cargo was destroyed but nothing of great value.

TRAGEDIES AND TRIUMPHS

One of the more unusual factors in the destruction of a boat involves the 139-foot schooner *Live Yankee*. The *Live Yankee*'s crew and a 14-year-old girl who was a passenger reached shore after the schooner was beached by a storm in early November 1869. The steward died, but the others were taken care of by local Indians. Were it not for the cargo, the *Live Yankee* may have been recovered. After the beaching, water surged over the deck, a problem that does not always lead to a ship's demise. Unfortunately for the *Live Yankee,* it was carrying a load of wheat. The cargo absorbed the lake water, expanded, and split the schooner's seams. The vessel was a total loss.

The 1870s were as unkind to mariners and their families as they were to owners and insurance companies. The first wreck of the decade was the double-masted schooner *Carrington,* washed up on Beaver Island during an October storm in 1870. The schooner was broken apart by wave action. Six of those on board and a cargo of pig iron were lost. The following month saw three more wrecks, including the three-masted barkentine *Badger State* at Sleeping Bear Point a short distance south of North and South Manitou Islands. The *Badger State* was involved in a collision the previous year with the schooner *Dolphin* during a storm. The *Dolphin* sank but the crew was saved by the *Badger State.*

One of the worst tragedies off the coast of northern Michigan involved the three-masted schooner *Charles H. Hurd.* On September 22, 1871, the *Hurd* foundered in the vicinity of South Manitou Island, the victim of a storm and leak. Only one of 12 persons on board survived and he was Captain W.O. Harrison. Among those lost were Harrison's wife, children, and brother. Waugoschance Point[2] also claimed a heavy toll that year. The bark *Maitland,* steamer *Free State,* and schooners *Thomas Kingsford* and *W.S. Lyons* sank on or near the shores of the point that juts into the lake southeast of the Straits of Mackinac.

Nearly half of northern Michigan's shipwrecks in the 1870s took place between 1870 and 1872. More than half the loss of life happened between 1872 and 1879. The worst wrecks were those of the schooners *Jennie and Anne, Gilbert Mollison, William Sanderson, J.P. March,* and *W.B. Phelps.* The *Mollison* and *Sanderson* went down with all hands. The *Phelps* took four of the crew and a cargo of beer.

[2] Known by generations of sailors as "Wobble Shanks."

An early wreck during this decade involved the three-masted schooner *R.P. Mason,* which went aground on Waugoshance Point on October 8, 1871. The four-year-old ship had been built by H. Piersen of Grand Haven, Michigan, and was 115 feet long. A lighter was used to transfer the *Mason's* cargo of corn, oats, pork, beef, and flour while the tug *Leviathan* labored to work the stricken schooner free. Six days after the *R.P. Mason* stranded, the *Leviathan* took the *Mason* under tow and the two vessels started for Little Traverse Bay. As the boats and their crews were under way, a storm blew up. At some point, the towline broke or was caught in the propeller of the *Leviathan.* Either way, the *R.P. Mason* was cast adrift.

Captain Thomas Phall and four others on board the *Mason* were lost after the schooner capsized. Four other crew members survived and were picked up by another boat. The battered and abandoned remains of the *R.P. Mason* made it to Cross City, between the Straits of Mackinac and Charlevoix, where the vessel was salvaged and returned to service.

This was not the last time the *R.P. Mason* would wreck. The schooner stranded in May 1883, near Chicago and went ashore yet again in 1905 in the vicinity of Marinette, Wisconsin. On June 20, 1917, fifty years after its construction, the *R.P. Mason* caught fire on Lake Michigan during a storm. This was the last blow that fate would deal the *Mason,* which sank as a result of the fire.

Common to the 19th century were many shipwrecks where the crew could either float to safety or escape from the sinking vessel as it foundered on shore. Obviously, this was one of the advantages of sailing close to land. One such incident involved the three-masted schooner *Bridgewater.* Built as a bark, the *Bridgewater* stranded at Waugoschance Point on December 1, 1875. The crew abandoned their ship and attempts to release the *Bridgewater* met with equal success. It was towed across Lake Huron, traveled the breadth of Lake Erie, and entered the waters of Lake Ontario, where the schooner was taken to Buffalo for repairs. While repairs were under way the *Bridgewater* burned and was declared a total loss.

THE 1880s AND 1890s

No decade witnessed a greater loss of lake boats in this region than the 1880s. While the loss of cargo was heavy, the loss of life was blessedly light. In 1880 the steamer *Fletcher* went ashore on South Fox Island with a load of corn. That same year the schooner *Thomas W. Ferry* stranded in the vicinity of Beaver Island. No vessels were lost in 1881. This interlude came to an abrupt end with the sinking of the steam tug *Uncle Sam* in the Straits of Mackinac in the spring of 1882. The *Uncle Sam* was abandoned; its wrecking added to the number of vessels lost due to ice. The *Uncle Sam* was followed later that same year by the wrecking of three schooners.

The *California* and the *Champlain*, lost in 1887, take credit for being the worst disasters of the decade. When the *Champlain* caught fire, it took 22 of the 57 on board to their deaths. The foundering of the *California* during a storm off St. Helena Island west of the Straits of Mackinac on October 3 cost nine people their lives and claimed a cargo of general merchandise. The *California* was raised shortly after the incident. Owned by a Canadian outfit, the vessel was abandoned to American interests, who rebuilt it as the *Pease* at Bay City, Michigan.

The last decade of the century was relatively peaceful yet there was still the occasional wreck of note. One of these was the *Annie Vought*, a 15-year-old schooner constructed by Bailey Brothers of Fairport, Ohio. On November 21, 1892, the *Annie Vought* was just north of South Manitou Island en route to Milwaukee from Buffalo with a load of coal. Fighting a storm, the schooner was washed up on the rocks. The men of the U.S. lifesaving service on Beaver Island rigged a breeches buoy to the *Annie Vought*. One by one, the eight crewmembers were brought to shore until everyone had been rescued.

The month prior to the loss of the *Annie Vought*, the schooner *Ostrich* went missing west of the Manitou Islands with the entire complement of six crewmen. The *Ostrich* was traveling light and high in the water. Two possibilities exist that might explain the schooner's loss. One of these holds that the *Ostrich* was claimed by the storm raging at the time. Another explanation maintains that the schooner was lost following a collision with the steamer *W.H. Gilcher* (an account of the *Gilcher's* sinking was at the beginning of this chapter). Both vessels disappeared in the night. The *Ostrich* was the greatest tragedy of a decade that was marked by mostly nonfatal wrecks.

The schooner *Northwest* was one of the larger wind-reliant vessels to venture onto Lake Michigan. With a length of 223 feet, a 38-foot beam, and 15-foot depth, this four-master was a proud sailing craft, eventually reduced to somewhat meaner estate as a schooner barge. In tow of the steamer *Aurora*, the *Northwest* struck an ice floe in Straits of Mackinac on April 6, 1898. The *Northwest* sunk, taking with it a load of corn; but the lake failed to claim any of the crew members, who were picked up by the *Aurora*.

THE INDUSTRIAL TWENTIETH CENTURY

Few areas of Lake Michigan have witnessed the number of wrecks that northern Michigan can claim in the 20th century. The vigorous industrial growth of the region during this time was reflected by the cargo many of these doomed ships carried: timber, iron ore, coal, grain, and petroleum, to name a few.

The schooner Mars.—*Courtesy of the Library of Congress*

The century was only seven months old when the scow schooner *John C. Bauer* stranded during a heavy fog on South Fox Island without loss of life. It was followed that November by the schooner *Manitowoc,* lost to a storm on North Manitou Island.

This was the era of the Christmas tree trade. Like the *S. Thal* three years before and the *Rouse Simmons* eleven years later, the schooner *Caledonia* went down with a load of Christmas trees and slabs on November 25, 1901, off Sleeping Bear Point. Here the similarity among the three ships ends, for not a single crew member of the *Caledonia* was lost. The crew of three was rescued by the schooner *Lomie A. Burton* and lived to continue working the lakes.

In 1903, the *Walter L. Frost,* a wood freighter, was fighting high winds, heavy seas, and a fog when it grounded on a reef off South Manitou Island. The *Frost* was abandoned but the lifesaving service rescued the crew. In the same year, the schooner *Mars* stranded, also on South Manitou Island. The *Mars* was pounded to pieces.

The decade of the First World War saw a large amount of lumber wash ashore, from battered wrecks and from the tremendous amount of timber carried during this ten-year period. At least 26 vessels wrecked in these ten years, proving how dangerous navigating the Straits of Mackinac and the Manitou Passage could be.

By the Roaring Twenties, new safety procedures, the use of the teletype machine, and the transition from wood to steel construction had a profound effect on the number of, and survivability of, shipwrecks. Only two wrecks are recorded for this entire period. They were the freighters *Niko* and *P.J. Ralph*, laden with lumber. Crews on both lakers were successfully removed. Perhaps it is not surprising that both freighters were constructed in 1889 when wood was the favored building medium.

As recounted earlier in this chapter, on November 18, 1958, the *Carl D. Bradley* broke its back in a storm near Gull Island. It is the largest laker to be lost on Lake Michigan and the second largest vessel to be claimed by the Great Lakes, surpassed only by the *Edmund Fitzgerald* less than two decades later.

In 1960, the steel freighter *Fransisco Morazan*, having recently departed Chicago, went ashore on South Manitou Island during a blizzard. On board was an expensive cargo of machinery. Efforts by the U.S. Coast Guard stationed on South Manitou Island, including three cutters and a helicopter, saved the entire crew. In death the *Fransisco Morazan* joined the steamer *Walter L. Frost*, which wrecked in the same area 57 years ago. The two boats, which wrecked on the same reef, now rest together, with the *Morazan* athwart the *Frost*.

The final two wrecks of the twentieth century off northern Michigan involved the tugs *Lauren Castle* and *Razel Brothers*. They sank following separate collisions in the 1980s with no loss of life.

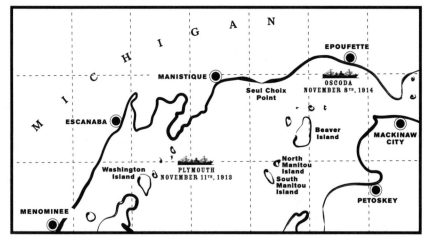

The shoreline of Michigan's Upper Peninsula.
—Courtesy of the National Oceanographic and Atmospheric Administration

MICHIGAN'S
UPPER
PENINSULA

Michigan's beautiful Upper Peninsula would fit any geologist's image of heaven on earth. The region has been blessed with an abundance of minerals and semi-precious stones, including copper, silver, and agate. Heavily forested, the Upper Peninsula's pristine wilderness encompasses an area greater in size than that of Rhode Island, Massachusetts, Connecticut, and Delaware combined, with a population smaller than that of any one of the New England states.

This northern expanse of Michigan has felt the blows of the miner's pick and the lumberjack's axe. Once primarily comprised of white pine, today the Upper Peninsula is covered with pine and a mix of deciduous trees, and most of the once-booming mines have been played out.

When the first explorers and settlers reached these shores, it was a region rich with virgin timber, pure copper, and high-grade iron ore. In the 19th century, lumber and mining operations dotted the landscape, extracting the area's natural resources and shipping them to ports around the Great Lakes and the world. Iron ore was shipped from the ports of Escanaba and Marquette, while the Keweenaw Peninsula became one of the biggest copper-producing regions of the world. To haul these resources south, boats typically docked at any of the ports along the Upper Peninsula's Lake Superior or Lake Michigan shorelines. Filled with as much cargo as they could safely handle, and often more, the lake boats would head into either Lake Michigan or Lake Huron.

Originally, the maritime industry was the sole means for timber companies and mines to transport their cargoes, but this mode of shipping goods was eventually forced to compete with other types of transportation, such as railroads and trucking. With the completion of the five-mile-long Mackinac Bridge in 1957, a new route to the Lower Peninsula was opened. Although far from eliminating the region's reliance on lake commerce, the bridge has reduced it. But the major reason for the Upper Peninsula's decline in port activity is the disappearance of the timber and ore that once flowed from of this region.

As a result, the Upper Peninsula is scattered with ghost towns; abandoned relics of a different age. These towns, once booming, now lie forgotten and overgrown. Piers, originally used for loading steamers and schooners, still jut into the lake waters before disappearing beneath the surface. These skeletal remnants are all that is left of a once thriving region. But the Upper Peninsula can boast of a rich maritime history, including numerous wrecks that brought out the best and worst in captains and crews who served as a lifeline to this isolated region.

I THE PLYMOUTH

The *Plymouth* was a decrepit vessel when it went down in the Big Storm of 1913. Originally propeller driven, the ship was 777 gross tons when Ira Lafranier of Ohio City, Ohio, launched it in 1854. It was 213 feet long, 35 feet in the beam, and 14 feet in depth. The *Plymouth* was rebuilt as four-masted vessel in 1884.

Fifty-nine years later, the *Plymouth* and its crew entered the teeth of the Big Storm of 1913. The vessel's fate was sealed on Saturday, November 8, when the tug *James H. Martin* cut it loose off St. Martin's Island, between Door County and the Garden Peninsula.

The owner of the tug was Donald McKinnon. Working for McKinnon was Captain Louis Setunsky, who was less than pleased with his new command. Captain Setunsky found the *James H. Martin* to be a boat prone to bouts of moodiness. Like the *Plymouth*, the *Martin* was an old boat and required constant repairs to the engine and continual pumping to keep it afloat. Neither vessel was up to the task of riding out the great storm.

Unable to keep the *Plymouth* under tow and flooding, the *Martin* retired to Summer Island, where Setunksy planned to repair the tug. This would also allow the pumps to operate in calmer waters, thereby reducing the flooding below decks. The wind was howling in from the north when the *Martin* signaled the *Plymouth* that the crew was releasing the towline. This signal was acknowledged by the *Plymouth,* which dropped anchor and watched as its tow disappeared in the driving snow.

Captain Axel Larsen of the *Plymouth* soon had a difficult job on his hands. The winds had increased to 80 miles an hour or more. With such strong winds, the snow was blowing horizontally. On board the *Plymouth* was Christ Keenan, a federal marshal. Ownership of the *Plymouth* was being contested by several parties, and Keenan was on board to prevent possible theft of the boat. Seven others were also on board and together the nine men fought to survive a bitter night.

The winds abated the following day, so the *James H. Martin* went to recover the *Plymouth* and tow it to port, only to discover that the schooner barge had disappeared. All nine crewmembers on board the *Plymouth* were lost during the storm as was the cargo of cedar posts. A week later, a note penned in Keenan's hand washed ashore in a bottle. It read:

Dear wife and children: We were left up here in Lake Michigan by McKinnon, captain of the tug James H. Martin at anchor. He went away and never said good bye or anything to us. Lost one man last night. We have been out in the storm 40 hours. Good bye dear ones, I might see you in heaven. Pray for me. Christ K. I felt so bad I had another man write for me. Huebel owes $35.00 so you can get it. Good Bye forever.

The note provides a poignant insight not only into the last hours of the *Plymouth*, but also into the thoughts of the shipwrecked as they awaited death.

Although the remains of the *Plymouth* were not located, wreckage indicated the probable cause of the disappearance. Captain McKinnon of the *Martin* later claimed that he was forced to leave the *Plymouth* to save his own crew. Hard-hearted as this may seem, it was common practice. Schooner barges were usually fitted with masts that could be relied upon if they were on their own.

Captain Setunsky claimed that the *Martin* was not seaworthy and that his actions in releasing the line were justified. Prior to examination of the *Martin* to verify this claim, the tug sank. The *Martin* was raised and evidence suggested that the boat had been scuttled.

Although McKinnon and Setunsky were experienced captains, there was doubt as to whether they were qualified to work the *Martin* and tow a vessel as large as the *Plymouth*. While neither was found criminally liable for the loss of the *Plymouth*, McKinnon had his license revoked as a consequence of the incident.

Captain Larsen's body and that of Deputy Marshall Christ Keenan eventually washed ashore, although those of the remaining seven crew members were never found. The wreck of the *Plymouth* remained lost until being discovered near Poverty Island in 1984.

Whatever the true story, Captain McKinnon was not a coward. Before the *Plymouth* was cut loose from the *Martin*, its cook, Margaret Olive, was taken on board the *Martin*. When she was washed over the side, McKinnon dove into the rough surf after her. The year after the *Plymouth* incident, Margaret Olive became Mrs. Margaret McKinnon.

II THE OSCODA

Lumber hookers had their origins in the lumber trade of the late 19th century. These boats specialized in carrying freshly cut wood for the building industry. Loaded with lumber from the mills of the northern Great Lakes, the hookers traveled south to the big cities of Chicago, Milwaukee, Detroit, Toledo, Cleveland, Buffalo, and other ports, where their cargoes were well received by these growing communities.

Into this trade came the wood bulk freighter and propeller steamer *Oscoda*. Built by S. Langell of St. Clair, Michigan, in 1878, it was intended for the lumber trade. A vessel of average dimensions, the *Oscoda* was built with a length of 175 feet, a 32-foot beam, and a 13-foot draft. Total, the vessel was 529 tons gross burden.

On Saturday, November 7, 1914, the *Oscoda* was serving as tow for two barges, the *A. C. Tuxbury* and the *Alice B. Norris*. Bound for the markets of Chicago from the lumber camps of Georgian Bay in Lake Huron, the steamer and its two charges were fully loaded on a westerly course through the Straits of Mackinac when they encountered foul weather.

Seeking shelter off St. Ignace, Michigan, near where the Mackinac Bridge would be built, the trio withstood the southwesterly gale that threatened shipping throughout the western lakes. While at anchor, a crewman discovered that the *Alice B. Norris* was leaking. The *Norris'* pumps went into action, but it was clear that they should resume their journey at the earliest convenience.

Conditions proved favorable around midnight when the wind shifted to the northwest. Opting to hug the shore, the captain of the *Oscoda* intended to lead his string of barges along the southern coast of the Upper Peninsula and then skirt the Wisconsin shoreline. Striking out shortly past midnight, the three hookers fought their way through a snowstorm so heavy that visibility was at times reduced to zero. Soon, the three vessels were in a heavy fog. It was rough going, but the *Oscoda* blindly led the two barges as best it could.

Mariners have many different sayings to predict and describe the weather and lake conditions. One such saying states that, "A winter fog will freeze a dog." The crewmen and three women working on board the *Oscoda*, *Tuxbury*, and *Norris* could attest to this cliche as they fought the elements.

West of Mackinac lies a submerged geographical feature known as Pelkie Reef. This hazard to navigation is three-quarters of a mile in length and lies just beneath the surface. It was approximately 3 a.m. when the *Oscoda* ran onto

Pelkie Reef with a groan of tortured timbers. Seeing what had happened to the *Oscoda,* the barges behind the steamer cut their towlines, dropped anchor, and waited for morning.

Morning dawned dark and dreary. The *Oscoda* was held firmly in place by the reef. The *Tuxbury* came alongside and the task of removing the *Oscoda*'s cargo of lumber was begun. While the sailors of both hookers labored, the storm around them grew in intensity. By 5:30 a.m., the *Oscoda* could take no more punishment and rolled onto its starboard side. The *Oscoda* crew abandoned the doomed vessel, and the men were taken on board the *Tuxbury.* Despite this safe transfer, the two surviving hookers and all on board were far from safe. Without the steamer to guide them, the barges were dead in the water.

By Monday morning, the storm was escalating in intensity, with high seas battering the anchored barges. In desperation, a boat was launched from the *Tuxbury* with the thought that a few of the crew might reach land and locate a tow. The boat had not gone far before it became painfully clear that the craft would never reach land. With difficulty, the men in the boat returned to the *Tuxbury.*

The position the *Tuxbury* held was becoming increasing untenable. Anchored just beyond the reef, the vessel was in danger of being swept shoreward and meeting the same fate as the *Oscoda.* For its part, the *Norris* was relatively safe, having anchored between the shore and Pelkie Reef.

A makeshift raft was constructed from lumber on board the *Tuxbury* and several men braved the surf crashing over the reef to reach the *Norris.* The transfer was successfully handled and another raft followed. By now, 12 of the 18 men and three women on board the *Tuxbury* were across the reef. The *Tuxbury*'s boat was lowered and the remaining nine reached the *Norris* without incident. Unknown to the three crews, now all on board the *Norris,* their plight had been observed from shore and a steamer, the *Schenk,* sent to assist. Soon the *Norris* was under the tow of the *Schenk,* which returned barge and crew to St. Ignace.

The following day, Tuesday, the tug *Gifford* came for the *Tuxbury.* As of Tuesday night, the storm that had been blowing for several days was showing little interest in subsiding. Shortly after a hawser was secured from the *Gifford* to the *Tuxbury* and the two vessels got underway, the towline snapped and the barge was again on its own. A search by the *Gifford* proved fruitless.

By Wednesday, the *Tuxbury* had been fighting the weather and lakes for five days. Despite the continuous beating, things were beginning to look up. By now, the storm had blown itself out. Furthermore, the *Tuxbury* was discovered by two tugs, the *Anabel* and the *Burger,* near Point Aux Barques, 60 miles east of Pelkie Reef and the community of Epoufette, Michigan.

The *Tuxbury* was towed to port. It and the *Norris*, as well as the crews of the three lumber hookers, survived. The only casualty was the *Oscoda*. Held prisoner by Pelkie Reef, the vessel proved impossible to salvage. The boat was abandoned. In short order, the *Oscoda* broke up and disappeared—another victim of the lakes.

OTHER SIGNIFICANT WRECKS

EARLY DISASTERS

The first boat known to have wrecked on the Lake Michigan side of the Upper Peninsula was the *Leander*. The tiny double-masted schooner was caught in a mid-November storm in 1857 and wound up beached near Gros Cap in the Straits of Mackinac.

On September 26, 1861, the steamer *Minnesota* stranded on Summer Island near the Garden Peninsula during a gale. The steamer was leaking heavily and was forced to dump its cargo of corn overboard. In an effort to save the *Minnesota,* the boat's master ran the vessel ashore on Summer Island. Had it not been for a storm that blew over the region soon thereafter, the *Minnesota* might have been recovered. As it was, the vessel became the first steamer to wreck in the waters of the Upper Peninsula.

It is no surprise to see that three of the four wrecks occurring after the *Minnesota* were loaded with iron ore. The only vessel not hauling ore was the sailboat *Lady Cornelia*, which capsized, taking four of the crew and passengers.

One of the more interesting wrecks to occur during the 1870s involves the side-wheel steamer *Queen City*. Originally built in 1856 by the Pringle Company of Oshkosh, Wisconsin, for carrying passengers and freight, the *Queen City* ended its days as a tug. On November 22, 1875, it was about ten miles south of Escanaba when the fire in the steamer's cook stove blazed out of control. Unable to beat back the flames and realizing there was nothing they could do to save their vessel, the crew lowered the ship's boat and headed for shore. All hands survived but the *Queen City* was a total loss.

THE TURN OF THE CENTURY AND BEYOND

In the years prior to 1880, there were probably no more than 16 shipwrecks in this region. But between 1880 and 1899, this number more than doubled. The period between 1900 and 1916 witnessed at least another 21 wrecks. Matters improved after 1916, with perhaps only four incidents occurring between 1940 and 1969.

November 29, 1881, was not the best of days for the New England Transportation Company. Two of their steamers, the sister ships *Lake Erie* and

Northern Queen, were sailing north from Chicago. Heading through a fog and late-November blizzard, the *Northern Queen* collided with the *Lake Erie* in the vicinity of Poverty Island, south of Summer Island. The *Lake Erie* sank as a result of the accident but the *Queen*'s captain saw to it that not a single crewmember or any of the passengers of the ill-fated steamer perished. The *Northern Queen* continued on to Manistique almost forty miles northeast of Poverty Island but struck a pier too hard and was wrecked. Despite their misfortunes, both vessels were later recovered.

No fewer than three different ships named *Monitor* wrecked off the Upper Peninsula coast. Two occurred in the 1870s; and on October 31, 1883, the schooner *Monitor* stranded off Seul Choix Point during a storm.[1] When it wrecked, the ship was carrying a cargo of iron ore. The tugs *Leviathan* and *Kate Williams* attempted to free the *Monitor* from the rocks, but abandoned the effort a month later. The *Kate Williams,* incidentally, was briefly seized by Canadian authorities in 1876 during a period when salvage vessels from the United States and Canada were illegally operating in one another's water. The tug sank at Washington Island in 1907.

Quite often a boat can wreck unexpectedly. This was the case with the *H.S. Hubbell,* which was destroyed by fire. The *Hubbell* was one of many propeller steamers working the northern lakes lumber trade when a galley lamp exploded on November 12, 1888. A good 20 miles east by northeast of Poverty Island, the crew took to the lifeboat and was eventually rescued by the steamer *New Orleans.*

---

[1] Seul Choix received its name from the early French voyageurs and means "only choice." It was the first harbor west of the Straits of Mackinac.

The Nahant.—*Courtesy of the Library of Congress*

The story of the *Erastus Corning* is significant for several reasons. Converted to a schooner, the *Corning* was until that time one of the last barks plying the lake trade. Furthermore, the vessel's namesake was the founder of the Corning Glass Company. On November 12, 1888, the *Corning* was under the tow of the steamer *Roumania* with a load of iron ore when it went ashore on Gull Island Shoal. The crew escaped serious injury but the ship did not, falling victim to the pounding of Lake Michigan's waves.

Despite the number of wrecks in the last two decades of the 19th century, deaths have been officially recorded for only three. These occurred to the crews of the schooners *Marinette* in 1886 and *William Home* in 1894, each with the loss of six on board. The steamer *Nahant* caught fire at its dock in Escanaba in Little Bay de Noc in late November 1897. The thermometer was hovering around the zero mark that day and made attempts to fight the blaze difficult. Two crewmen died.

A BRUSH WITH DISASTER

The Armistice Day Storm of 1940 wreaked havoc throughout the Lake Michigan region, resulting in enormous property damage and significant loss of life. One of the Upper Peninsula's most harrowing brushes with disaster occurred at Lansing Shoals during this monster storm.

Lansing Shoals is a desolate area of the Upper Peninsula, with the only visible feature above the surface of Lake Michigan a 59-foot navigational light atop a 20-foot-high and 74-foot-square concrete base. It is within this base that the machinery and equipment for the light are kept. The Lansing Shoals Light was completed in 1928 and replaced *Lightship Number 55*, which had been on station at the same location since 1900.

On duty at the lighthouse on November 11, 1940, were keeper G.L. Gordon and his assistant, W.L. Keller. Waves of at least 25 feet were slamming into the lighthouse, smashing in portholes and ripping the south door from its frame. With water pouring in, the engine room filled with water, thereby dousing the fire in the boiler and causing a loss of power. Despite all the water and debris washing around the room, Gordon started another fire in the boiler and returned power to the station.

Meanwhile, out on the lake, Captain Beganz, in command of the steamer *Thomas F. Cole*, was fighting to save his freighter and crew. Having steamed through the Straits of Mackinac, Beganz was heading the *Cole* for the Wisconsin side of Lake Michigan. The weather was so severe and visibility so limited that it was only after they had been fighting the storm for some time that the crew of the *Cole* realized they were along the Upper Peninsula coast.

Striking out for the Sturgeon Bay canal, the *Cole* attempted to enter the waters of Green Bay, but the snow was so thick that Captain Beganz turned toward Lansing Shoal instead. Later, Beganz reported that the ship encountered waves of 50 feet and winds of up to 125 miles per hour. Lacking radar and having a radio that could receive but not send, the *Cole* headed for Lansing Shoals. It was not long before the *Cole*'s lookout saw a light on the freighter's starboard side. Having heard over the radio that the Gray's Reef and Lansing Shoals Lights were not operating, Captain Beganz and the crew in the pilothouse could only speculate as to what the light might be.

The *Cole* closed the distance between it and the light. It was only when they were about a quarter of a mile away that the crew suddenly came to the conclusion that they were heading for the Lansing Shoals Light. Lacking time to change course, Captain Beganz watched as the shadow of the lighthouse loomed larger.

Just when it seemed as though a collision was inevitable, the *Cole* dropped into a trough. Simultaneously, a wave struck the lighthouse. As the mountain of water washed away from the light, it hit the vessel's stern, lending the freighter just enough force to propel it to safety. The *Cole* continued into the maelstrom. Twenty minutes later, the vessel and its crew were safely harbored at Garden Island.

As for the crew of the lighthouse, their ordeal was far from over. They remained on duty for three more days, when the Beaver Island Coast Guard relieved the two weary men, who had endured so much and come near death. In his log, Gordon reported considerable damage to the lighthouse, including the loss of the south door, the destruction of five porthole windows, the loss of many provisions from the storeroom, the presence of at least a foot of water in the engine room, water in the gasoline tanks, temporary loss of the antenna, and the subsequent loss of communicating with the outside world, with eight inches of ice coating the remaining doors and windows.

Although the wrecks on Lake Michigan continued well into the 20th century, this litany of disasters gradually grew less frequent. The last shipwreck off the Upper Peninsula occurred when the *Roen Salvage Derrick Barge No. 93* foundered near Rock Island Passage on October 20, 1969. It went down with approximately 60 tons of construction equipment.

LISTS OF SHIPWRECKS

WISCONSIN

NAME OF VESSEL	TYPE OF VESSEL	LOCATION OF LOSS	CARGO AT TIME OF LOSS	CAUSE	CREW & PASSENGERS	DATE OF LOSS
Alvin Clark	schooner	Chambers Island	light	C/S/R	3	6/29/1864
Appomattox	prop steamer, wood freighter	Milwaukee	coal	A/FG	0	11/2/1905
Art Palace	schooner	Green Bay	brothel	A/S/R	0	8/14/1869
Australasia	prop steamer, wood freighter	Whitefish Bay	coal	FI	0	10/18/1896
Berwyn	schooner	Death's Door	?	A/S	0	11/25/1908
Blue Bell	scow schooner	Sturgeon Bay	lumber	F/S/R	0	11/11/1887
Boston	side-wheel steamer	Milwaukee	?	A/S	0	11/24/1846
Bridgebuilder X	tug	Sturgeon Bay?	none	?	2-all	12/15/1959
Buccaneer	catamaran	Eagle Harbor	none	F	0	7/1/1981
Buckeye State	bark	Milwaukee	?	A/S	?	11/5/1852
C.C. Trowbridge	side-wheel steamer	Milwaukee	none	A/S	0	12/5/1842
Cambria	steel freighter	Sturgeon Bay	?	F	?	12/4/1924
Collingwood	schooner	Milwaukee/midlake	posts, poles	C/S	4 or 5	11/25/1882
Columbia	brig	Death's Door	copper	A/S	0	6/7/1859
D.A. Van Valkenburg	schooner	Whitefish Point	corn	A	9	9/15/1881
Daniel Lyons	schooner	Foscoro	wheat	CO	0	10/18/1878
Delaware	steam propeller	Sheboygan	gen. merch.	A/S	10 or 11	11/3/1855
E.G. Crosby	iron steamer, pass. freight	Sturgeon Bay	none	FI/R	0	12/3/1935
E.M. Ford	steel freighter	Milwaukee	cement	F/S/R	0	12/24/1979
Ebeneezer	schooner	Baileys Harbor	?	A/S	?	10/16/1880
Ella Doak	scow schooner	Hedgehog Harbor	stone	A/S	0	8/5/1875
Erie L. Hackley	prop steamer, yacht	Green Island	gen. freight	F/S	11	10/3/1903
Fairfield	schooner	Baileys Harbor	light	A/S	0	9/29/1869
Francis IV	motor yacht	Chambers Island	none	EX	3	8/6/1927
Frank O'Connor	prop steamer, wood freighter	Cana Island	coal	FI	0	10/2/1919
Gallinipper	schooner	Sheboygan	?	C/S	?	7/7/1851
Griffon	brig	Death's Door?	furs	?	?	8/1679
Halstead	schooner barge	Washington Island	?	F/S/R	All	11/11/1913
Howard	schooner	Racine	?	F	?	8/1850
Humko	oil screw	Two Rivers	?	FI	?	7/22/1956
J.G. McCullough	schooner	Clay Banks	pig iron	CO/S	0	7/3/1869
Joseph G. Masten	schooner	Two Rivers	coal	A/S	?	12/4/1897

WISCONSIN

NAME OF VESSEL	TYPE OF VESSEL	LOCATION OF LOSS	CARGO AT TIME OF LOSS	CAUSE	CREW & PASSENGERS	DATE OF LOSS
Josephine Lawrence	schooner	Baileys Harbor	?	A/S	0	10/16/1880
Kate Williams	tug	Washington Island	none	F	?	8/1908
Lac La Belle	prop steamer, wood freighter	Racine/midlake	grain	F/S/R	8	10/13/1872
Lakeland	steamer, steel freighter	Sturgeon Bay	automobiles	F	0	12/3/1924
Leland	schooner	Death's Door	lumber	A	?	1855
Lilly Amiot	gas launch	Washington Island	dynamite, gas	EX	0	6/6/1909
Linda E.	fishing tug	Port Washington	fish	?	3	12/11/1998
Little Sarah	schooner	Green Bay	passengers	C	1	11/17/1854
Lottie Cooper	schooner	Sheboygan	lumber	C/S/R	1	4/9/1894
Louisiana	prop steamer, wood freighter	Washington Island	light	FI	0	11/8/1913
Lumberman	schooner	Milwaukee	light	C/S	0	4/20/1893
M.J. Bartelme	steel freighter	Cana Island	?	A/S	0	10/4/1928
Maria Hilliard	schooner	Death's Door	?	A	?	1856
Merchant	prop steamer, pass., freight	Racine	lumber	A/FI	0	10/6/1872
Milwaukee	car ferry	Milwaukee	rail cars	F/S	52	10/22/1929
Niagara	side-wheel steamer	Port Washington	pass., freight	FI	70?	9/24/1856
Nile	side-wheel steamer	Milwaukee	?	FI	0	9/6/1850
Ocean Wave	scow schooner	Baileys Harbor	stone	CO	0	9/23/1869
Our Son	schooner	Sheboygan/midlake	wood	F/S	0	9/26/1930
Peoria	schooner	Baileys Harbor	lumber	A/S	0	11/12/1901
Perry Hannah	schooner	Jacksonport	?	?	?	10/15/1880
Phoenix	prop steamer, pass., freight	Sheboygan	pass.	FI	161– 190	11/20/1847
Polynesia	schooner	Sheboygan/midlake	coal	F/S	0	10/23/1887
Pride	schooner	Death's Door	?	?	?	11/1905
Prins Willem V	propeller, steel freighter	Milwaukee	TVs, gen. freight	CO	0	10/14/1954
R.G. Peters	prop steamer, wood freighter	Milwaukee/midlake	ballast	FI/S	14 – All	12/1/1882
R.J. Hackett	steamer	Whaleback Shoal	coal	FI	0	11/12/1905
Reciprocity	schooner	Foscoro	?	A/S	0	10/16/1880
Resumption	schooner	Plum Island	?	A/S	?	11/7/1914
Rouse Simmons	schooner	Kewaunee	Christmas trees	A/S	17–All	11/26/1912
Rudolph Wetzel	tug	Oak Creek	none	EX/PR	3–All	10/28/1882
Seaman	scow schooner	Death's Door	potatoes	A/S	0	11/15/1908

WISCONSIN

NAME OF VESSEL	TYPE OF VESSEL	LOCATION OF LOSS	CARGO AT TIME OF LOSS	CAUSE	CREW & PASSENGERS	DATE OF LOSS
Sebastopol	side-wheel steamer	Milwaukee	metals	A/S	4-7	9/18/1855
Senator	steel freighter	Port Washington	240 automobiles	CO/FG	10?	10/31/1929
Silver Cloud	scow schooner	Port Washington	wood	C/S/PR	3	7/7/1891
St. Albans	prop steamer, pass., freight	Milwaukee	gen. merch., cattle	CO/Ice	0	1/30/1881
St. Lawrence	schooner	Milwaukee/midlake	timber	FI	2	4/30/1878
St. Mary	schooner	Kewaunee?	pig iron	F/S	11- All	9/7/1860
Sumatra	schooner barge	Milwaukee	railroad ties	F/S	4	9/30/1896?
Toledo	brig	Baileys Harbor	?	?	0	1848
Toledo	steamer	Port Washington	gen. freight	F/S	40 to 55	10/22/1856
Two Friends	bark	Death's Door	salt	A/S	0	10/16/1880
Vencedor	sailing yacht	Fox Island	none	A/S	0	7/23/1911
Vernon	steamer	Two Rivers Point	gen. freight	F/S	36 to 41?	10/25/1887
W.G. Buckner	schooner	Ozaukee	lumber	C/S	5?	9/28/1849
William J. Livingstone	propeller, tug	Sturgeon Bay	?	F	?	10/1880
Windham	schooner	Death's Door	lumber	A	?	12/1855
Wisconsin	prop steamer, iron freighter	Kenosha	passengers	F/S	18	11/29/1929
Wollin	schooner	Sheboygan	wood, potatoes	A/S	0	4/29/1897

ILLINOIS

NAME OF VESSEL	TYPE OF VESSEL	LOCATION OF LOSS	CARGO AT TIME OF LOSS	CAUSE	CREW & PASSENGERS	DATE OF LOSS
Alnwick	schooner	Chicago	?	FI	0	10/4/1871
C.G. Mixer	schooner	Calumet River	railroad ties	A/S	0	5/18/1894
Calumet	prop steamer, wood freighter	Ft. Sheridan	coal	A/S	0	11/28/1889
Citizen	schooner	Chicago	?	A/S	?	5/18/1853
David A. Wells	schooner	Chicago	iron ore	F/S/R	8	10/16/1880
Eastland	prop steamer, steel pass. liner	Chicago River	passengers	C/R	835	7/24/1915
Evening Star	schooner	Chicago	?	CO/S	0	5/18/1894
F.L. Danforth	schooner	Chicago	corn	A/S/PR	0	4/20/1893
George W. Morley	prop steamer, wood freighter	Evanston	light	EX	0	12/5/1897
Heartless	schooner	Chicago	?	A	?	1824
Hercules	schooner	Calumet River	whiskey, gen. merch.	A/S	6–All	10/3/1818
J. Loomis McLaren	schooner	Chicago	lumber	A/S	1	5/18/1894
Jack Thompson	schooner	Chicago	lumber	CO/S	1	5/18/1894
Lady Elgin	side-wheel steamer	Winnetka	passengers	CO	297	9/7/1860
Lem Ellsworth	schooner	Chicago/midlake	stone blocks	F/S	7–All	5/18/1894
Mary D. Ayer	schooner	Grosse Point	light	CO/FG	5–All	5/17/1896
Mercury	schooner	Chicago	lumber	A/S	0	5/18/1894
Myrtle	schooner	Chicago	lumber	F/S	6–All	5/18/1894
Navarino	prop steamer, pass., freight	Chicago	?	FI	0	10/9/1871
Newburyport	side-wheel steamer	Chicago	?	A/S	?	10/1834?
Oregon	side-wheel steamer	Chicago	?	FI	0	1849?
Philo Parsons	side-wheel steamer	Chicago	none	FI	0	10/4/1871
Post Boy	schooner	Chicago	gen. merch, gunpowder	EX	10	1841
Rainbow	schooner	Chicago	lumber	C/S	0	5/18/1894
S. Thal	schooner	Glencoe	lumber	F/S	5–All	11/10/1898
Seabird	side-wheel steamer	Waukegan	gen. freight	FI	72- 102	4/9/1868
Seneca	tug	Chicago	none	EX/R	2	10/16/1855
Tioga	steamer	Chicago	?	EX	?	7/1890
Tuscarora	brig	Chicago	coal	A/S	0	10/16/1855
UC97	German submarine	Highland Park	none	Gunfire	0	6/7/1921
Valetta	bark	Chicago	?	FI	0	10/8/1871
Wisconsin	side-wheel steamer	Chicago	?	A/R	?	11/1842

INDIANA

NAME OF VESSEL	TYPE OF VESSEL	LOCATION OF LOSS	CARGO AT TIME OF LOSS	CAUSE	CREW & PASSENGERS	DATE OF LOSS
Beloit	schooner	Michigan City	?	A/S	?	1882
Charlotte	gas screw	Michigan City	?	F/S	?	7/1945
David Dows	schooner barge	Whiting	coal	F/S	0	11/25/1889
Eureka	propeller steamer	Michigan City	?	A/S	?	10/1873
Flying Cloud	schooner	Gary	?	A/S/R	7–All	11/1857
J. Barber	propeller steamer	Michigan City/midlake	fruit?	FI	5	7/19/1871
J.D. Marshall	propeller, wood freighter	Michigan City	machinery	C/S	4	6/11/1911
Martha	fishing tug	Michigan City	none	C/S	4–All	12/1933
Michigan City	scow schooner	Michigan City	?	F/S	?	10/5/1889
Muskegon	propeller, freighter	Michigan City	sand	FI	0	10/6/1910
Ray S. Farr	schooner	Michigan City	?	F/S	0	12/1/1886
Richard H.	fishing tug	South Lake Michigan	none	F/S	3	11/11/1940
Superior	side-wheel steamer	Michigan City	wheat	A/S	?	10/22/1843
William F.P. Taylor	side-wheel steamer	Michigan City	?	A/S	?	9/1838

MICHIGAN

NAME OF VESSEL	TYPE OF VESSEL	LOCATION OF LOSS	CARGO AT TIME OF LOSS	CAUSE	CREW & PASSENGERS	DATE OF LOSS
A.D. Patchin	side-wheel steamer	Skillagallee Reef	gen. merch.	A	0	9/27/1850
Albany	brig	Straits of Mackinac	passengers	A/S	?	10/1/1843
Alert	brig	Waugoschance Point	?	A/S	?	1844
Alpena	side-wheel steamer	Holland?	passengers	FI	100?/all	10/15/1880
Andaste	steel propeller	Holland/midlake	gravel	?	25-All	9/29/1929
Anna C. Minch	propeller, steel freighter	Pentwater	coal	F/S	24- All	11/11/1940
Annie Vought	schooner	South Manitou Island	coal	A/S	0	11/21/1892
Arab	schooner	Arcadia	none	C/S	1	11/13/1883
Arabian	bark	Point Betsie	none	F/S/PR	0	11/29/1856
Arcadia	prop steamer, wood freighter	Big Sable Point	wood	F/S	14- All	4/12/1907
Argo	schooner barge	Big Sable Pt./Manistee	?	A/S	14	4/1907
Asia	schooner	Grand Traverse Bay	corn	CO	0	9/21/1855
Badger State	bark	Sleeping Bear Dune	corn	A/S/R	?	11/16/1870
Black Hawk	brig	Point Betsie	stained glass	F/S	All	11/1862
Bridgewater	schooner	Waugoschance Point	?	A/FI/R	0	12/1/1875
Caledonia	schooner	Glen Haven	Christmas trees	F/S	0	11/25/1901
California	prop steamer, pass., freight	Straits of Mackinac	gen. merch.	F/S/R	9 to 14	10/3/1887
Carl D. Bradley	steel propeller, freight	Gull Island	none	F/S	33	11/18/1958
Caroline	schooner	Grand Haven	none	F	0	1855
Carrington	schooner	Beaver Island	pig iron	A/S	6?	10/30/1870
Champion	schooner	Waugoschance Point	?	A	?	12/1844
Champlain	prop steamer, pass., freight	Charlevoix	pass., horses, merch.	FI/R	22	6/16/1887
Champlain	side-wheel steamer	St. Joseph	gen. merch.	A/S/R	0	5/3/1840
Charles H. Hurd	schooner	South Manitou Island	corn, posts	F/S	11	9/22/1871
Chicora	propeller, pass., freight	St. Joseph	flour	F/S	25- All	1/21/1895
City Of Grand Haven	schooner	North Manitou Island	?	?	?	10/12/1916
Columbia	prop steamer, wood freighter	Frankfort	corn	F/S	16	9/10/1881
Davy Crockett	stern-wheel steamer	St. Joseph	?	A/S	?	5/9/1834
Daylight	side-wheel steamer	Grand Haven	?	FI	0	10/7/1870
Dolphin	schooner	Waugoschance Point	coal	CO/S/PR	0	7/6/1869
Driver	schooner	South Manitou Island	hardwood	C/S	0	8/30/1901
Empire State	steamer	Sleeping Bear Dunes	?	A	?	1849

MICHIGAN

NAME OF VESSEL	TYPE OF VESSEL	LOCATION OF LOSS	CARGO AT TIME OF LOSS	CAUSE	CREW & PASSENGERS	DATE OF LOSS
Energy	schooner	Petoskey	wheat	A/S/R	1	10/5/1854
Equinox	prop steamer, pass., freight	Big Sable Point	salt	F/S	25	9/10/1875
Erastus Corning	schooner	Poverty Island	iron ore	A/S	0	11/12/1888
Experiment	schooner	St. Joseph	?	C/S	?	1840
Fletcher	prop steamer, wood freighter	South Fox Island	corn	A/S	0	11/21/1880
Forest City	propeller	Grand Traverse Bay	gen. merch.	CO	0	9/21/1855
Forester	schooner	Straits of Mackinac	gen. merch.	F/S	0	10/1846
Francisco Morazan	propeller, steel freighter	South Manitou Island	machinery	A/S	0	11/24/1960
Free State	prop steamer, wood freighter	Waugoschance Point	cereals/grains	A/FG	?	9/30/1871
Free Trader	schooner	Manitou Passage	?	A/S	2	1835
Gilbert Mollison	schooner	Manitou Islands	corn, grain	F/S	8 or 9-all	10/27/1873
Governor Mason	side-wheel steamer	Muskegon River	?	A/S	?	5/3/1840
Granada	schooner	Muskegon	lumber	F/S	4	10/17/1880
H.C. Akeley	prop steamer, wood freighter	Holland	corn	F/S	6	11/13/1883
H.S. Hubbell	prop steamer, wood freighter	Poverty Island/midlake	lumber	FI	0	11/12/1888
Havana	schooner	St. Joseph	Iron ore	F/S	3	10/3/1887
Helen	scow schooner	Muskegon	Lumber	A/S	7?	11/18/1886
Hippocampus	prop steamer, pass., freight	St. Joseph	?	A/S	25 or 26	9/8/1868
Hurricane	schooner	St. Joseph	rye	F/S	9-all	11/23/1860
Indian	fishing tug	South Haven	none	F/S	5-all	11/11/1940
Ironsides	prop steamer, pass., freight	Grand Haven	gen. merch.	A/S	18 or 28	9/15/1873
J. Oswald Boyd	steel fuel tanker	Beaver Island	gasoline	S/FI	0	11/11/1936
J.H. Rutter	schooner	Ludington	grain	A/S	0	11/1/1878
J.P. March	schooner	Sleeping Bear Point	coal	A/S	4	10/30/1878
James McBride	brig	Sleeping Bear Point	wood	A/S	?	10/19/1857
Jennie and Anne	schooner	Empire Bluffs	grain	A/S	6 or 7	11/13/1872
John C. Bauer	scow schooner	South Fox Island	light	A/FG	0	7/6/1900
John Lillie	scow schooner	Grand Haven	?	F/S	?	1870
John V. Jones	schooner	Ludington/midlake	wood	F/S/R	2	10/20/1905
John V. Moran	propeller, wood freighter	Muskegon	flour, freight	F	0	2/9/1899
Keystone	prop steamer, wood freighter	Big Summer Island?	coal	A/FI/S	0	9/12/1898
Kitty Grant	schooner	Little Sable Pt./midlake	lumber	F/S	4-All	10/8/1884

MICHIGAN

NAME OF VESSEL	TYPE OF VESSEL	LOCATION OF LOSS	CARGO AT TIME OF LOSS	CAUSE	CREW & PASSENGERS	DATE OF LOSS
L.J. Conway	schooner	Whitehall	corn, oats	A/S	5-All	11/17/1886
L.M. Hubby	bark	Point Betsie	ballast	C/S	10	8/8/1855
Lady Cornelia	sailboat	Escanaba	none	C	4	11/3/1865
Lauren Castle	tug	Grand Traverse Bay	none	CO	1	11/8/1980
Leander	schooner	Gros Cap	?	A/S	?	11/17/1857
Lester R. Rockwell	schooner	Muskegon	?	F/S	?	1855
Live Yankee	schooner	High Island Reef	wheat	A/S	1	11/5/1869
Lomie A. Burton	schooner	South Manitou Island	lumber	F	0	11/17/1911
Lydia	schooner	Muskegon	?	A/S	0	10/20/1905
Maitland	bark	Waugoschance Point	corn	CO	0	6/11/1871
Manitowoc	schooner	North Manitou Island	?	A/S	?	11/10/1900
Marinette	schooner barge	Fairport	lumber	A/S	6	11/19/1886
Marold II	steel ferry	Beaver Island	gasoline	EX	5-all	1/1/1937
Mars	schooner	South Fox Island	?	A/S	?	11/19/1903
Menekaunee	schooner barge	Frankfort	lumber	A/S	7-all	11/19/1886
Michigan	propeller, iron, pass.	Holland	light	S	0	3/20/1885
Milwaukee	prop steamer, pass., freight	Straits of Mackinac	wheat	CO	5	11/29/1859
Milwaukee	propeller, wood freighter	Grand Haven	ballast	CO	1	7/8/1886
Milwaukee Belle	schooner	Straits of Mackinac	lumber	F/S	?	11/18/1886
Milwaukee	side-wheel steamer	Grand Haven	gen. freight	A/S/R	0	10/9/1868
Milwaukie	side-wheel steamer	Kalamazoo River	gen. merch.	A/S	9	11/17/1842?
Minnesota	side-wheel steamer	Summer Island	corn	A/S	0	9/27/1861
Monitor	schooner	Peninsula Point	?	?	?	10/1875
Monitor	schooner	Seul Choix Point	iron ore	A/S	0	10/31/1883
Monitor	tug	Muskegon	?	F	?	10/1873
Muskegon	side-wheel steamer	Muskegon	gen. freight	A/S	29	9/22/1919?
Nahant	prop steamer, wood freighter	Escanaba	?	FI	2	11/30/1897
Naomi	prop steamer, pass., freight	Grand Haven	gen. freight	FI	7	5/21/1907
Neptune	brig	Little Sable Point	gen. merch.	A/S/PR	18	11/25/1839
Niko	propeller, wood freighter	Garden Island	lumber	F/S	0	11/2/1924
Northern Queen	prop steamer	Manistique	?	A	0	11/29/1881
Novadoc	propeller, wood freighter	Pentwater	powdered coke	A/S	2	11/11/1940

MICHIGAN

NAME OF VESSEL	TYPE OF VESSEL	LOCATION OF LOSS	CARGO AT TIME OF LOSS	CAUSE	CREW & PASSENGERS	DATE OF LOSS
Orphan Boy	schooner	Big Sable Point	lumber	A/S	8 or 12 – all	12/5/1885
Oscoda	prop steamer, wood freighter	Epoufette	lumber	A/S	0	11/8/1914
Ostrich	schooner	Manitou Islands	light	F/S	6–all	10/1/1892?
P.J. Ralph	propeller, wood freighter	South Manitou Island	lumber	A/S	0	9/8/1924
Pere Marquette #18	car ferry	Ludington/midlake	loaded RR cars	F/S	25	9/8/1910
Pioneer	side-wheel steamer	St. Joseph	?	A/S	0	7/9/1834
Plymouth	schooner barge	St. Martin's Island	cedar posts	F/S	9–all	11/11/1913
Post Boy	prop steamer, pass., freight	Holland	?	FI	0	8/8/1905
Prince Eugene	schooner	Big Sable Point	?	A/S	?	11/1834
Protection	tug	Holland	none	A/S	1	11/14/1883
Queen City	side-wheel steam tug	Ford River	?	FI	?	11/22/1875
R.P. Mason	schooner	Unknown, Michigan?	?	F/S	?	6/20/1917
Razel Bros.	fishing tug	Whiskey Island	none	CO	3	8/20/1986
Reindeer	side-wheel steamer	Big Sable Point	?	F	23	11/1857
Roen Salvage Derrick #93	barge	Rock Island	construction equip.	F	0	10/20/1969
Souvenir	schooner	Ludington	shingles	A/S/R	6	11/26/1872
Spray	scow schooner	South Haven	?	C/S	3–all	6/2/1875
Sylvanus Marvin	schooner	Grand Haven? Racine?	?	F	9	5/22/1851
Thomas Kingsford	schooner	Waugoschance Point	corn	F	?	4/18/1871
Thomas W. Ferry	schooner	Beaver Island	?	A/S	?	11/17/1880
Three Brothers	propeller, wood freighter	South Manitou Island	lumber	A/S	0	9/27/1911
Troy	schooner	North Manitou Island	glass	A/S	?	10/1843
Uncle Sam	tug	Straits of Mackinac	none	F	?	Spring, 1882
W.B. Phelps	schooner	Glen Arbor	beer	A/S	5	11/19/1879
W.H. Gilcher	prop steamer, steel freighter	N. Lake Michigan	coal	F/S	21 – all	10/1/1892
W.S. Lyons	schooner	Waugoschance Pointe	iron ore	A/S	0	10/11/1871
Walter L. Frost	prop steamer, wood freighter	South Manitou Island	gen. merch.	A/FG	0	11/4/1903
Welcome	sloop, warship	Mackinaw City	?	A/S	0	Fall, 1787?
Westmoreland	propeller, pass., freight	Manitou Passage	Mackinac Is. provisions	C/S	17	12/7/1854?
William B. Davock	propeller, wood freighter	Pentwater	coal	F/S	33– all	11/11/1940
William Home	schooner	Seul Choix Point	?	F/S	6	9/25/1894
William Sanderson	schooner	Sleeping Bear Point	wheat	F/S	7-10 all	11/25/1874

GLOSSARY OF TERMS

aft: Toward the stern

aftermast: In a sailing ship carrying multiple masts, the mast set closest to the stern; also called the mizzenmast in a three-masted sailing vessel

barge: Large, flat-bottomed boat used chiefly for the transport of goods on inland waterways and usually propelled by towing

barkentine: A three-masted ship with the foremast square-rigged and the mainmast and mizzenmast fore-and-aft rigged

barque (bark): A three- to five-masted ship with foremast and mainmast square-rigged and mizzenmast fore-and-aft rigged

beam: The extreme width of a ship at its widest point

boat: Common name for a vessel in the Great Lakes region

boom: A long spar used to extend the horizontal foot of a sail

bow: Front end of the boat

brig: A two-masted square-rigged ship

brigantine: A two-masted ship with a square-rigged fore mast and fore-and-aft rigged aft mast

centerboard: A retractable keel used for stability in sailing vessels

Coast Guard cutter: Generic term for a Coast Guard vessel over 65 feet that serves as a buoy tender, ice-breaker, and search-and-rescue vessel

consort: An unpowered Great Lakes cargo vessel, usually a schooner barge, towed by a steam barge or a steamer; also a pair of such vessels

depth: A measurement inside the hull from the underside of the deck to the top of the keel

draft: Depth of water required for a vessel to float

fathom: A unit of length equal to six feet

flicker: Crew's quarters

fore-and-aft: Lengthwise on a ship, from stem to stern

forecastle: The forward part of a merchantman where the crew is housed, pronounced "fo'-c's'l"

foremast: The mast nearest the bow of a ship

gaff: The upper spar of a fore-and-aft sail

gale: A strong wind, rated depending on its velocity; moderate (32 to 38 mph), fresh (39 to 46 mph), strong (47 to 54 mph), and whole (55 to 63 mph)

gross tonnage: Internal volume of a ship below decks equaling 100 cubic feet

hold, holds: The interior compartments of a ship used for carrying cargo

hull: The body of a ship

jib: A triangular sail set in front of the foremast

knot: One nautical mile (6,080 feet or 1853.2 meters) per hour

lake bulk freighter: Lake boat without any special self-unloading rig above deck

laker: A ship or boat built for travel on the Great Lakes

Lifesaving Service: Federal agency tasked with providing rescue service to ships and crew; it became part of the U.S. Coast Guard in 1915

light: Carrying no cargo

lighter: A large, usually flat-bottomed barge used in unloading or loading ships

lumber hooker: Vessel used to carry timber

mainmast: A sailing ship's principal mast, usually second from the bow

mainsail: The principal sail on the mainsail

mast: A long vertical pole or spar rising from the keel or deck of a ship and supporting the yards, booms, and rigging

metacentric height: A measure of a boat's stability in water based on the relationship of weight and height to equilibrium

mizzenmast: The third mast from the bow or the mast directly aft of the mainmast on a sailing ship

net tonnage: Gross tonnage less crew cabins, storerooms, and machinery spaces

port: The left side of the boat

rating system: System of rating the quality of vessels for insurance purposes. The three classes, from highest quality to lowest, are A, B, and OO, which are further subdivided as A-1, A-1.5, A-2, A-2.5, B-1, B-1.5, B-2, and OO

sail: A piece of cloth used to catch the wind and power a boat

schooner: A two- to five-masted fore-and-aft rigged vessel having the foremast and mainmast stepped nearly amidships.

schooner barge: A schooner used as a barge; may or may not be able to move under its own power

scow: A large flat-bottomed boat with broad square ends used chiefly for transporting bulk material

seacocks: A valve used for taking on or discharging water

self-unloader: Lake boats equipped with self-unloading equipment with enormous cargo capacity

side-wheeler: A steamer with paddle wheels on both sides

sloop: Fore-and-aft rigged boat with a single mast

spars: A stout rounded wood or metal piece such as a mast, boom, gaff, or yard used to support rigging

squall: A sudden violent wind, often with rain or snow

square-rigged: A vessel with the sails rigged perpendicular to its length

starboard: Right side of the boat

steam barge: An early Great Lakes wooden steamer used for carrying bulk cargo

steamer: A ship propelled by steam

stem: The upright post of the bow

step: Refers to both a frame on a ship that receives a mast and the process of raising the mast into place

stern: Rear end of the boat

stern-wheeler: A steamer with a paddle wheel placed in the stern

topmast: The second mast above the deck

tugboat: A strongly built boat used for towing and pushing other vessels

unstep: Removing the mast from the mast "step"

whaleback: A steamer or barge with a convex upper deck, at one time used on the Great Lakes

yawl: Popular rig for pleasure sailboats, has two masts, the after mast is much smaller and stepped behind the rudder post; also refers to a small rowing boat carried on lake vessels

BIBLIOGRAPHY

Baillod, Brendon. *Frank O'Connor.*
http://www.mailbag.com/users/bbaillod/frkoconn.html

Baillod, Brendon. *The Remains of the* Lottie Cooper.
http://www.execpc.com/~bbaillod/sheboygan/l_cooper.htm/

Baillod, Brendon. *Sebastopol.*
http://www.mailbag.com/users/bbaillod/sebastopol.html

Baillod, Brendon. *A Tale of Two Ships.*
http://www.execpc.com/~bbaillod/SchoonerX/2ships.html/

Baillod, Brendon. *The Wreck of the Steamer* Lady Elgin.
http://www.execpc.com/~drewitz/elginh/

Baulch, Vivian M., "Ship Sinks in '58, Killing 33," The *Detroit News*
18 Nov. 1999: Metro C9.

Beaver Island Virtual Tour. *Lansing Shoals.*
http://www.beaverislandtour.com/lansing_shoals.htm

Bevier, Thomas, "Expedition Rediscovers 'Ship That Time Forgot,'"
The *Detroit News* 11 May 1997: Metro B3.

Bonevelle, Mary J. *The* Eastland *Disaster of 1915.*
http://www.novagate.net/~bonevelle/eastland/

Bowen, Dana Thomas, *Lore of the Lakes.* Cleveland: Freshwater Press, 1940.

Bowen, Dana Thomas, *Memories of the Lakes.* Cleveland:
Freshwater Press, 1946.

Bowen, Dana Thomas, *Shipwrecks of the Lakes.* Cleveland:
Freshwater Press, 1952

Boyd, Dr. Richard, "The Dark Voyage of the Propeller *Vernon – Part 1,*"
Wisconsin's Underwater Heritage June 2000, Vol. 10 No 2.

Boyer, Dwight, *True Tales of the Great Lakes.* New York: Dodd,
Mead & Company, 1971.

Buelow, Andrew. *Lake Michigan Car Ferries.*
http://www.execpc.com/~abuelow/ferry.html

Bukowski, Doug, "Chicago's Other U-Boat," *Chicago Tribune* 28 Jan. 1998: 1.

Burton, Pierre, *The Great Lakes.* Toronto, Canada:
Stoddart Publishing Co., 1996.

Chapman, Kirsten, "Ship of Trees Laden With Memories of
Christmases Past," *The Columbus Dispatch* 14 Dec. 1995: Features Accent
& Entertainment 1G.

Chicago Public Library. *Chicago Timeline.*
http://www.chipublib.org/004chicago/chihist.html

Creviere, Paul J. Jr., "A Confederate Yankee in King Arthur's Court"
Wisconsin's Underwater Heritage May 1998, Vol. 8 No 2.

Creviere, Paul J. Jr., *Wild Gales and Tattered Sails.* Creviere, 1997.

Dabe, Christopher, "Brewing Up History," *Marquette Tribune* Jan. 2000.

Davis, Marc, "Norfolk Man Hailed as Hero," *The Virginian Pilot* 5
May 1995: B1.

Dillon, Karen, "Remembering the *Eastland*," *Chicago Tribune* 5 June 1989:
Chicagoland 1.

Donahue, James L., *Schooners In Peril: True and Exciting Stories About Tall Ships
On The Great Lakes.* Cass City, Michigan: Anchor Publications, 1995.

Donahue, James., *Terrifying Steamboat Stories: True Tales of Shipwreck, Death
and Disaster on the Great Lakes.* West Bloomfield, MI: Altwerger and Mandel
Publishing Co., Inc., 1991.

Door County Chamber of Commerce. History in Door County.
http://doorcountyvacations.com/HISTOR~1.HTM

Drewitz, Adrian. *Milwaukee.*
http://www.execpc.com/~drewitz/milwaukee.html

Drews, Richard C. *The* David Dows, *First Lady of Chicago Shipwrecks.*
http://www.xnet.com/~acpinc/dows.html/

Ferguson, Brian. Great Lakes Fleet Page Vessel Feature – E.M. Ford.
http://www.oakland. edu/boatnerd/pictures/rburdick/fleet/emford.htm

Flesher, John, "Survivor to Visit Site of Ship Wrecked in 1958,"
The Ledger 11 Aug. 1995: 2B.

Franklin Moore, George Foot, and George F. Bagley,
Plaintiffs In Error v. The American Transportation Company,
65 U.S. 1 (U.S. Supreme Court 1860).

Gladish, Dave, "An Explosion In Island Development"
Beaver Island Historical Society Vol. 4.

Government of Canada and the United States Environmental Protection
Agency, The Great Lakes: An Environmental Atlas and Resource
Book, 1995.

Great Lakes Update, "Lady Elgin" *Wisconsin's Underwater Heritage*
Summer 1996, Vol. 6 No 2.

Grossman, Ron, "The Flow of History," *Chicago Tribune* 29 Aug. 1995: 1.

Haberski, Jim and Moureau, Jonathan A. *S.S. Wisconsin.*
http://www.blclinks.net/~sshort/shipwrecked/grtlakes/michigan/wisconsn.htm

Heise, Kenan, "Borghild Carlson, *Eastland* Survivor," *Chicago Tribune*
3 Aug. 1991: 15.

Historical Collections of the Great Lakes, Bowling Green State University,
Bowling Green, OH.

Jones, Meg, "Diving Into the Past," *Milwaukee Journal Sentinel* 9 July 1999: 1.

Jones, Meg, "Shipwreck Can Be Dangerous Lure," *Milwaukee Journal Sentinel*
26 October 1997: 3.

Jones, Meg, "Wisconsin's Titanic," *Milwaukee Journal Sentinel* 25 June 1998: 1.

Knoche, Eldon, "Fishing Melded the Lives of Missing Lake Crew,"
Milwaukee Journal Sentinel 28 December 1998: 1.

Lapeer, Jack. Historical Notes on the "Erie L. Hackley."
http://www.rootsweb.com/~migls/hackley.html

Lapeer, Jack. History in Door County.
http://doorcountyvacations.com/HISTOR~1.HTM

Mahr, Joe, "Case Adds New Chapter to Lady Elgin Saga,"
The State Journal Register 19 April 1999: 1.

Martin, Jennifer, "Time Running Out," *South Bend Tribune* 25 May 1998: A1.

McCann, Dennis, "From Ashes, New Lives Were Built,"
Milwaukee Journal Sentinel 9 Nov. 997: Travel 1.

McCann, Dennis, "Load Full of Christmas Trees Went Down With the Ship,"
Milwaukee Journal Sentinel 11 Jan. 1998: 2.

Michigan City Public Library. *Lakefront Legacy*.
http://www. mclib.org/lakefron.htm

Morey Norris, Libelant v. Harvey D. Goulder, Claimant, 79 F. 378
(Distict Court, N.D. New York 1897).

National Park Service. *Sleeping Bear Dunes National Lakeshore*.
http://www.nps.gov/slbe/SMI_page.htm

Oleszewski, Wes., *Ghost Ships, Gales and Forgotten Tales*. Marquette:
Avery Color Studios, 1996.

Oleszewski, Wes., *Mysteries and Histories*. Marquette:
Avery Color Studios, 1997.

Oleszewski, Wes., *Sounds of Disaster*. Marquette: Avery Color Studios, 1993.

Page, Shelley, "His Quest for Ancient Vessel Sends Scuba Sleuth Seeking
Sunken Proof of Lost Voyages," *The Vancouver Sun* 2 Jan. 1992: A8.

Page, Shelley, "The *Titanic* of the Great Lakes," *The Vancouver Sun* 29
Sept. 1991: Our Planet E1.

R.L. Polk and Company, *Directory of the Marine Interests of the Great Lakes*.
Detroit: R.L. Polk and Company, 1884.

Ratigan, William, *Great Lakes Shipwrecks and Survivals*. Grand Rapids:
William B. Eerdmans Publishing Co., 1977.

Rich, Craig R. *Alpena Goes Missing!*.
http://www.macatawa.org/~crich/alpena.htm.

Rich, Craig R. *Chicora*.
http://macatawa.org/~crich/chicora.htm

Rich, Craig R. *The Steamer Ironsides*.
http://www.macnet.org/~crich/ironside.htm

Sander, Phil, "Christmas Tree Ship" *Wisconsin's Underwater Heritage*
Dec. 1998, Vol. 8 No 4.

Sandler, Larry, "Report: Barge Hit *Linda E.*," *Milwaukee Journal Sentinel*
15 October 2000: 01A.

Sandström, Fredrik. *Sailing Ships*.
http://www.infa.abo.fi/~fredrik/sships/

Sawyers, June, "The Greatest Disaster on the Great Lakes,"

Chicago Tribune 27 July 1986: Sunday Magazine 5.

Stonehouse, Frederick. e-mail to Shelak, Benjamin, 1, December, 2000.

Stonehouse, Frederick. e-mail to Shelak, Benjamin, 1, January, 2001.

Stonehouse, Frederick, *Great Lakes Lighthouse Tales.* Gwinn, MI: Avery Color Studios, Inc. 1998.

Swayze, David A., *SHIPWRECK!.* Boyne City: Harbor House Publishers, Inc. 1992.

Switzer, John, "Confederate Plan to Seize Gunboat Fizzled," *The Columbus Dispatch* 21 Sept. 1994: 22D.

Taylor, Troy. *Great Lakes Ghost Ships: The Shores of Michigan.* http://www.prairieghosts.com/glgship.html

Triebe, Richard, "Queen of the Lakes." *Skin Diver.* Feb. 1984: 106.

Triebe, Richard, "The Reluctant Prins; Salvaging the *Prins Willem V.*" *Skin Diver.* Aug. 1985: 52.

University of Wisconsin Sea Grant Institute. *History of the Frank O'Connor.* http://www.seagrant.wisc.edu/Shipwrecks/Michigan/frankOconnor/history.html

University of Wisconsin Sea Grant Institute. *History of the Louisiana.* http://www.seagrant.wisc.edu/shipwrecks/Michigan/Louisiana/history.html

University of Wisconsin Sea Grant Institute. *The Palace Steamer Niagara.* http://www. seagrant.wisc.edu/shipwrecks/michigan/Niagara/index.html

U.S. Army Corps of Engineers, Detroit District. *The Soo Locks* http://huron.lre.usace.army.mil/SOO/lockhist.html

U.S. Coast Guard. *Waiting for the Christmas Tree Ship.* http://www.uscg.mil/news/Christmasship/Christmasship.htm

Volgenau, Gerry, "Pirates, Spies, and Song," *The Record* 12 Sept. 1999: Travel T11.

Watia, Vic, "Skeletons From 1903 Shipwreck Get Burial," *United Press International* 10 May 1986: Domestic News.

Webster's Ninth New Collegiate Dictionary, Merriam Webster, Inc., 1991.

Whipple, Hank, "Schooner Christina Nilson" *Wisconsin's Underwater Heritage* May 1998, Vol. 8 No 2.

INDEX

More Great Titles from Trails Books & Prairie Oak Press

Activity Guides

Great Cross-country Ski Trails: Wisconsin, Minnesota, Michigan & Ontario, Wm. Chad McGrath

Great Minnesota Walks: 49 Strolls, Rambles, Hikes, and Treks, Wm. Chad McGrath

Great Wisconsin Walks: 45 Strolls, Rambles, Hikes, and Treks, Wm. Chad McGrath

Acorn Guide to Northwest Wisconsin, Tim Bewer

Paddling Illinois: 64 Great Trips by Canoe and Kayak, Mike Svob

Paddling Southern Wisconsin: 82 Great Trips by Canoe and Kayak, Mike Svob

Paddling Northern Wisconsin: 82 Great Trips by Canoe and Kayak, Mike Svob

Wisconsin Underground: A Guide to Caves, Mines, and Tunnels in and around the Badger State, Doris Green

Travel Guides

Great Little Museums of the Midwest, Christine des Garennes

Great Minnesota Weekend Adventures, Beth Gauper

The Great Wisconsin Touring Book: 30 Spectacular Auto Tours, Gary Knowles

Tastes of Minnesota: A Food Lover's Tour, Donna Tabbert Long

Wisconsin Lighthouses: A Photographic and Historical Guide, Ken and Barb Wardius

Wisconsin Waterfalls, Patrick Lisi

Wisconsin Family Weekends: 20 Fun Trips for You and the Kids, Susan Lampert Smith

County Parks of Wisconsin, Revised Edition, Jeannette and Chet Bell

Up North Wisconsin: A Region for All Seasons, Sharyn Alden

Great Wisconsin Taverns: 101 Distinctive Badger Bars, Dennis Boyer

Great Weekend Adventures, the Editors of Wisconsin Trails

The Wisconsin Traveler's Companion: A Guide to Country Sights,
    Jerry Apps and Julie Sutter-Blair

Nature Essays

Wild Wisconsin Notebook, James Buchholz
Trout Friends, Bill Stokes
Northern Passages: Reflections from Lake Superior Country,
    Michael Van Stappen
River Stories: Growing up on the Wisconsin, Delores Chamberlain

Home & Garden

Creating a Perennial Garden in the Midwest, Joan Severa
Wisconsin Garden Guide, Jerry Minnich
Wisconsin Herb Cookbook, Suzanne Breckenridge & Marjorie Snyder
Bountiful Wisconsin: 110 Favorite Recipes, Terese Allen
Hometown Flavor: A Cook's Tour, Terese Allen

Historical Books

Prairie Whistles: Tales of Midwest Railroading, Dennis Boyer
Barns of Wisconsin, Jerry Apps
Portrait of the Past: A Photographic Journey Through
    Wisconsin 1865-1920, Howard Mead, Jill Dean, and Susan Smith
Wisconsin: The Story of the Badger State, Norman K. Risjord
Wisconsin At War: 20th Century Conflicts Through the Eyes
    of Veterans, Dr. James F. McIntosh

For a free catalog, phone, write, or e-mail us.

Trails Books
P.O. Box 317, Black Earth, WI 53515
(800) 236-8088
e-mail: books@wistrails.com
www.trailsbooks.com